in the Stars

Wicked & Uncensored Astrology Advice

for Getting

the (Almost) Perfect Guy

Love Is in the Stars

(Formerly *He's Just Not in the Stars*)

JENNI KOSARIN

AVON

An Imprint of HarperCollins*Publishers*

FIRST PAPERBACK EDITION
MORROW HARDCOVER EDITION: NOVEMBER 2006

Designed by Susan Yang

Library of Congress Cataloging-in-Publication Data is available upon request.

ISBN 978-0-06-088729-2

08 09 10 11 12   ID/RRD   10 9 8 7 6 5 4 3 2 1

Contents

Acknowledgments

Endless telephone conversations later, thank you to Melissa DuShane, who kept the ideas flowing and the support ready at handheld. A sincere thank-you, also, to Jason Goldberg, who missed his writer calling. Your precious wit, talent, and time were given selflessly, yet you still made every flight. To my fantastic editor, May Chen, for your bottomless, indefatigable wisdom, patience, and savvy: You're a Scorpio goddess. To Mauro DiPreta, *grazie* for believing in this—I'm so lucky to have you in my corner. To Craig Stanton, you're like the sun itself—your playfulness, brilliance, purity, compassion, and warmth are truly inspiring. You were there for me. I'll always be there for you. To Joelle Delbourgo and Molly Lyons, for your clever input and savoir faire. And to Selina McLemore for helping get this writing party started. Last but not least, to Donna and Paul Kosarin, my rocks, my inspirations for love and in life, my sounding boards. How could I do it without you?

Finally, I'd like to thank the cheese police for not holding me accountable when I say that though this book may be filled with celebs, the people I've listed above are the real stars.

Love Is
in the Stars

Intro Induction

Here 'tis. Not all men in love are created equal. That's why there's Oprah (as addictive as potato chips), free will, and *Love Is in the Stars*.

Outrageous, gossip-filled, and wicked advice for you. Only for you. All for you.

How to deal with men of all kinds, shapes, sizes . . .

(Get your mind out of the gutter.)

What to do when the going gets tough. And *he* gets going.

Truth is, this relationship-for-the-long-haul thingy: it's all about getting the lowdown, the core, of a man's hidden psyche.

What's a modern man's worst fear? Being discovered for who he is.

What's a modern man's deepest desire?

Uh, being discovered for who he is.

So you're doing both yourself *and him* a favor. Knowledge is power. And with knowing *this*, you can take the advice here, and go from there. In other words, if you don't want to get rid of him, at least you can see what you're up against, then figure out how to successfully navigate his *Rocky Horror Picture Show* personality.

The suggestions given in this book are clear-cut and unambiguous. Obnoxious, yes. Incorrect, no.

You know. Everyone knows. When you're in a truly sucky relationship, or about to start one, you wonder if you're just rubbernecking *a really bad accident*. Like with Howard Stern—you just can't get yourself to change the station. It's disturbing, right? See. Sometimes you're too shocked and revolted—to get a hold on that dial.

That's love, too.

You want to move on, but you can't manage it. *Love Is in the Stars* will help steer you through the scary gridlock traffic to smoother roads ahead.

Love astrology—this successful, precise new designer brand of potential-man judging—works. And if he's not emotionally all there, time to kick it to the curb.

Without a man's Venus combined with his Sun—explained in-depth, no holds barred, for the first time—you're getting a cardboard, cookie-cutter version of who a man really is. His Love sign combined with his Sun will tell you if he's more like Woody Allen or Woody Harrelson in a relationship.

Who would *you* rather have in your bed?

Don't answer that.

Avoiding a bad relationship is a lot simpler than you think. From *Sex and the City:* "Men are like taxis. When they're ready, the light is on. If they're not, you're just a stop along the way . . ."

Here's to putting ourselves in the driver's seat.

THE LOWDOWN: HOW IT WORKS

Love Is in the Stars will help you assess your boyfriends, your potential boyfriends, your husbands, potential husbands, and even your ex-boyfriends and ex-husbands. The concept of this book is radical: With a birth date and a chart—provided for you at the back of this book, with explanation of how to use it on page 273—you'll discover your man's predisposition in love. The trick is in considering the combination of his Sun (the "sign" people ask you about in bars) and his Venus (where Venus, his real love sign, was hanging out on the exact day of his birth)—together.

Shockingly, pairing his Venus sign with his Sun sign is a concept that's never been done before. But it's staggeringly effective. You don't have to know what time he was born (many astrology books cruelly make you ferret this out of his mother)—just his day, month, and year. Look him up on the easy chart provided. Read about him. Then determine if you want him or if you can, uh, change him.

> Some of us are becoming the men we wanted to marry.
>
> GLORIA STEINEM

This book gives you the know-how that you'd normally have to figure out on your own, the hard way. Now, by way of wicked and revolutionary means, *you* have the advantage.

It's not that astrology books on the market today don't include the twelve Venus signs: they do. But they don't relate your Venus to your Sun sign. In other words, you're given a Venus without being told what's really important—how it relates to his real personality, his Sun sign. And (of course) one significantly influences the other. *In fact, the method used today works about as well as a cocktail umbrella in a hailstorm.*

But by pairing the two signs, you'll find out how he'll treat you if you have a big, blow-out fight. Or how you should act if you break up, so you can walk away with dignity *and* the upper hand. You'll be stunned at how much of his behavior is innate; how much his personality (Sun) influences the way he behaves in love (Venus), and vice versa.

Of course each man is different, and the analysis here takes that into account—examining each man based on his sign combinations, giving in-depth evaluations instead of sweeping generalizations; saving you from big head- and heartaches down the line.

It can help dispel doubts and reduce your chances of making foolish, reckless moves that can potentially backfire. It tells you what his instincts are, how he'll react, and what to do if he's more, um, Freddy Krueger than Freddie Prinze, Jr. Natch.

> The appropriate age for marriage is around eighteen for girls and thirty-seven for men.
>
> ARISTOTLE

These points are illustrated with real-life celebrities—examples that are clear, ironic, and even SHOCKING.

In the current age of blind dates and Internet dating, women don't want to be cast out without a net. Nothing but a man's Venus and Sun sign combination will give us what we need to understand him: how he thinks, what his next move'll be. And how to counteract it. There are sixty combinations, meaning you can get super-specific results, not outdated stereotypes. This book is easy to use.

> Smart women love smart men more than smart men love smart women.
>
> NATALIE PORTMAN

No day-to-day schedules, no manipulative strategies, no *Rules*. Just helpful information and cut-to-the-chase expert advice.

Here's an example. Remember, we're putting together Sun with Venus to judge a man in love. The following celebrity men are all Sun sign Leo combined with Venus in Virgo—signs they were born with and never change:

Robert De Niro (August 17, 1943)
Sean Penn (August 17, 1960)
Antonio Banderas (August 10, 1960)

Not only do these three guys have the same Sun and Venus combination, but they're all . . . big, hot studs. It's eerie. Yes, these guys will woo their women the same way. And advice to you—the potential girlfriend—is going to be similar for all three. These are men who are masters of physical expression, who have all been married twice and all had excellent long-term second marriages.

But astrology books on the market say that a Sun sign Virgo, Venus in Virgo—the same Venus but a different Sun sign—is going to woo you the same way as Robert De Niro, Sean Penn, and Antonio Banderas because they all have the *same Venus*. And that's not correct. Look below.

Plain women know more about men than beautiful women do.

KATHARINE HEPBURN

Different Sun in Virgo combined with *same* Venus in Virgo:

David Arquette (September 8, 1971)
Adam Sandler (September 9, 1966)
Bill Murray (September 21, 1950)

Do these guys look like they belong grouped together? Yes, they do. They're all funny-guy, ironic wiseasses. But should they be combined with the big, hot studs above just because they have the same Venus? No. They're not going to be the same in love at all. You see, contrary to what other astrology books claim, a simple Venus doesn't work. It's the *combination* of Sun and Venus that gives the only accurate picture. Sun Leo, Venus in Virgo (De Niro, Penn, Banderas) is going to romance you with one sexy, smoldering *I'm taking you now* look. Sun Virgo, Venus in Virgo (Arquette, Sandler, Murray) is gonna woo you by blowing snot through his nose. The difference? Titanic.

A man cannot be defined by his Sun sign.

He cannot be defined by his rising sign.

He cannot even be judged in love by his Venus, his actual love sign.

There's no right love match—as other astrology books claim—without examining his Sun and Venus—together.

Read this book and discover that Chris Noth (aka Mr. Big), Ike Turner (ex of Tina), Larry Flynt (creator of *Hustler*), and Ethan Hawke (Uma Thurman's ex)—all ladies' men, on- as well as offscreen (check the tabloids)—have the same Sun (Scorpio) Venus (Scorpio) combination. Coinkidink? What do *you* think?

Or how about Sun in Cancer and Venus in Cancer combo:

O. J. Simpson (July 9, 1947)
Curtis Jackson aka rapper 50 Cent (July 6, 1976)
Lizzie Borden (July 19, 1860)

Wait . . . Now change the sun to Taurus—keep the Venus in Cancer (remember, other astrology books say these guys should be the same in love as O. J. Simpson)—and you've got:

Ricky Nelson (May 8, 1940)
Jimmy Stewart (May 20, 1908)
Harry S. Truman (May 9, 1884)

Look how different. To bring home the point, current astrology books categorize Ricky Nelson with O. J. Simpson because they have

> The more I see of men, the more I like dogs.
>
> CLARA BOW

> I met this wonderful girl at Macy's. She was buying clothes and I was putting Slinkies on the escalator.
>
> STEVEN WRIGHT

the same Venus. Yeah. Pair Ricky with Lizzie Borden and you hardly get a match made in heaven.

But here's more. How about slightly intimidating, brawny hulks who, in reality, are just big pussycats (with an abiding fondness for kids):

Leo combined with that same Venus in Cancer:

> **Men are pigs. Too bad we own everything.**
>
> TIM ALLEN

Hulk Hogan (August 11, 1953)
Dean Cain (July 31, 1966)
Arnold Schwarzenegger (July 30, 1947)

Or how about serious bad boy rebels who somehow manage to project that good guy, appealing image, too? These guys are romantic souls with a certain self-mocking side. Sun Aquarius combined with Venus in Capricorn:

Robbie Williams (February 13, 1974)
James Dean (February 8, 1931)
Paul Newman (January 26, 1925)
Justin Timberlake (January 31, 1981)
Chris Rock (February 7, 1966)

Men who cannot get enough of different women (buyer beware):

Aries sun combined with Venus in Pisces:

Marvin Gaye (April 2, 1939)
Vincent van Gogh (March 30, 1853)
Hugh Hefner (April 19, 1926)

And men you should stay away from at all costs. Seriously, these guys have no problem playing psychotic, religious nuts on-screen . . . Isn't that hint enough? *Stay away.*

Aries Sun combined with Venus in Aquarius:

Quentin Tarantino (March 27, 1963)
Alec Baldwin (April 3, 1958)
Gary Oldman (March 21, 1958)
William Shatner (March 22, 1931)

And men who have weird relationships with sex:
Virgo Sun combined with Venus in Leo:

Michael Jackson (August 29, 1958)
Leo Tolstoy (September 9, 1828)
Mickey Rourke (September 16, 1953)

Get the picture? (Ladies, in regard to the above group: um, run.)

And seriously, isn't it odd that strong political or religious ideas that influence the masses follow in the wakes of those listed below? (Or, ironically enough, hideously corrupt totalitarian governments???)

Sun Taurus combined with Venus in Taurus:

Niccolò Machiavelli (May 4, 1469)
Adolf Hitler (April 20, 1889)
Karl Marx (May 5, 1818)
Oliver Cromwell (May 5, 1599)
Michael Moore (April 23, 1954)
Muhammad (April 3, 570)
Pope John Paul II (May 18, 1920)

Now. If you change the Venus and keep the Sun in Taurus (astrology books also say this should be the same guy in love as the men above; they're all Taurus), you actually have someone who's a good love candidate.

Sun in Taurus combined with Venus in Gemini:

William Shakespeare (April 26, 1564)
Andre Agassi (April 29, 1970)
David Beckham (May 2, 1975)
Enrique Iglesias (May 8, 1975)
Jason Biggs (May 12, 1978)
Tony Danza (April 21, 1951)

Who would *you* rather be in a relationship with? Romantic, sweet guys: Enrique Iglesias and Andre Agassi or Niccolò Machiavelli and Adolf Hitler? If you go by current astrology books, the two groups are the same. Look again. Are they kidding? Isn't it time someone tells the real story about how you should define men in love? Don't take my word for it. Look at the celebrity examples I've provided: It's so *clear*.

The beauty of this book, too, is that it's so easy—just a quick glance at a chart provided in the back. You don't need to know the hour a man was born, his placements or planetary alignments, or other confusing information that only stumps. You just need to know his birth date: month, day, and year. Easy. You don't even need to know your own combination—combos are different for men.

Listen. Each man has words he uses to describe himself—ones you'll probably ascribe to him when you two first meet; ones he'll claim and swear to till his deathbed. I've included the amusing, spot-on, terrifying descriptions of what they *truly mean*.

Let men have their porn. This is the real hard core.

CHAPTER 1

Aries, Ex or Next
(the Ram, March 21–April 19)

ARIES RUDE-IMENTS

I'm sorry to be the one to break this to you but, when it comes to men—and whether or not they have good relationship potential—you have to look at two things: first, his Venus (love sign). And then his Sun sign (the basis for his personality in general). But with Aries it's different. There are *three* things you must consider. Lucky you. After you've sorted through the first two—and have thrown out the last of the used tissues—you must ask yourself one necessary, though frightening, question: Is he an Aries with his birthday in March or in April?

Listen to me. Astrologers don't give you this one *big* piece of information. Maybe they're protecting you. Maybe they just don't want you to throw the baby out with the bathwater (ha!—actually a fitting reference, considering who we're dealing with here). But you've gotta know. You simply must:

If he's an April Aries, okay. Maybe you'll be okay. If he's a March Aries (especially one near the Pisces cusp), run! Get out of town! Hop on the bus. Make a new plan, Fran. Be coy, Joy. And set yourself free.

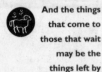

And the things that come to those that wait may be the things left by those that got there first.

STEVEN TYLER

You should know that it's gonna take your March Aries a little more time to grow up than you'd hoped (like 120 to 130 years longer . . . you'll be dead by then), and in the meantime he might even just be a little *psychotic* and an *insensitive bastard* (oh, but he may also be good at convincing you, at first, that he's not). That's right. He's Chucky and Chucky Returns. Combined.

I'm not playing around here. There *may be* a difference between your March guy and your April Aries guy: a straitjacket, designed especially for you.

So I just thought you'd want to know this now, going in. Consider yourself forewarned. Read on, knowing that there's some hope to make him a decent boyfriend, and I'll tell you how. Go. Go in peace.

Just remember that Luke resisted the Dark Side. And so can you.

ARIES TONGUE LASHING

"You want me. You know you do."

I'm not sure that acting is something for a grown man to be doing.

STEVE MCQUEEN

"No I don't!" you insist, lips pursed. It kills you that this man's got you. You hate it. You hate him. You're beginning to hate yourself.

Aries man licks his lips, penetrates you with his eyes, and smiles so cockily you'd like to smack him. But you don't.

Damn, he's good.

"I'm going to kiss you. Now."

"No you're not!" you hear yourself whimper, impressed.

Damn, he's sexy. Your head whips around to check if others are listening in on the unfolding scene. You almost wish they were. You giggle, feeling ridiculous for imitating a fourteen-year-old virgin. (Get real. You know he's gonna do it anyway, but it's—let's face it—*fun* to let him charm the pants off you. *Literally*.)

"I'm going to caress you with my tongue and make your loins ache for me."

"Not in front of all these people!" you assert, louder now, with conviction. But you're smiling. Unabashedly. Swooning. Pretending that you don't like the public displays of affection when, in fact, your knees are jelly under the table. You wish he'd just do it already and shut up.

You love it. You love this man. You see yourself walking down the aisle to him. You see him as the father of your children. You imagine him in the future as the romantic, spontaneous, charismatic fool for you he is now. The love of your life. THE ONE. Showering you with love and affection. Rocking your world in bed and in life.

> It was so nice to go into this fake courtroom on *Ally McBeal*. I immediately went up into the judge's chair. Nice view. A preferable perspective.
>
> **ROBERT DOWNEY, JR.**

WAIT! (Record scratches. Violins abate.)

Not so fast. Are you sitting down? Really? Good. Take a deep breath and listen. About your Aries man: Six months of erotic, sexy quicksand. A sinking ship made of lead. Seriously. In the beginning, he's soooo charming. Then something *changes*. All of a sudden . . .

He wants to be pampered. He wants you to think like he thinks. He wants you to be perfect. Always. He wants his mommy. He wants you to be his mommy and to put him in his place. He wants to see you as his lover, his confidante (his webcam partner—he's so *big* . . . on political issues). The absolute love of his life. *He wants. He wants. He wants.*

Are you noticing a pattern?

Aries are the children of the zodiac. Make no mistake. That "grounded," "super-smart," "sensitive," "moralistic," "self-assured" "man" you've just nabbed (or are dying to) will cry, whine, and stamp his feet if you take his ducky from the tub.

ARIES: IS HE *INTO* YOU?

Out of nowhere (and you're privy to the inane consequences of your actions) you start flipping coins, wondering if it's going to last. You feel it won't. You absolutely do. But there's that little voice inside you saying, "Shut up, Goddamn it! I'm doing the best I can here!"

I don't think silicone makes a girl good or bad.

JAMES CAAN

Because you just can't help yourself. Because Aries men are like those little boys who are so cu-uute, you just can't stop staring at them: You know the ones. They make you want to have kids and dress them up in snappy little overalls with preppy starch-collared shirts and parade them all around the park in front of the other jealous mothers.

"Look at *him*!" you screech gleefully, unable to contain yourself. "Don't you just wanna pinch his cheeks and take him home?"

And they do want to. Because he's *got* something. He's special. And he knows it.

And so do you. Damn it.

Life is a tragedy when seen in close-up, but a comedy in long shot.

CHARLIE CHAPLIN

Aries guys can make awful boyfriends because they're just so easy to fall in love with. They have their good points. The power thing *is* sexy. The righteousness thing they've got going on gives you a sense of security. And it may just be a false sense.

He *seems* like he's a take-control guy. All roads point to the fact that he *can* take care of you. This is, alas, perhaps an illusion. Financially, he can. Emotionally, he may just have problems—serious ones. And you need to know this, friend, right now. Listen up: *You* need to take control.

Neuroses with this guy? Try the following. Get Aries to open up sometime . . . really open up. Tell him you're gonna do a role-playing thing. Tell him you're his mommy and you'd like him to be your baby—your little goo-goo gah-gah wittle boo-boo baby—and you want him to nuzzle your breasts like he's your little boy. Go ahead, tell him. "I'm you mooommmmy." Coo to him. See what he does. Do it.

Aries wants *you* to be his mommy. And his real mommy, betcha anything, was the strong, in-charge one of the two 'rents. And though he's actually frightened, terri-fied of his mother, he's always fantasized of having a woman just like her.

> I can't say I gave up totally my passion for women but almost.
>
> **OMAR SHARIF**

In truth, Aries man's entire agenda is to con-vince you, for the sake of his overindulged, over-inflated ego, that he's the one with the pants in the relationship. But (see above) that's not really what he wants. Instead, he wants you to be numero uno domination woman—everywhere but in bed. 'Cause he hates feeling like a wuss. Truly hates it. But, as with every rebellious man-child, it's his innermost desire.

As the girlfriend of an Aries man, you're secretly surprised how much influence he's got over you. Nobody else did such a thorough, bang-up job of it. You kinda like it. His flair, charm, and boyish good looks keep you panting like a horny though misguided teenager. He tells you what to do *and how to do it.* Shockingly enough, you listen to him. He brings out a side of you you've never seen before. He's just plain fun. And a pervert, too . . . in a good way.

True, you know he just likes to hear himself talk. But you don't mind. You know he's a total control freak. You let him be.

You despise the way he barks at others and orders around his posse and those who work for him (though he somehow does it with charm). But it thrills you, too. And you suc-cumb. Because he's your future. He's your Future Man in Life . . .

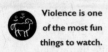

Violence is one of the most fun things to watch.

QUENTIN TARANTINO

Well, I have good news for you. Aries men are romantic, loving, sweet, and extremely attentive.

And even Aries men marry, eventually. Some even get married early on (it's rare but it happens). You *can* win his heart. If that's what you truly want. And if Aries is an ex, I've got startling advice for you, too.

ADVICE TO THE FUTURE MRS. ARIES

Here's a story. I have a good friend who nabbed an Aries man who was many years her junior; kind of young for marriage, especially for an Aries: twenty-six. Know how she did it? She worked hard, saved her money, bought a house (without waiting for him), and, once the documents were signed, dated, and stamped, turned to him and said, "You in?"

If you make a fool of yourself, you can do it with dignity, without taking your pants down. And if you do take your pants down, you can still do it with dignity.

WILLIAM SHATNER

He was impressed. In fact, he wanted to live with her in her new house. "No way," she told him. "Marry me or forget it." He did. Two babies, seven years, and a mortgage almost paid off later, he pays all the bills, she owns the house, and they're still very happy.

Bottom line: If you're waiting for Aries to sweep you off your feet, you're going to wait a long time. *You* have to take charge and have some balls. Aries is all talk in the beginning. But after he's conquered you, he can, easily, and without remorse, walk away.

If you do your own thing, though, Aries will follow you like an obedient duckling. Under the bottom line: Aries wants a woman who's going to stand up to him. He's the one sign in the zodiac who will not be intimidated by a strong woman. *Au contraire, that* makes him feel secure.

ADVICE TO THE EX MS. ARIES

If you've broken up with an Aries man, I've got news that shouldn't be a huge shocker for you: DO NOT SLEEP WITH HIM. This may work with some other signs, but not him. (Taurus or Pisces, maybe.) I mean it. His complex messed-up sex/(self)-respecting women issues are on par with Cancer or even Gemini man. Just forget it. He'll be tempted to leave money on the dresser, *after,* when he leaves.

> I'm a pretty quiet guy, but if people want to think of me as a lady-killer, I guess that's good.
>
> JAMES WOODS

Instead, I want you to do something: Put the book down. Do it. Put it next to you. Step away from the book. Hands in the air. Slow-ly.

Now go outside. Run around. Wave your arms. Flap them like a pterodactyl. You heard me. Yell "Squawk, squawk." Bare your teeth. *Grrrr.* Jump on one foot. Yell it again, "SQUAWK, SQUAWK!" Repeat five times. Hop around in a big circle.

Did you do it? Did anyone laugh at you? Now, why is that? 'Cause what you did was silly, immature, and you looked dumb doing it? Right. Now, okay. I'm going to be straight here. Going after an Aries man who doesn't want you—whether it be a phone call or an e-mail or registered letter, whatever—is as futile as you going outside and squawking like a prehistoric bird with an attitude problem. I mean it.

Futile with a capital F.

(And please, please, please, read this whole chapter, at least, before you do anything else stupid. Like plan the wedding before you've seen the way he interacts with his mother.)

(Yeah, babe. That's how he's gonna treat *you*.)

> I wish they would only take me as I am.
>
> VINCENT VAN GOGH

So . . . You want to know why you can't chase after him? Because Sun sign Aries knows what he wants. Or at least he *thinks* he does. And there is nothing you can do to change his mind. He is completely *inflexible,* and I don't mean in bed. He is the fetus of the zodiac. He's still running around showing off his neat little toys when he's thirty, forty, or even fifty. He's aggressive. He takes. He takes what he wants. He's a hunter—a caveman, still holding a stone-carved knife—and he's not comfortable unless he's out getting his own meat.

Capisce?

Listen, you going after him will bring up his *biggest* deep-seated fear. And he will instantly be nauseated by your attempts to get him back. Here's your answer: You know how we reject what we see in ourselves that we can't stand?

> You have to love the guy that you play; even if you play the villain, you've got to love him.
>
> ANDY GARCIA

Yeah. With Aries it's weakness. Pathetic, whiny weakness. Wimpiness. *Please-come-back-to-me-y-*ness. Gag. It revolts him. And he'll cut you off completely when he sees it in you because it absolutely disgusts him when he sees it in himself.

Walk away with some dignity. If you call him—or call him and call him—I guarantee you he will never take your phone call again. He'll rewrite history. He'll say, "Maybe I used to love you. *Maybe.* But I have no feelings for you anymore." And that'll be the end of it. And then you'll feel like a worthless schmuck instead of the way you should feel—like you've just won the ten-million-dollar scratch-off sweepstakes. You now have a chance to find a *good* boyfriend. 'Cause let's face it. Aries man is charming, affable, and dastardly, wickedly fun. But did you really want to live with a total control-freak dictator for the rest of your life?

Don't answer that.

Now brace yourself: I guarantee you—GUARANTEE you—that if you don't call Aries after you're broken up, he will call you. The problem is, he'll call you to:

> Marriage is miserable unless you find the right person that is your soul mate, and that takes a lot of looking.
>
> **MARVIN GAYE**

A. Sleep with you
B. Tell you how miserable he is without you (and how he's *so* disappointed that you're, *sigh*, not good enough for him)
C. See if you're still pining for him (out of curiosity)
D. Check whether anyone's snatched you up yet (and, by the way, the answer is yes. Hey—you're not lying. You're dating yourself. Take a hot bath tonight and pour yourself a glass of Chardonnay. And stop mourning him. Aries man has radar; he'll sense when you're not living and breathing solely for *him* anymore.)

BUT: DO NOT TAKE THIS PHONE CALL. The only way Aries guy will want to get back together with you is if you *continually* don't take his phone calls. Seriously. One day, a year from now, he'll call you out of the blue like nothing happened. He'll invite you to his office to have sex. And you'll tell him to go call a 900 number.

And he'll think about it.

SUN/VENUS COMBINATIONS:
THE TRUE LOVE POTENTIAL TEST

Now, remember. Venus can only land in five different signs for each of the twelve Sun signs. The descriptions for Aries are forthcoming. First, go look at the Sun/Venus chart in the back of the book. Find his birth date. Write down his Venus. Read the following. If his Venus is in Aries or Aquarius, be afraid. Be very afraid.

Aries Sun, Venus in Aries

I swear to you that this is the worst placement for an Aries man, next to Venus in Aquarius. His idealism in love is quadrupled. He is looking for the PERFECT woman—that is, someone who will never falter; never pass gas, never forget a line from the script he's so carefully written and crafted for her, never show her weaknesses. She has to be warm and caring, sensible and sensitive, strong and domineering—except with him. (Don't ever order *this* Aries around—he'll ask you to go get him something at the corner deli and then—aw, sh*t, really??—change all the locks.)

> He wasn't a great father. He was a great musician. That's always been a touchy one, and it will be until I can find the answer, but I don't know if there is one.
>
> JULIAN
> LENNON

Be the strong, silent type, subtle and practical. Never the needy drama queen. Things need to be focused on him—get it? Um, why else would he be in a relationship?

In the beginning he is THE PERFECT CATCH. He's *hot and masculine,* yet "a nice guy." A hint of slick, but it's under the surface, so, strangely, it's a turn-on. That's what makes him so crafty. Don't ignore blazing red flags that'll pop up from the very beginning. He'll inadvertently uncover some of his flaws on your first date. Actually, he may even brag about them outright, then you'll never hear him speak of them again. This is him getting stuff off his chest. He's a real sincere, "honest" guy, this one. File it away if your two neuroses match. But don't forget. Ever.

No, it's not *you. It's him.* This man will make you jealous of someone who doesn't exist: his perfect woman, his ideal goddess. He may even talk incessantly about "her." Hey—he's with you, right? If he does this, get out quickly. Don't be masochistic. Say to him, in a singsong Glinda-the-Good-Witch-of-the-East voice: "Oh-ho. Rubbish. Be gone before someone drops a house on you, too." Then leave.

Maybe that goes along with my personality—it's white or black, never gray.

WAYNE NEWTON

Ever see *Xena? Wonder Woman? Weird Science?* Yeah. He wants a mythical creature. I'll tell you something, though. If you're faking it—pretending to be his powerful, independent love goddess—and that's not the real you, he'll find you out and it'll be over when he does.

He's intuitive. He can smell a lie like that big-shnozzed ugly villain guy in *Chitty-Chitty Bang Bang* can smell kiddies. In fact, lie to him and he'll delete you from his life with one swift keyboard stroke of his souped-up top-of-the-line Mac.

He is a dictator. I'm telling you, Stalin would look up to this guy.

So do this: Agree with everything he says. Let him repeat himself like he has Alzheimer's. He does. He will forget your birthday—know this, my friend—and anything remotely important that has been said. In fact, let the whole eerie Groundhog Day–thing work for you. He'll be impressed that you "guessed" things he already told you twelve times. He doesn't even listen when *he* talks, for God's sake, so don't be offended when he doesn't listen to *you.*

Oh, one last word of advice: Don't ever get jealous with this man. Tell him to go out, have fun. He'll *run* back to your side. If

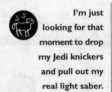

I'm just looking for that moment to drop my Jedi knickers and pull out my real light saber.

EWAN
MCGREGOR

you're too possessive, instead, his little-boy I-wanna, I-wanna rebel thing will come out, full force, and he'll *start* flirting with other women, just to show you that *he can*. He'll turn off his cell phone so that you can't reach him. Sadly childish, right? Right. This is what I'm saying.

One last thing: The little-boy, funny, sweet thing is so attractive, you may just be severely spoiled by romantic gestures and soul-mate kinda BIG love.

BOYFRIEND POTENTIAL RATING: High if you make it past the six-month mark; that's a good sign for things to come. Extremely low until he grows up; usually in his forties. Very high scary factor because he's truly deceptive. When he's young, he talks on and on about how he wants to get married and start a family. In reality, he's a better magician than David Copperfield: *This is an illusion. . . .* So good, he believes it himself.

CELEBRITY CORRESPONDENTS
WITH ARIES SUN, VENUS IN ARIES

Eddie Murphy (April 3, 1961) Caught with a transvestite hooker.

Steven Seagal (April 10, 1952) Married three times; his youngest child with Kelly LeBrock is named after the nanny; he then got the nanny pregnant.

Steve McQueen (March 24, 1930) Ladies' man; married three times, including to actress Ali McGraw.

Kevin Federline, aka the first-ex Mr. Britney Spears (March 21, 1978) Left first wife when she was pregnant with his child.

Robert Downey, Jr. (April 4, 1965) In and out of jail for drugs. On second marriage since 2005.

Napoleon III (April 20, 1808)

Adrien Brody (April 14, 1973)

DJ A.M., born Adam Goldstein (March 30, 1973) On-again, off-again with Nicole Richie ended in 2006.

Steven Tyler, Aerosmith (March 26, 1948) Had problems with drug abuse. Liv's mother covered up the fact that he was her father because of it.

Vince Vaughn (March 28, 1970)

Aries Sun, Venus in Taurus

Well, here you may have something to work with. Aries with Venus in Taurus will want real love. He'll want to go slow and seduce you big-time. Venus, by the way, rules Taurus. And he's a sensual beast, unlike Aries with Venus in Aries—who talks a good game, but performs like a machine drill.

Want Aries with Venus in Taurus? Drive a Mercedes. Or an Aston Martin. Tell him you just finished hanging your clothing outside with clothespins and you now have a daisy-print cotton apron on (with your initials on it) and are chopping his favorite vegetables.

In fact, tell him you're about to cook a full-course dinner of risotto with white truffles and porcini mushrooms, veal chops with a tarragon-mustard cream sauce, and death-by-chocolate cake. For the mayor. And your nanna. And he's invited but he doesn't have to bring anything because it's just *such a privilege* to cook for him.

I'm exaggerating here. But do you see the rub? You have to be flashy but prudent. Have expensive taste, but stay home and cook. Wealthy and powerful, but domestic and frugal, too. Aries Sun, Venus in Taurus can also have this weird, paranoia thing that you want him for his money or that you're using him ('cause he can be an opportunist to the *n*th degree). Just make sure you don't let him spend too much on you in the beginning, even if he offers. He'll think you can be bought ('cause *he* can be—and he'll get funky about seeing it in you).

This guy's a lady-killer who doesn't know what he wants early on in life. Eventually, he'll realize what he's looking for: stability. He wants his woman to be grounded. Be his rock. Get his ironic humor. And you'll get him.

This one's easier to catch than many other Aries men. Just follow my counsel. And say your Hail Marys ten times. Even if you're Jewish. Or a Jehovah's Witness. Or agnostic.

F*ck it. Just pray.

BOYFRIEND POTENTIAL RATING: High. Not a bad catch either. Except for the paranoid/delusional/thinks-you're-using-him thing, sometimes.

CELEBRITY CORRESPONDENTS
WITH ARIES SUN, VENUS IN TAURUS

Marlon Brando (April 3, 1924) Married three times.

Charlie Chaplin (April 16, 1889) His last marriage was a long one. He was fifty-four when they married, though; she was seventeen.

Christopher Walken (March 31, 1943) Happily married since 1969.

Warren Beatty (March 30, 1937) Known for his love 'em and leave 'em style. Roster: Joan Collins, Madonna, Julie Christie, Leslie Caron, Carly Simon (rumored to have written "You're So Vain" about him), Diane Keaton, Elle Macpherson, Cher, Goldie Hawn, Brigitte Bardot, Britt Ekland, Liv Ullmann, Candice Bergen, and Stephanie Seymour (who dumped him for Axl Rose). Finally married Annette Bening, with whom he has four children.

James Caan (March 26, 1940) Married and divorced five times.

Eric Clapton (March 30, 1945)

Anthony Perkins (April 4, 1932)

Leonardo da Vinci (April 15, 1452)

Zach Braff (April 6, 1975)

Hayden Christensen (April 19, 1981)

Aries Sun, Venus in Gemini

Aries with Venus in Gemini will live for love . . . at least, his version of it. He's so lost that he doesn't know which end is up. Actually, he likes being abused. That's right. You heard it here. When Aries/Gemini is tortured in love, he's happy. He doesn't really want to suffer, but, let's face it, it's the drama quotient working overtime . . . not unlike a Shakespeare play where swords are drawn and somebody dies in the end with lots of fake blood. It's what he wants. It *makes* him want. And it'll make him want *you.*

So, here's my advice. Tell him you need your space. Then pop over with a bottle of wine. Tell him you want to go out. Then call him at the last moment and say you really didn't really mean it—you don't feel like it—you've changed your mind. Tell him you two should go on vacation, and then tell him you just got a call from Mr. Big and you're going, instead, to visit the wine estate he still has in Napa.

Wait. That was fictional. No, no. Tell him you got a call from your ex, who needs to talk about his current girlfriend and—but, oh!—he's a good guy and you just want to help. (And by the way, sweetie, don't worry that I'm going to meet him in his hot tub. And that I'm packing a thong bikini. And nothing else.)

Do you see where I'm going here? Actually, you only have to do this for a few months. In other words, by the time you're ready to commit to your Aries/Gemini, he'll be ready to be committed.

To an asylum, true. But he'll be all yours.

BOYFRIEND POTENTIAL RATING: High if you dose him with your best impression of Lady Macbeth (Out, out, damned spot). Low if you don't.

P.S. These guys just can't seem to function like the rest of us mere mortals. They're passionate, yes. But like a fire you just can't put out, the damage keeps spreading.

CELEBRITY CORRESPONDENTS
WITH ARIES SUN, VENUS IN GEMINI

Russell Crowe (April 7, 1964) Pleaded guilty to misdemeanor for throwing a phone at a hotel clerk. (Though also helped French police arrest, identify, and convict a thief he saw on the street—*kewl.*)

Andy Garcia (April 12, 1956) Well-known for his disinterest in Hollywood and marrying his college sweetheart. It's possible to get a good one.

Omar Sharif (April 10, 1932) Sued for "assaulting and battering" a valet in a restaurant and calling him pretty nasty racist names.

Brian McFadden (April 12, 1980) The Westlife star has been in rehab a couple of times to stop drinking.

Gregory Peck (April 5, 1916)

Dudley Moore (April 19, 1935) Never kicked the rumors of his habit for going into debt due to his affinity for prostitutes, cocaine, and alcohol.

Aries Sun, Venus in Aquarius

Danger. Alarm. Break out the bomb squad. Danger. DANGER WILL ROBINSON. Entering the most terrifying, *terrifying* love zone. Just stay away. Do it. I'm warning you. This guy, within a month or two of you dating him, will swear up and down that you're "it." He'll be ready to bring the priest or rabbi or judge around and just get it over with. He'll show you how committed he is by throwing out all his beloved photos of Jenna Jameson (the famous porn star, y'know?—if this isn't your first red flag, what is?). He'll sigh and look at you like you're the last sip of water in the Mohave.

Fawn. Worship you. Sigh and shed tears.

He's the evangelist Jim Bakker of passion (and look what happened to Tammy Faye). He's a really bad episode of *The Love Boat*, a trip back and forth to Fantasy Island; and all the while with that *Won-*

der Years innocent, Mister Rogers–trustworthy mug staring back at you with pure *loving*, sappy adoration in his eyes. Just for you. He is exactly, EXACTLY, what you've hoped for all your life . . .

But listen. LISTEN. It is very likely that one day, soon, he will break up with you, so coldly, so ruthlessly, so brutally, it would make Mussolini wince and go "Ooh, that's harsh." He'll take the lace cloth you've had in your hope chest since birth (that your dear great-grandmother passed down to you) and use it as toilet paper. And he'll have no remorse for it because *he's never wrong*. Sadly, no one is good enough for him.

Sigh. Double sigh.

Sure, this open, gregarious, exciting man is unimaginably fun to be with. But admit it. You kinda knew it going in. He seemed so whipped that you were never really sure if he was in love with *you* or the *idea* of you.

And there you have it in a cracked nutshell. Look. This is for your own good. Don't take it personally. This guy is a survivor— all Venus in Aquariuses are, but especially Sun sign Aries (and Aquarius)—and so it goes. He needs to use women to boost his ego so he doesn't have to deal with what a pathetic (romantic, ide- alistic, though horribly misguided), righteous loser he is.

Your only hope is when he finally moves out of his mother's house. At forty-two. And has been sufficiently potty trained. And needs to set- tle down because he must produce progeny who are *exactly like him*.

God help us, everyone.

BOYFRIEND POTENTIAL RATING: Do I have to say it again? Stay away. Do it . . . I know you're attracted to him like Courtney Love is to getting her name in the tabloids: but for something wrong and stupid. Listen. Listen to nice, smart ex-first lady Nancy Reagan: "*Just say no.*" Oh—if he's got his financial act together and he's hit- ting his forties, he may—may—be okay. Just be careful. *Really.*

CELEBRITY CORRESPONDENTS
WITH ARIES SUN, VENUS IN AQUARIUS

Quentin Tarantino (March 27, 1963)

Alec Baldwin (April 3, 1958) Note on the biggest divorce/child custody battle in decades . . . Kim Basinger is a Sagittarius/Sagittarius—he's an Aries/Aquarius. Their Sun signs go together (both fire), but their Venuses don't (Sag and Aquarius—fire and air).

Elton John (March 25, 1947)

Richard Chamberlain (March 21, 1934)

Gary Oldman (March 21, 1958) Married three times, once to Uma Thurman.

Wayne Newton (April 3, 1942)

William Shatner (March 22, 1931) Married three times. Third wife, sadly, drowned in their backyard pool.

Aries Sun, Venus in Pisces

I hate to say this, but you're dealing with potluck here. It can go either way: romantic, artistic poet who resembles the heartthrob wooing the nerdy-and-schlumpy-turned-knockout-gorgeous girl in all those corny teen movies you'd never admit to liking. Or: total, utter *PSYCHO*.

Yup. It's true. Freddie Prinze Jr., or Freddy Krueger.

It really depends on the guy. It's up to you to make sure which before it's too late.

These guys can be dangerous in love. You wouldn't expect it, because they're ultra-, ultra-sensitive—and *therefore, can go the womanizer route or, on the other side, become obsessive and masochistic.* It's a defense mechanism. Examples: Vincent van Gogh (uh . . . cut off ear); Marvin Gaye (known for his obsessive, love/hate addiction to women); Hugh Hefner . . . (need I say more??)

So, here's my advice. Don't get too close. That's right. Keep him at a distance. See if he uses his powers for good or evil. Watch him.

True, he's nice to the waiter and the bellboy, and is incredibly charming with your mother. But he does seem a little quiet, doesn't he? Hmmm. He's almost too perfect. He's even a good listener. And his eyes are so liquidy intense. You're wondering if he's really listening to you or just measuring your neck to see what size machete he needs . . . Oh no! Did I give it away? (Hey, confess. Your friends are a little freaked out about this guy.)

Now, he might just be fine. Let's just see. But if you sleep with him, make sure it's after the ring. Really? Too long? Then go interview his ex-girlfriends. I mean it. I know, I know. Over the top. Let the critics loose on me. But go anyway. Do it. Subtly. Or not.

Put on your best Jackie O glasses, wig, and trench coat. Usually I wouldn't advise this. But with this guy—if you have access, do it . . . and you can even tell him *after* the fact.

He'll be offended. He'll kind of admire you for it, though, too. You've now got bigger balls than he does. And he likes that. 'Cause he always kind of suspected that everyone else in the world does. *This* will make him fall for you. Having that certain kind of oomph he so craves. Yin-yang. Get it?

And if his ex-girlfriend admits that he used to watch her through the shower curtain . . . and she suspects his real initials are N.B. (right, Norman Bates), that just might be a sign.

P.S.: If he manages to stay away from the dark side (he's easily swayed)—and you decide he's really more Freddie Prinze, Jr., than Freddy Krueger, then, um—keep him.

BOYFRIEND POTENTIAL RATING: Extremely high if he's emotionally balanced and mature—and over that I-only-want-her-'cause-I-can't-have-her thing. Very low if he keeps an old lady's wig hidden in his closet.

CELEBRITY CORRESPONDENTS
WITH ARIES SUN, VENUS IN PISCES

Hugh Hefner (April 19, 1926) The Ultimate "Playboy."

Vincent van Gogh (March 30, 1853) Almost as famous for his psychotic behavior as for his ingenious artwork.

Julian Lennon (April 8, 1963)

James Woods (April 18, 1947) Has an IQ of genius: 180. Married twice. Marriage to second wife lasted four months.

Ewan McGregor (March 31, 1971) Married since '95.

Dodi Al Fayed (April 15, 1955) With Princess Di when he died.

Heath Ledger (April 4, 1979)

David Letterman (April 12, 1947)

Conan O'Brien (April 18, 1963)

Kenny Chesney (March 26, 1968) Married Renée Zellweger after knowing her four months. The marriage lasted only a few months, and was annulled.

ARIES DIC*-TIONARY

GROUNDED <GRUND-ED> Having two feet on the ground and touching metal while dangerous, live wires flail around you, threatening to end your life.

Translation for potential girlfriend: As long as he's not the one being dumped, he's okay with turning *you* into a neurotic, psychotic, insecure, and desperate PSYCHO. He already suspected as much. Now it's simply confirmed. And he can't wait to tell his mother.

SUPER-SMART <SUP-ƏR-SMAHT> Knowing enough about everything to talk knowledgeably about it. Depending on *his assessment* of these things, making up the rules (until they're not recognizable anymore) and expecting those around him to abide by them.

Translation for potential girlfriend: He is never wrong. This can be a problem when *he actually is wrong*.

SENSITIVE <ZEN-SEE-TIV> Having one eye on his instant messenger on the computer, listens to everything you say. He won't *hear* it, but he will listen. *God, how she likes to blab,* he thinks. But he knows he's got to do it if he wants some. And his mother taught him that this is very important. And Mom's always right. (Even if she's also incredibly f*#ked up and irritating, surreptitiously, in his mind).

Translation for potential girlfriend: He will listen to your side of it *if he's into you*. Only because he knows he must. If not, he will call you a manipulative, sneaky, ignorant, whiny female who doesn't know how to listen. Then he'll end it without so much as a glance back . . . until he's interested in a one-night romp for old times' sake. (See "Advice For Ex Ms. Aries")

MORALISTIC <MOR-A-LITH-TIC> Championing a noble cause.

Translation for potential girlfriend: Anything that relates directly back to him. In other words, if he happens to be well off and a staunch Republican, he'll go around the issues and never admit that he's really in it for the tax break.

SELF-ASSURED <SELF-ASSUUUURED> Possessing such incredible narcissism that—if he stopped to consider himself for a moment (and was forced to truly look in the mirror—and not just to check his receding hairline)—would crumble into a heaping pile of crying, blubbery, pathetic mess.

Translation for potential girlfriend: Aries man is a born dictator. Don't believe me? One name: *Adolf* (April 20, 1889, Aries/Taurus cusp).

MAN <MAN> Homoerectus.

Translation for potential girlfriend: Closet metrosexual.

CHAPTER 2

Taurus, Ex or Next
(the Bull, April 20–May 20)

TAURUS RUDE-IMENTS

 Pity the woman who falls in love with Taurus guy before he falls in love with her. If this is you, take ten steps back. Hold the phone. Climb off the cloud. Alert the media. And stop defending him. Shht. You're still talking. Just listen.

Speaking from experience, I've never seen so many perfectly smart women get taken by a more unworthy cause.

> **After doing One Fine Day and playing a pediatrician on ER, I'll never have kids. I'm going to have a vasectomy.**
>
> **GEORGE CLOONEY**

Why? Because Taurus men, once they know they've got you, will milk it for all it's worth. They love adoration. Okay, yes—all men do (your mother told you so). But you need to know exactly how it's taken: not well.

It's slurped up greedily like the last drink of water in the desert. Drawn out like oil from an old crone's face. Bled dry like leeches on a fresh cadaver.

Oh, ew. Did I have to go there?

Yup. It's true: Taurus guy uses the ego boost you give to make him feel powerful enough to win the *other* object of his affections—namely, not you.

Unless you know how to work it.

Chil', this one actually gets off on playing with you the way we torture poor kitty with a string: Come, come here. (Evil laugh as we pull it away.)

And here's something else you didn't want to know: May 6 men are the ultimate brutal Taurus birthday. They're the most romantic—and the most cruel. It's the influence of the number 6 in numerology—they live for love. But they're not really psychologically equipped for it because they're so scared of suffering themselves. Hence, they wind up breaking hearts and tormenting women . . . until they find The One.

Powerhouses—larger than life. Yet horrors. Unless they're completely gone in love, they're gonna bat you around like the Mets in 1986: They'll win the World Series with you, then leave you sitting in the dugout till the end of time. (And it's such a heady ride, it will ruin you for boring, tedious future mates to come.)

Proof: George Clooney, Sigmund Freud, Orson Welles, Stewart Granger (swashbuckling actor from the forties and fifties), Rudolph Valentino: all May 6.

Taurus guys in general: Potent. Compelling. Brilliant. But dumb like the floor when it comes to communicating their true needs for happiness to their intendeds. (This isn't a coincidence, incidentally. It's how they maintain control—over you and over themselves.)

> I'd think, "In a relationship, we should never have this kind of fight." Then, instead of figuring out how to make it work, I looked for a way to get out of it. The truth is, you shouldn't be married if you're that kind of person.
>
> GEORGE CLOONEY

> We are ready to sacrifice our souls, our children, and our families so as not to give up Iraq.
>
> SADDAM HUSSEIN

So, first, let me tell you the good news: Taurus guy can be had. Even love-starved bad boys like May 6. You just have to figure out his raison d'être. His M.O. His game. For him, the game is Monopoly: He wants Park Place. He's not sure why. He just knows it's the best. And since he doesn't want to buy something on the Lower East Side—a real fixer-upper that'll need work—he'll go for the polished choice. He's not into rescuing. *He's* the damsel in distress.

One is very crazy when in love.

SIGMUND FREUD

He wants a prize. And if that's you, you'll get him.

TAURUS TONGUE LASHING

Ring, ring.

Taurus guy picks up his cell. "Yes, yes . . . I'll be there," he says. "Yes, please tell the queen of Spain I can attend."

Taurus smiles smugly at you and drops a casual "Oh, sorry. That was just (fill-in-the-blank important person)." You sense that he's playing it down: no biggie. Yet that he fixed it to have someone call him at precisely *this moment* in hopes of making a good impression. Sadly, you're not mistaken.

Sometimes a cigar is just a cigar.

SIGMUND FREUD

On the other hand, there's that other strain of Taurus. Y'know—the one who tells you things only when you ask. Or beg. Strangely, this one is low-maintenance. And a woman who's frivolous in any way will turn him off bigtime.

Wanna lose him and also get him to never shut up in one swift motion? Insult his masculinity. Ask him if he bats for the other team. Better yet, order for him in a restaurant. Pick the quiche. Get a sloe gin fizz (with a frilly cocktail umbrella in it) and leave him holding it as you sashay off to the bathroom. Ditto that with your purple suede fringy clutch purse during the Super Bowl—while his buds are standing by *watching*.

You only require two things in life: your sanity and your wife.

TONY BLAIR

"Come closer," he beckons. "I don't bite." But he does. He does. Biting is definitely an accepted form of foreplay for him. You slide closer and he whispers in your ear. Taurus guy knows that it's not really *what* he says but *how* he says it (i.e., with *his* lips against *your* skin).

Sexually, you're probably overwhelmed by this guy. But you're not completely sure if you respect him. Or—it's the opposite. You absolutely adore his semi-pedigreed soul, but the thought of kissing him excites you about as much as the thought of making out with his pet bulldog.

Sadly, it's usually either/or.

SO, if you're in the minority—and are *actually* in love with this guy . . . really in love, NOT obsessed because you just want to get him—or bed him (think about it), I've got good news. Follow my advice, read this chapter and then . . .

I have an unfortunate personality.

ORSON WELLES

Just know that one day very soon, you may just find out that this "composed," "proud," "sensual," "romantic," "curious," "financially secure" guy who keeps pictures of himself on the mantel does so only because he has no clue who he really is.

TAURUS: IS HE *INTO* YOU?

If you've done your job, you're now pleasantly enjoying the benefits of Taurus guy secretly adoring and worshipping the ground you walk on. He should be pulling out all the stops. If he's spending money on you, good. Well done. He can be incredibly generous—or as cheap as a polyester pin-striped suit from Sears *if he doesn't trust your motives.* He MUST trust you.

And to do this, you need to keep him guessing—yet show him that you're not going to bear his love child, then run away to Guatemala with his best man. That big love-crazy cocktail is scary for him. His fear is so tangible, it's like how Michael Jackson would feel, were he forced to take a *paternity test.*

And you should know this: If he doesn't respect your wishes to wait for sex, he's not into you. Ironically, though, you should respond subtly to his advances when he puts it out there. But not too much. Balance.

He may be offended if you push him away, but he'll be back. I promise.

In fact, just when you think he's pulling away, remember my words: Uh-uh. No way. If things are going as planned, he's off formulating another scheme to get you. And if you take *this* job away from him, I guarantee, he'll have no choice but to torture you instead. He needs a hobby. Give it to him.

Sadist. Masochist. It's up to you to decide which. It's all in there, wrapped up into one pretty, brooding Taurus package. Let him suffer or you will.

He's good at playing the cool guy until he falls. Oh, and you won't miss the signs when he does. But along the way, you may be confused. You'll wonder about his honorable (or dishonorable) intentions. You should.

> Now comes the part where I relieve you, the little people, of the burden of your failed and useless lives. But remember, as my plastic surgeon always said: If you gotta go, go with a smile.
>
> JACK NICHOLSON

> People who speak in metaphors should shampoo my crotch.
>
> JACK NICHOLSON

This guy will evaluate and categorize you—both judge and jury. But, it's easy to trick him into thinking you're perfect. *He's almost never on the mark.* In other words, many men are good at sizing up women; Taurus man is not.

So read on, woman. You can get him.

Pay attention.

> They say Elvis is dead. I say, no, you're looking at him. Elvis isn't dead; he just changed color.
>
> **DENNIS RODMAN**

ADVICE TO THE FUTURE MRS. TAURUS

Here's a story for you. I know a woman. I'll call her Sam. She had a boyfriend. And then there was Taurus guy—waiting in the wings for some crumbs.

Taurus guy was enamored with her, and she wasn't sure what she wanted. One night, she threw caution to the wind. And kissed him. From that moment on, he considered her *his.* A kiss by any other name would not taste as sweet, rationalized Taurus. When he's serious, he instantly marks his territory. Like a dog.

So when he found out that Sam was surreptitiously hovering between him and the other guy, he flew into a rage. Secretly. See—he didn't tell her. Instead, he opted for vengeance and plain ol' in-your-face jealousy.

> I think I was the best baseball player I ever saw.
>
> **WILLIE MAYS**

For instance, when they went out to a restaurant, and her best friend joined them, he waited till Sam went to the bathroom, then put the moves on her friend. In fact, he found out the best bud's phone number and started calling her, asking her out.

So after, when Sam confronted him, he admitted that he wasn't even interested in the friend. He just wanted to see if he could get a rise out of Sam—and get her back for what she'd "done to him." (This, after a casual work friendship, one smooch, and her indecision.) But hey, he was seriously smitten. And that's big stuff for Taurus.

So when Sam finally decided she *did* want him, he didn't trust her anymore. And didn't want her. She had committed the ultimate sin in his eyes: not being on the same page as him at the same time; not giving him the security he *needed,* at precisely the moment *he* knew *he* wanted it. Holy deliberate smokescreen, Batty guy.

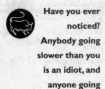

> Have you ever noticed? Anybody going slower than you is an idiot, and anyone going faster than you is a moron.
>
> GEORGE CARLIN

Bottom line: This is true whether you're just starting out with Taurus or preparing to walk down the aisle: This man has an extremely fragile ego. He gives all if he loves you. And he expects it back in return. *When he's ready.*

Under the bottom line: Confused or capricious women need not apply. You can get him, but heed my words if you want to keep him. (Gemini girl, be careful. Yes, I'm talking to you, toots.)

ADVICE TO THE EX MS. TAURUS

Bizarre thing. Most guys *cannot* be swayed by sex after a breakup. Instead, Taurus **can**. He *wants* to forgive. Poor, beleaguered, pigheaded Taurus has invested in you. And since he's done all that work already, he doesn't want to see it go to pot.

> I have as much authority as the pope, I just don't have as many people who believe it.
>
> GEORGE CARLIN

Here's how it's gotta go, though. Listen carefully. In order to seduce Taurus back into your life, it cannot be a wham bam. Ringing him at midnight for a booty call will only throw him back into the arms of . . . anyone but you.

But wait—you can't be too serious either. Tears are okay, but he's gotta know that you miss him on a *friendship* level. Pretend that you're his wife already. And that you married him twenty years ago. The honeymoon's over, baby. Here's your mantra: Calm, rational. Nice, steady.

Here's how it should go down. If he doesn't call you, wait three weeks. I know it's hard, but do this right. Call and ask, "How're you feeling?" No big deal. Keep it light. Businesslike, even. How's his sister? His mother? Some deal he's been working on at the office? He'll probably get fidgety after less than five minutes. He's worried that you're gonna start bringing up things he can't deal with.

> Success is the sole earthly judge of right and wrong.
>
> **ADOLF HITLER**

That's normal. If he says he wants to call you back, tell him, "No. No problem. Just wanted to see how you're doing. Bye." Hang up. (Don't say "Don't bother." It's too manipulative. He'll know you're playing a game, and trust me, he'll beat you at it.)

If he doesn't want to deal with you, leave him be. Just remember the "leeches on a fresh cadaver" analogy. Again: ew. He'll suck the self-respect right out of you.

Instead, if he stays on the phone, tell him you've been practicing cooking a new pasta recipe or hearty steak dish. If he's interested, you'll make it for him.

> Catch a man a fish, and you can sell it to him. Teach a man to fish, and you ruin a wonderful business opportunity.
>
> **KARL MARX**

Here's what NOT to say: anything related to sex; anything related to how you miss him *as a boyfriend—boo-hoo;* anything about what *you* need, like fixing something in your house or helping you make a decision on this or that. Do not use the phrases "hang out" or "it would be cool."

You have to be humble, sober, sincere. Grounded. Not needy or dramatic in any way. (That's *his* job.) Crisp like new sheets. Soft like cotton.

If this doesn't work, you can call him and give him a list of *his* faults. He's no great catch, either. But wait at least two or three weeks after you try the first approach.

All I know is I'm not a Marxist.

KARL MARX

Oh, and if he comes over, cook for him and wait for the connection. Bring up good times. Think sentimental, not sexual. Show him some photos of Granny and you—with pigtails. He'll most likely take the bait.

Last story: One Aquarius woman I know snagged a Taurus man big-time. But her method makes *The Bold and the Beautiful* look plausible. Surreal, this. She got pregnant after the first month they were together. She was thirty-three; he was thirty-two. He flipped and stopped trusting her; she told him she wanted to have the child.

Whoa. He was shocked. To add chaos to mayhem, he was Israeli, she was Apple Pie. His family expected him to marry someone of his heritage—and threatened to cut him off if he didn't comply.

At the age of six I wanted to be a cook. At seven I wanted to be Napoleon. And my ambition has been growing steadily ever since.

SALVADOR DALÍ

She was so cool and composed. To this day, all are stunned as to how she did it. Taurus guy felt manipulated and roped in—a humungo faux pas. But, throughout the pregnancy, she just gave him the subtle digs, let *him* call (mostly out of guilt), made him aware of what was going on, never asked for money (even though he was a well-to-do lawyer), and just knew he would return.

He did.

Sure, she freaked him out a few times. Placed a couple of psychologically f*cked-up phone calls, with lots of name calling. But she chalked it all up to hormones. Explained it as such. And didn't apologize too much for her behavior.

Last tip: this story says it all. Get Taurus man by going slowly through the back door. And not wanting or asking for too much. That's how *he'd* do it. And that's how you should, too.

I don't do drugs.
I am drugs.

SALVADOR DALí

SUN/VENUS COMBINATIONS: THE TRUE LOVE POTENTIAL TEST

Taurus Sun, Venus in Aries

If there hadn't been women, we'd still be squatting in a cave eating raw meat—because we made civilization in order to impress our girlfriends.

ORSON WELLES

This one has a presence so commanding, so intense, you have to look at him. He's like a total eclipse of the sun: You can stare at it, but (oh sh*t) . . . it's reeeally bad for you. Meanwhile, he has to be sure that you're his future. He's the Martha Stewart of love—so efficient, with a get-out-of-jail-free card to boot. (Are you listening, Martha? Don't you wish you knew that *before?*)

There are some days when I think I'm going to die from an overdose of satisfaction.

SALVADOR DALí

Yeah, it's true. He's got contacts up the wazoo. And he's not afraid to use them at precisely the right time. Precisely. Listen up, though. There has to be a ground-base reason for him to be with you. Security. Mutual interests. Shared taste . . .

A trust fund in your name.

Oh, all right. Damn it. I didn't mean to let the cat out of the bag. This one's just a little obsessed with money—like in an OCD way. Like checking his wallet every hour to make sure Lincoln didn't run off the five-dollar bills to go free the slaves or some-thing. Look, truth is, it's not all that bad—but he's gotta believe that you have a decent, steady-paying job, or backup money from another source—at least. If not, this guy will freak.

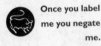

Once you label me you negate me.

SØREN
KIERKEGAARD

He has to know that you're in it *for him,* not for what he can give you. And he'll be able to read the truth of that . . . well, he *thinks* he can read the truth of it. He's an analyzer, this one. Thinks too much.

Bottom line: He doesn't want the responsibil-ity of obsessing over his financial tab and yours. That means, well, no staying home and raising the young ones. Leave 'em with the babysitter. She'll do a fine job. Even if she only speaks Swahili. Or Urdu. And learned her child-rearing tactics from Bertha, the stalwart women's criminal cor-rection center warden.

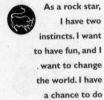

As a rock star, I have two instincts. I want to have fun, and I . want to change the world. I have a chance to do both.

BONO

Actually, when this guy's relaxed with his money situation, though—which he is almost never—he's extremely devoted, loving, and childlike sweet. That's why he needs to keep on top of things. He falls in love and it's all over. He sees things (meaning: you) through rose-colored glasses. But oh, what a pretty, shiny pink diamond you make.

BOYFRIEND POTENTIAL RATING: High if you feed him through his ego and don't stress his wallet. Extra high if he stays with you, 'cause he's not gonna unless he's really, truly in love. A done deal if you're a billionaire heiress. Anorexic. Or one of the Hilton sisters—both. And love him for *him.* But last tip: You *can have* this guy big-time if you really, *truly* know in your heart that money's not part of it. Then this guy will latch on to you and be incredibly generous—like a celebrity in third-world-country crisis-time.

One more thing: This guy's charm can con-
quer whole nations—think Saddam Hussein,
Tony Blair—or just the entire female population:
George Clooney.

I don't listen to
myself very
much.

JOE COCKER

CELEBRITY CORRESPONDENTS
WITH TAURUS SUN, VENUS IN ARIES

George Clooney (May 6, 1961) Is George scared of marriage?
Nahhh. It's the Aries-baby Venus. He wants what he wants
(Taurus is this way, too). He figures life doesn't get any better.

John Wilkes Booth (May 10, 1838)

Saddam Hussein (April 28, 1937)

Sigmund Freud (May 6, 1856) According to him, sex was the root
of everything.

Jack Nicholson (April 22, 1937) Legendary womanizer.

Zubin Mehta (April 29, 1936)

Isiah Thomas (April 30, 1961)

Tony Blair (May 6, 1953) Married since 1980.

Orson Welles (May 6, 1915) Married three times, once to Rita
Hayworth. Third marriage lasted.

Taj Mahal (May 17, 1942)

Dennis Rodman (May 13, 1961)

Jean-Paul Gaultier (April 24, 1952)

Ronald Reagan, Jr. (May 20, 1958)

Willie Mays (May 6, 1931)

George Carlin (May 12, 1937)

Taurus Sun, Venus in Taurus

There's something you need to know about Taurus sun, Venus in
Taurus: Besides Taurus, Venus in Aries, no other sign claims such

an extensive collection of persuasive men. It doesn't matter who they are—it's just frightening.

Sometimes they're morally PC, but most times, they don't see beyond their own totalitarian-dictatorship agendas. They want to control the masses with their political ideals, found in their songs, their paintings, their work—whatever. Just look at the influence these guys have over their peers. That's a good indicator. *You* must be the rational one. But beware of scary-guy factor.

> My first language was shy. It's only by having been thrust into the limelight that I have learned to cope with my shyness.
>
> AL PACINO

Deep down, this man can be controlling. When he's got the upper hand, though, you wouldn't even know it. He's like a Ziploc in the fridge: cool and contained. But that's not his true self. And you've got to put him off his guard to make him off his rocker. For you.

Here's the one thing you need to be careful of, though: Since he's so averse to talking things out, he's prone to sneaking around (with others, Mammy) so that he doesn't have to confront any problems. He goes out and does *bad things*. Risky, he is. Just sayin'.

It all comes down to character. Or lack of. This Taurus can be soulless. Definition: Without a soul. And this can be dangerous because he seems like such a fun, down-to-earth, charming guy. Perilous.

> Being number two sucks.
>
> ANDRE AGASSI

Bottom line: There's a tendency for this Taurus to go over the edge to Psychoville if he's had a rough past. He can be completely unethical. *Completely.*

He's like a volcano, ready to blow. And you don't want to be there for it. 'Cause Mount Etna doesn't erupt often—but it *does* erupt.

BOYFRIEND POTENTIAL RATING: Low if you let him master you—as he so deftly does others. Mezzo-high if you can stand your ground. Unbelievably high if he knows you're the only one he can trust—'cause he's made so many enemies in the past, he needs at least one person he can rely on.

CELEBRITY CORRESPONDENTS WITH TAURUS SUN, VENUS IN TAURUS (CHECK OUT THE POLITICAL SCARY GUYS)

Niccolò Machiavelli (May 3, 1469)

Adolf Hitler (April 20, 1889) Cusp, also sometimes considered Aries.

Karl Marx (May 5, 1818)

Oliver Cromwell (April 25, 1599)

Michael Moore (April 23, 1954)

Muhammad (April 3, 570)

Pope John Paul II (May 18, 1920)

Søren Kierkegaard (May 5, 1813)

Salvador Dalí (May 11, 1904)

Busta Rhymes (May 20, 1972)

Bono (May 10, 1960)

David Boreanaz (May 16, 1969)

Joe Cocker (May 20, 1944)

Billy Joel (May 9, 1949) On third marriage. She's thirty-one years younger than he is.

George Lucas (May 14, 1944)

Rande Gerber (April 27, 1962)

Taurus Sun, Venus in Gemini

This guy's heart is in the right place. He's a good guy, and the most fun of all Tauruses, with a quick wit. Self-mocking. To others, he seems exceedingly sociable. He can start up a conversation and keep it going (even if the other person isn't talking—talented, really). But what makes him happiest? An audience of one. He just wants to be in love—poor thing—and has a tough time making up his mind, committing.

I always respect a woman.

ENRIQUE IGLESIAS

Remember that board game Risk? Yeah, that's NOT what he's into.

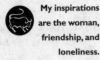

> I prefer love over sex.
>
> ENRIQUE IGLESIAS

Here's the big bummer: It's a precarious situation. He wants to know that when it's Game Over, aka marriage, you're going to be his Rock of Gibraltar. Faithful. Loyal. Ideal.

But wait—getting there must be a rocky *climb* or he'll discount you like a Chinese knockoff of an Italian designer label.

Again, he's clueless as to what he wants, exactly. So you have to show him.

For now, just keep in mind that all it takes is a little cruelty to get the ball rolling; that is, a boyfriend he can steal you from. A big, hairy challenge.

Jerry Seinfeld is the perfect example of Taurus, Venus in Gemini. Jerry, in real life, met a woman at the gym *two weeks after she was already married.* Wanted her. Courted her. (I couldn't make this stuff up if I tried.) When she finally left her husband and got together with him, rumors swirled that she wasn't the first married lady Jerry had gone after. But at least she wasn't sixteen, like Shoshanna. He MARRIED her. End of story.

> My inspirations are the woman, friendship, and loneliness.
>
> ENRIQUE IGLESIAS

Just make sure he knows that you're a possibility. Sorta. That you *may* be interested. Difficult, nearly impossible, but doable. "Fate." Russian roulette with four bullets instead of one. Play your ace. Then show him the deuce. Luxuriate here. Obviously, when he gets you, it's necessary: Pull away. Game, but Jeopardy-justified. He's a romantic—but confused. He has to win *you.* And he's got to work for it.

BOYFRIEND POTENTIAL RATING: High if he's extremely solvent and you still agree to sign the pre-nup. (It's really not about money, it's all about "trust"; (that is, his lack of it.) Also very high if you're Judge

Judy and can give it to him straight. Cinched if you play him as big and dramatic as Angelina Jolie's lips rock the free world. And also as promising. Low if these analogies are registering just about as much as scandals dealing with the British Royal Family being offered coffee at high tea.

> A man should control his life. Mine is controlling me.
>
> RUDOLPH VALENTINO

CELEBRITY CORRESPONDENTS
WITH TAURUS SUN, VENUS IN GEMINI

Al Pacino (April 25, 1940)

William Shakespeare (April 26, 1564)

Andre Agassi (April 29, 1970) Want an example of a great couple? Here 'tis. Andre is Taurus, Venus in Gemini. Steffi Graf is Gemini, Venus in Taurus. When your Venus matches his love sign and vice versa, it's a SOULMATE connection.

Luther Vandross (April 20, 1951)

Bing Crosby (May 3, 1903)

Oskar Schindler (April 28, 1908)

Malcolm X (May 19, 1925)

David Beckham (May 2, 1975) Married to Victoria Beckham, ex-Posh Spice.

Enrique Iglesias (May 8, 1975)

Charlie O'Connell, aka the Bachelor, 2005 (April 21, 1975)

Jason Biggs (May 12, 1978)

Hank Azaria (April 25, 1964)

Tony Danza (April 21, 1951)

Jerry Seinfeld (April 29, 1954)

Rudolph Valentino (May 6, 1895)

Emilio Estevez (May 12, 1962)

Taurus Sun, Venus in Cancer

He wants a stable home life, yet his business ambitions keep him away a lot. Use this. Work it. Make him feel guilty. But threaten to have a life of your own. He'll be Silly Putty in your hands—without the newspaper imprint stuck to it.

He wants to possess you.

One thing you should be careful of, though: it seems like this guy cares more about what his "public" thinks of him than about what you think. Not true. He simply *expects* you to be his grounding force, his spiritual guru, his unfailing supporter. That's your duty. To him, it's your *job*.

More High Expectations: Eventually, he'll have you cook all his favorite meals, host his social gatherings with the higher-ups, be his siren—without being too sexy (so as to be mistaken for anything but a good girl). And never EVER contradict him in public. It's all about treading a fine line between exciting and stable. Sexy and saintly. Domestic and haggardly.

This Taurus is a pretty confused puppy. If he gets it into his head that he wants something, he'll cling to it desperately. It's pretty pathetic, y'know, having to pump, pump up his ego like that air mattress from the infomercial you watched at four in the morning in an insomniacal haze. As with the mattress, you keep putting in the juice, it just keeps leaking out.

But I guess that can be okay, too. See, he needs you. And if you play the stable force in his life and get him, he'll cling to you like that nerdy girl in ninth-

> You can have either the Resurrection or you can have Liberace. But you can't have both.
>
> **LIBERACE**

> This is a busy time for President Clinton. Not only does he have that thing in Kosovo, it's also prom season.
>
> **JAY LENO**

grade algebra. Not a bad deal, either, because you won't have to do everything he asks, like, um, make sure your locker is next to his.

He'll still come after you like Freddie or Jason. Sequels 1–45.

BOYFRIEND POTENTIAL RATING: Very low if you don't revel in his flair for the stylish and utterly "moral." And aren't just a little into he-worship and joined-at-the-hip kinda love. Extra high, period. Many of these guys are in it for the long haul (especially if you've read the above and have ingested it like a gluttonous dog hoovers the ground at a 10th Street food fair).

> Today is Valentine's Day—or, as men like to call it, Extortion Day.
>
> JAY LENO

CELEBRITY CORRESPONDENTS WITH
TAURUS SUN, VENUS IN CANCER

Harry S. Truman (May 8, 1884) The only U.S. president to use the atomic bomb (Hiroshima). Married his childhood sweetheart and remained with her till his death.

Jimmy Stewart (May 20, 1908) Married for forty-five years to the same woman, until her death.

Socrates (May 14, 466 B.C.)

Christian Lacroix (May 17, 1951)

Sugar Ray Leonard (May 17, 1956)

Ricky Nelson (May 8, 1940)

Steve Winwood (May 12, 1948) On second marriage since 1987.

Liberace (May 16, 1919)

Valentino Garavani (May 11, 1932)

Bronson Pinchot (May 20, 1959)

Ayatollah Khomeini (May 17, 1900)

Taurus Sun, Venus in Pisces

He's an analyzer, this one. He'll test you like a new mommy, for the first time, with that freshly warmed baby bottle. He's critical. Philosophical. Quixotic. Impractical—yet with a good business sense. Creative, but has it in his mind that he's gonna make dollars from it if it kills him. Indulge him.

Today, one year after their divorce, Pamela and Tommy Lee announced they're getting back together. You know what that means? There's still hope for Ike and Tina Turner.

JAY LENO

Problem is, he'll only stick to what he's good at. (P.S., though, he won't be successful at it until he's told a million times that he's amazing.)

Speaking of bottles and infants, you may discover that this Taurus guy is only one step above the other baby: Aries, Venus in Aries. He's not as fickle, not as much of a closeted metrosexual, but he's definitely as ridiculously immature. Oh, but he hides it well. Just wait. It's coming.

See, the problem just rears its ugly head differently. Fact is, at least Aries/Aries knows what he wants. And makes no secret of it. (Even if he changes what that is every five minutes.) You might notice it right away. Unfortunately, with *this* Taurus, it's not blatant.

Bottom line, here: He needs to know that you fit into his plan.

One thing my wife says is bad about me, is that I still care too much.

AARON SPELLING

Concurrent with his emotional needs. He's convinced that no one does it better than he does. Like 007. Bond. Shaken, not stirred. And he'll rate you based on *his* assessment of how you *handle* things—everything from nights out at the theater and sports events to, ah, his joystick.

Just make sure that you don't let him know you're dying for him. He's gotta know he's snagged crème de la crème. Top hat. "It."

Things have to be slow and steady for this guy: like grandma's stew. He needs time to decide. Push—and it's over. Think of him like chocolate soufflé: take it out of the oven too soon and it falls into a big, gooey mess.

BOYFRIEND POTENTIAL RATING: High if you realize that his dream is to be Brawny, the macho quicker picker-upper. He wants to be the dominant one. (Tough, this, because he's so unsure of his prowess out of the client's den. Work stuff.) Low if you're too aggressive with him. Quiet simmer: passion, tempered with restraint. For example, if you don't give him control in the bedroom, you'll leave him as cold as Madame Tussaud's finest. (Dibs on him, by the way, if you can't hack it.)

> I have lived in a flurry of images, but I will go out in a freeze-frame.
>
> **ANTHONY QUINN**

    Kidding.

CELEBRITY CORRESPONDENTS
WITH TAURUS SUN, VENUS IN PISCES

Jay Leno (April 28, 1950) Married to the same woman—women's rights activist Mavis—for decades. They have no children.

Aaron Spelling (April 22, 1923) Was married to Carolyn Jones (Morticia Addams) before he married Candy and had Tori.

Keith Haring (May 4, 1958)

James Brown (May 3, 1933) Allegedly beat wife.

Peter Frampton (April 22, 1950)

Iggy Pop (April 21, 1947)

Frankie Valli (May 3, 1934)

Lee Majors (April 23, 1939) Married to Farrah Fawcett before he married a *Playboy* Playmate. Here's gossip for you: He was so jealous and protective of Farrah that once, when he went out of town, he asked his best friend to watch her. Know who that best friend was? Ryan O'Neal (also a Taurus. She's an Aquarius).

Ryan and Farrah had an affair and stayed together for seventeen years. They never married.

Ulysses S. Grant (April 27, 1822)

Anthony Quinn (April 21, 1915) Quinn conceived all of his children while married to *other women*. First two children were with an Italian costume designer, so he divorced his wife and married *her*. They were together for thirty-one years—until he fathered another with his secretary, Kathy Benvin. Oh. Then he married *her*.

TAURUS DIC*-TIONARY

COMPOSED <COM-POZED> Together. Grounded. Socks matching. Shirt not turned inside out.

Translation for potential girlfriend: Inside, his mind is as tortured as a performance artist's canvas.

PROUD <PROWD> Um. Narcissist.

Translation for potential girlfriend: His vanity can be like the worst cheap cologne: It costs him almost nothing, but you smell it before he even enters a room.

SENSUAL <SEN-SHOO-ALL> He can be great in bed.

Translation for potential girlfriend: But it all comes back to ego. Sadly, his masculinity is tied into it. Just make sure you have an orgasm every time, or he'll go out and find someone who fakes it better than you do.

TRADITIONAL <TRAH-DISH-AH-NAHL> This one's got a good-girl complex. He's ridiculously old-fashioned. Don't be surprised if you find him sitting out on the porch with your folks, talking about "kids these days."

Translation for potential girlfriend: The three-date sex rule does *not* apply here. Wait ten. Or twenty. Or a hundred. Wait a year. Go to bed with

---

him in your next life. This guy, when he's in love, will wait for a nun. If you sleep with him too fast, though, he'll run like a turkey the day before Thanksgiving.

CURIOUS <KYOUR-EE-US> He'll ask you questions about your past and pretend everything you say is fine, even though it's not.

Translation for potential girlfriend: Be careful. In actuality, he's just handing you the noose and letting you hang yourself with it.

FINANCIALLY SECURE <FY-NAN-SHUH-LEE SEE-CURE> So obsessed with money that he's been counting coins instead of sheep since he was a toddler.

Translation for potential girlfriend: Tell him you're even a little in debt and he'll make off like a new bride's dress after the wedding.

CHAPTER 3

Gemini, Ex or Next

(the Twins, May 21–June 20)

GEMINI RUDE-IMENTS

 Da-da-da dah dah dah dah! (I'm singing. Plug your ears if you like.)

PRESENTING . . . *The Dating Game.*

Bachelor number one hails from Dysfunctional, North Dakota. He's kind, generous, curious, clever, and funny. Yet he's also paranoid, neurotic, and hides his insecurities under his Members Only jacket. (Y'know the one. It's got a fake Armani label sewn into it.)

 You know that look women get when they want sex? Me neither.

DREW CAREY

Bachelor number two is from Codependent, Utah. He claims his worst fear is being lonely. Yet he goes through periods when he's a workaholic, then comes out of his shell and socializes like a man on fire. (He also tells our female producers that his bed is about to collapse from all the notches on it. *Nice move.*)

Bachelor number three is from Megalomania, Massachusetts. He cares deeply about others . . . until he gets so wrapped up in himself that—wait. He's backstage and can't tear himself away from the full-length three-way mirrors.

Right. Fooled you. Bachelors number one, two, and three are all Gemini guy. He's a big mishmash of many products (of his creation). He wears all kinds of chapeaus. He's dashing, sympathetic, witty. Sometimes dangerous to damsels in distress . . .

Do not fear mistakes. There are none.

MILES DAVIS

He saves women by tossing his coat over a puddle. Then tramples them as he runs headlong *toward the nearest reflective surface*.

Accidentally pushing them into the mud in the process.

Looky here. Gemini man never means to hurt anybody, and can be incredibly devoted to helping the world and spurring on political change. But unless your plight is directly tied into his current love direction, he can be as faithful and as caring as Hugh Grant in a parked car.

Sorry, pumpkin.

Well, the good-guy-with-a-bad-boy-edge thing works for him. He apologizes and moves on. Carries the charming-cad card. We can't help but forgive 'im.

Men are what their mothers made them.

RALPH WALDO EMERSON

Actually, Gemini guy likes to *think* he's a rock star. He imagines it. Pretends he's one. Big, bad, and famous, requesting fifty gallons of Evian in his dressing room so that he can shower with it. And twenty-nine bendy straws to drink it with—twenty-nine, mind you. Not twenty-eight. Pay attention.

Although . . . then he knows (as all famous rock stars do—because they're almost *too* famous), he'll just whip out those dark hipster sunglasses, tell the paparazzi "No pictures, no pictures,

PUH-LEEASE!" and become a recluse, appearing in public only
when his publicist makes him—or when he hears thunderous ap-
plause he just can't resist—like the kind necessary
for Tinker Bell not to die. "I believe in fairies! I
believe in fairies! (And you're the neatest and the
bestest!)

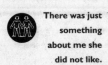

There was just
something
about me she
did not like.

ANDY
GRIFFITH

Right. Gemini guy is . . . you guessed it: Peter
Pan. Green getup and all (it's under his clothes).
It's absolutely true. Besides the fact that we sus-
pect he has his personal plastic surgeon on call, locked away in his
basement (he always looks about ten years younger than the rest of
us), he is a child. And despite your best intentions, he ain't never,
ever gonna leave Neverland and grow up. At least not willingly.

Waah.

Double-edged sword, though: children are cute. Especially
when you can hand them back to mommy when they're bad. (Unfortunately, you can't. She wants him off and married. Tough tit-
ties.)

He's also rash, irrational, hasty, fidgety, wants what he can't
have, impatient, indulgent . . . Go on? But, like every adorable tot,
he gets away with it most of the time—and gets his
way almost all of the time. If he doesn't, and if he's
not especially mature, brace yourself for a fist-
waving, macaroni-throwing temper tantrum worthy of the rottenest three-year-old.

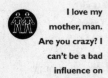

I love my
mother, man.
Are you crazy? I
can't be a bad
influence on
anybody!

MARK
WAHLBERG

Memo to potential mate: He's also incredibly
persuasive, enchanting with arresting allure, a
natural-born comedian, inquisitive, interesting, a
wild card, bright, innovative . . . and the list goes
on. Yet he wreaks havoc on poor, unsuspecting young maidens
who don't wish to have their hearts crushed like a can of beer at
halftime.

Seesaw action. (I hope you're weighing it out now. Up. Down. Want him. Don't.)

You've heard that Gemini, sign of the twins, has two sides? Not true. He has at least 147—at last count. He's closed and private, yet extroverted and Grimm-like storyteller fascinating. He embellishes and exaggerates—yet may never truly let you in on what he's really thinking. May not know it himself. He says one thing, means another. Changes his mind every four seconds. Ten, on a good day. He demands loyalty and fidelity—yet has trouble putting his money where his mouth is. Like Peter Pan, he'd like to live forever and make his mark. But he starts things all the time and never finishes them.

> I never lie. I believe everything I say, so it's not a lie.
>
> **MARK WAHLBERG**

Gemini guy will be only as mature as he's forced (himself) to be. If he's got a high-ranking job, he'll be responsible. And if he loves what he does, he'll excel like no other. However, if he's just been fired from his job, he'll sit around moaning in his jockey shorts, watching Oprah reruns and Christie Brinkley infomercials (*Hey, she's still hot!* he'll cry).

> Men are liars. We'll lie about lying if we have to. I'm an algebra liar. I figure two good lies make a positive.
>
> **TIM ALLEN**

If he's done some introspection and quotes Dr. Phil off the cuff, you may just have it made. Plus, if he admits to his feelings, and actually expresses them out loud, well—that'd be good. (Gemini guy only believes he's in love when he hears it from his own mouth.) But be warned. They never told you, when you were a kid, what actually happened to Peter Pan. He came back to the present to live out his life. One day he got old, his fantasies of Neverneverland were trampled, dreams were shot. He discovered he was a mere mortal.

And he didn't like it one bit.

GEMINI TONGUE LASHING

Let's play a game (Gemini's favorite sport, besides tongue lashing).

Make Gemini guy a puppet. You be the ventriloquist. He's, ah, the dummy.

Sit him on your lap and crank up the soundtrack to the Broadway hit show *Chicago*. Song: "Razzle Dazzle." (The gist of the ditty is: give 'em a good show and they'll never catch on to the truth. That's Gemini's M.O.)

Get the picture? Good.

> Women are like cars: We all want a Ferrari. Sometimes want a pickup truck . . . and end up with a station wagon.
>
> **TIM ALLEN**

Back to it. Gemini guy will pull your pigtails to show you he likes you. He's the original "I'm not jealous" (when he is) and "I'm not interested" (when he is). Though he's as spontaneous and impetuous as a sloshed college freshman girl at a fraternity party, he's also capable of rationalizing you away if he doesn't think you'll fit into his Playboy Bunny agenda-book.

And once he's got you, all bets may be off.

"I know you want me," Gemini coos. (But he secretly wonders whether you truly do.) The way to hang on to a Gemini is to keep him hungry and off balance—more than he keeps you, ditto. Be a Slinky. The toy. He grabs you and your coils drop down and bounce. Slip and slide and spring and walk downstairs and make a clinkety sound. A spring, a spring, a marvelous thing.

> Women now have choices. They can be married, not married, have a job, not have a job, be married with children, unmarried with children. Men have the same choice we've always had: work, or prison.
>
> **TIM ALLEN**

Be the bomb, then throw a few grenades, too.

Gemini man loves the chase maybe even more than he loves the actual getting. It all comes back to ego. He's *so* sensitive and defensive. That's why he freaks when you don't want him. But give him this: When he's truly jumped over the edge, he's romantic, loving, and even faithful. Most of the time.

Just remember that most of the time is not all of the time—and that this "magnetic," "sexual," "generous," "charming" "stud" was a child once—and might just still be.

GEMINI: IS HE *INTO* YOU?

Can you say *ladies' man,* kids? Lay-diss man. Gooood. He's incredibly insecure, deep down where he stuffs a sock in his pants.

Gemini guy will go to great lengths to not show you his cushy side. He's developed that hard, crusty pink-eye shell that takes the form of joke-telling and self-mocking so that you never suspect that, when he's in love, he's as unsure as a scrawny prepubescent with a fourteen-pound bowling ball (his aim is good, but it's a little too much for him to handle).

So do yourself a favor: praise him and his great moves. Well, yeah—he *is* good, so it shouldn't be hard. (Get your mind out of the gutter.) Then just walk away and let him follow. Trouble is, with all that air and superficiality, he gives capriciousness a new name. Namely: <insert his name here>. Just keep it light. That's what he's looking for. He has to be the one to get serious first. Oh—but don't trust everything he says. Keep your options open. Consider his actions, not his words. Gemini talks a good game but fails to play by the rules (and changes them all the time to fit *his* needs).

Keep him at arm's length. Make him work for it. Again, tell him how wonderful he is, then hang a "Gone Fishing" sign on your door, even though he knows you detest the smell of earthworms and live bait.

> You might say I'm a philosophic nut, or a nutty philosopher. It doesn't matter. Words don't mean anything. If you dig into anybody's character, you can find eccentricities you can characterize as nutty.
>
> JACK KEVORKIAN

Puzzle him. Draw him in. Then push him away. Ask him lots o' questions. He loves to hear himself expound and wax poetic.

Also, watch him like a hawk—but don't let him know you're doing it. Out of all the signs, Gemini is the most likely to run if he thinks you're trying to box him in. In fact, you'll have to be able to take him or leave him when it gets down to it. If he thinks you're bluffing, you'll lose your bargaining chip. And he'll win the pot.

> I'm always open for people saying I'm wrong because most of the time I am.
>
> PRINCE WILLIAM

This guy will stay and be faithful to you as long as he believes you're the Bonnie to his Clyde, the yin to his yang, the Siegfried to his Roy. If not, you're just a bump on his long and winding road.

ADVICE TO THE FUTURE MRS. GEMINI

I know a woman. I'll call her Jules. Jules was dating Mr. Gemini. He was actually a rare breed of Gemini—a little reserved. Modest. A bit of a workaholic. His spatial relations were off (meaning he needed space, almost all of the time). Granted, he was bright, mentally agile, hysterically funny but with a somber edge. He wasn't a showoff like many Geminis, and his sense of humor was ironic, not in-your-face. But he was indecisive in love: the typical Gemini virus strain.

> I just think the funny response would be that I think there needs to be a Bride of Freddy. I think Freddy needs a woman in his life.
>
> ROBERT ENGLUND

So, Jules was getting tired of seeing him only twice a week. He had control of the relationship. But she also knew that he was completely in love with her (with Geminis, you just know it—they can't fake it for long). So, she got smart. After two years of winging it, she conceived a plan. And carried it out with the cold precision of General Patton. No hesitation.

She left him. Told him she loved him but that she had someone else waiting in the wings (true) who loved her and wanted to get married. Gemini man said okay (they always do, out of pride) and let her go.

In the end, the love you take is equal to the love you make.

PAUL
MCCARTNEY

She was clever. Kept in touch. *But she never let on to Gemini guy that she missed him or regretted leaving him.* Eventually, Gemini guy brought in a close friend to intervene. Since he felt he couldn't really put his heart on the line alone (r-i-i-i-ght), he set up a meeting with Jules and the friend, and they negotiated the terms of the relationship, all three, as if it were a house deed. It worked.

Bottom line: If he's older, in his late thirties or forties, he's probably already set in his independent ways. This will take the form of a spoiled child who wants to eat ten candy apples, then go ride the negative G-force gargantuan upside-down roller coaster. (You know it's gonna make him throw up, but you have to let him do it anyway.)

Am I a romantic? I've seen *Wuthering Heights* ten times. I'm a romantic.

JOHNNY DEPP

Under the bottom line: Gemini guy will never move to the next step unless he's forced to—and believes you'll actually leave him when you threaten to. If he doesn't respond, just do it. He'll also stay in a relationship that's over far too long if the sex is good. Save yourself; get a life raft, row to shore. He may just follow—and if he doesn't, at least you're safe on dry land.

ADVICE TO THE EX MS. GEMINI

Gemini guy has got to be the one to get you back. If you call him, chase him, or go after him, he'll think *I'm too sexy for Milan. Too sexy for Milan. New York. And Japan.*

Here's the baby lotion rub: Gemini guy *does* realize he's made a mistake after he's broken it off with you. But you have to be a disappearing act. Houdini.

If he hears from friends that you're dating someone else, so much the better. Don't worry. If he cares (and if he doesn't, to hell with him—he's worth nil), he'll call. He'll find you. But let him make the move. In fact . . . don't pick up the phone the first few times he calls. If he's a little desperate, he'll confess his undying love when he finally gets you on the horn. That's worth the pain and suffering of singing "Lah, lah, lah, not listening" to drown out his pleas on your answering machine.

> Your intellect may be confused, but your emotions will never lie to you.
>
> ROGER EBERT

Expensive French Manicure Tip: Please, please don't show him that you've been waiting by the phone like a computer geek for that new, ultra-techy groove software you just ordered. He'll change his mind that he wants you faster than a playah changes his sheets.

Here's the catch. Gemini guy has trouble focusing on the task at hand. There's a one-month limit to his love when you break up. Two months, tops. After that, he's probably not coming after you. In fact, you may not hear from him or see him again—until someone has crushed his heart three years later and he comes around looking for an ego boost.

> I love knowing that I'm not better than any other person on the planet.
>
> THOMAS HAYDEN CHURCH

Truth is, Gemini can only see as far as his own situation. If you're wrapped up in that, and he believes your destiny intertwines with his, he'll do anything to have you. If not, you're just a shot of tequila: He'll take it, make a face, suck the lime, and smile at the hot bartending actress-model-singer-songwriter as he moseys on

out through the swinging doors (that hit you right in the face as you follow behind him).

Truly, if there's any sign in the zodiac who can move on and never turn back, it's Gemini. He has no problem turning the Love Boat around faster than Captain Steubing on speed. And he's not looking behind, he's looking in front of him . . . for another pretty, new port to explore.

> I can do anything. In GQ, I appeared as a man.
>
> BOY GEORGE

SUN/VENUS COMBINATIONS: THE TRUE LOVE POTENTIAL TEST

Gemini Sun, Venus in Aries

Humble, modest, a true innovative thinker—with a genius-like mind. Most likely a guy's guy, but despises that reference because he actually *is* sensitive to women's needs. Could be a professional if they offered money for it.

> Family is not an important thing, it's everything.
>
> MICHAEL J. FOX

Yet he doesn't want to be categorized. He wants to leave an imprint on the world: subtly. You wouldn't expect it. He uses calm force—has people (or heads of state) convince you *for* him.

He also has a dead-on sense of what gets to you, with humor, tact (odd, for Gemini), and a genuine curiosity about what makes you tick. He'll rephrase questions several hundred times to get the answer he's looking for. Then he'll utilize it in spades. (If your intuition is a little keen, you'll begin to feel the push-pull power play.)

What makes no sense is that this Gemini has Venus in fire: Aries. You'd expect him to be a ball-buster. Instead, his humility surprises you. He doesn't claim to be anything he's not. At first glance.

He's crafty. (He gets around. Yeah, Beastie Boys—what's it to ya?) This guy is principled, in a weird way. Has morals, structured to his cause *even if they're wrong by any other standards*. Weighs his actions—sometimes too much. He might even back away from you to save you the grief. Thanks, buddy. Yeah. He knows how powerful he is—even if you don't get it . . . yet.

> I am careful not to confuse excellence with perfection. Excellence, I can reach for; perfection is God's business.
>
> MICHAEL J. FOX

He believes in "the truth." But twists it around like a debutante's thong in the backseat of her boyfriend's car.

Real patience, *for him,* is actually another word for indecision. It's not truly patience. Potato. Potahto. Or Dan Quayle's spelling. Whatever. He can call it anything he wants—make it like a spiritual "let's wait and see, kitten" Dalai Lama tact, but it all boils down to an excuse. He wants his space to think as he pleases, do as he pleases, when he pleases.

> I'm going to marry a Jewish woman because I like the idea of getting up Sunday morning and going to the deli.
>
> MICHAEL J. FOX

Again, ironically, he's a romantic. But when *he wants to be.* On *his* terms. He also has a strange relationship with money. He likes material things, but hates to admit it. Wants the best, but detests flaunting it. He's cool and copasetic—but has fire simmering below the surface. So intense—like a tsunami: you don't see it from a distance, or even when it's close, but it hits you with full force when it's already upon you.

BOYFRIEND POTENTIAL RATING: High if he's analyzed himself—and marries ten years later than he thinks he should. His early for-

ties can work. Low if he suits up too early—he'll lose by pure bad fencing tactics. He'll let his opponent strike him down, then scream do-over. (He'll claim he wasn't ready.)

CELEBRITY CORRESPONDENTS
WITH GEMINI SUN, VENUS IN ARIES

Pat Boone (June 1, 1934)

Miles Davis (May 25, 1926) Married three times.

Muammar Al-Qaddafi (June 1, 1942)

Ralph Waldo Emerson (May 25, 1803)

Andy Griffith (June 1, 1926) Married three times; twenty-three years, first one; second one, eight years; third, since 1983.

Drew Carey (May 23, 1958) Never married. A word about Drew. Venus in Aries is always a little wary of commitment (example, George Clooney—Taurus, Venus in Aries). But when they have bad things happen to them in childhood, this flat-out doubles. Drew made several suicide attempts and suffered bouts of depression . . .

Gemini Sun, Venus in Taurus

If this guy can attain his good-guy status the nice-guy way, he'll do it. If not, he's as risky as a ten-year-old condom.

Actually, he's not afraid to go to the ultra-weird dark side route . . . if he can't get attention by any other means. He MUST be large—and incredibly respected by his peers (oh, and by you). *Even if it's for his antisocial or nonconformist ways. Yeah, it can go that way, too.*

To you—in love—he can be as hazardous as smoking: you might like it, be addicted to it even, but it'll kill you in the long run if you do it too much.

> I am being frank about myself in this book. I tell of my first mistake on page 850.
>
> HENRY A. KISSINGER

When popularity comes easily to him, he can be saint-like. Sweet. But when he's not heard . . . he can be as creepy as a dust-infested attic.

If I had to live my life over again, I would have a different father, a different wife, and a different religion.

JOHN F. KENNEDY

Be forewarned. He'll air your dirty laundry to friends, and justify himself because the "right" detergent wasn't used; i.e., *you* messed up. (Shoulda used Wisk.) It's your fault, never his. Sob. (*Now, where's my mistress??* He'd like to know.)

Look, if this guy learns how to be out-there interesting (or, um, strange) to others, he may just be capable of being really good to you. Especially when he's older and can't get anyone else.

Take that back. On the upside, he also has a true, amorous heart, and will want love and idealistic, supersonic devotion. If he doesn't go Batman-psycho, and vow to avenge all who have wronged him, he could just . . . ah, be a good potential Robin dependable-guy future for you.

As long as his "public" is satisfied, you may just have a chance.

BOYFRIEND POTENTIAL RATING: This all depends on him. High if he's made it in life, and has truly figured out what he wants. And

Chaos is a friend of mine.

BOB DYLAN

that's you. Low if he's been scarred by parents who didn't give him the time of day—and has unlocked the safe where he keeps his Barbie doll (i.e., his ideal woman—he can take her out to play when he wants, put her back: she never complains). P.S. He hates gossip, but likes being well known (revered) . . . Under the radar. When he's pursued, he huffs, indignantly, like a just-got-her-nose-done newly-turned-hot cheerleader. How *dare* they snap my profile? (That's not my good side.)

CELEBRITY CORRESPONDENTS
WITH GEMINI SUN, VENUS IN TAURUS

Robert Englund, a.k.a. Freddy Krueger (June 6, 1947)

Paul McCartney (June 18, 1942)

Johnny Depp (June 9, 1963) Kate Moss and Vanessa Paradis are both Capricorns.

Prince (June 7, 1958)

Rudolph Giuliani (May 28, 1944) Married three times; nasty divorce.

John Hinckley, Jr., a.k.a. attempted assassin of ex-President Reagan (May 29, 1955)

Roger Ebert (June 18, 1942)

John D. Rockefeller IV (June 18, 1937)

Kurt Browning (June 18, 1966)

Mark Wahlberg (June 5, 1971)

Jeffrey Dahmer (May 21, 1960) Serial killer and cannibal.

Jason Patric (June 17, 1966)

Tim Allen (June 13, 1953) Was married nineteen years. Divorced.

Jack Kevorkian (May 26, 1928) Nickname, "Dr. Death."

Mister T. (May 21, 1952) Married and divorced once.

Mike Myers (May 25, 1963)

John Wayne (May 26, 1907) Married three times; seven children.

Frank Lloyd Wright (June 8, 1867)

Griffin Dunne (June 8, 1955)

Louis Gossett, Jr. (May 27, 1936)

Douglas Fairbanks, Sr. (May 23, 1883)

Jackie Mason (June 9, 1931)

Cy Coleman (June 14, 1929)

Noah Wyle (June 4, 1971)

Thomas Haden Church (June 17, 1961)

John Edwards (June 10, 1953)

Al Unser (May 29, 1939)

Michael J. Fox (June 9, 1961) Happily married since 1988 to
Tracy Pollan (TV girlfriend from *Family Ties*); four children.

Boy George (June 14, 1961)

Henry Kissinger (May 27, 1923)

Cole Porter (June 9, 1891) Suffered many tragedies; married to
the same woman for thirty-five years.

Gemini Sun, Venus in Gemini

This guy sooo gets away with being a playboy. And it's not fair.
'Cause he's so good at doing it, that it's annoying when he's handsome . . . And more annoying when he's not. Deep down, it pisses
you off. You think—why bother with the okay-looking guy?
Every other girl is on the same page. And the ugly guy is just as

> All of the
> women on *The
> Apprentice*
> flirted with
> me—
> consciously or
> unconsciously.
> That's to be
> expected.
>
> DONALD
> TRUMP

BYOB: Bring Your Own Bastard. So if you've
picked this guy, he might as well be a hottie. The
ugly one's equally as Bad, Michael Jackson–like.
Yeah. Scary.

It's the nerd clause. This guy can be so like-
able, that when he gets to the age (thirties, forties,
and so on) when girls are ready (a.k.a., ah: desperate) to get hitched, he can get any damn Tori, Dana,
or Harriet he wants.

That's it. This guy has "it." He may be tactless
with you, and have difficulty looking inward to
see his own faults, yet he appears so altruistic and for-real when
he's smitten that it's nearly impossible to resist his Elvis pelvis-
roll/lip-curl.

Adaptable—he fits into any circumstance, with anyone. He can
make friends with a bum on the street, then rub shoulders with the
Secretary of Defense. (Maybe that's where he picked up all his
paranoid relationship-war tactics.)

It's hard not to respect him. But you become a sucker when he disparages himself . . .'cause he's waiting for you to say, "No, no. You're perfect." (It's so annoying. Like wall-to-wall traffic and the guy behind you who's got his hand glued to the horn when you've nowhere to go.)

He'll stay with you only when you don't agree that he's a loser when he looks for ego-elevating. The best way to deal with this is to mock him. "Yes, you do make me want to regurgitate my breakfast. But I'm like a kid in a candy store. I keep coming back for more even *with* my tummy ache." Now give him a big, toothy, silly-like grin. He'll believe you're kidding even if you're half *not*.

> Money was never a big motivation for me, except as a way to keep score. The real excitement is playing the game.
>
> DONALD TRUMP

Private, quiet, lively, sociable, temperamental, naïve—yet worldly. Sensuous. Removed, where love is concerned (if it comes too easily). Attractive to all, though, all the same.

Damn.

He can reel you in with his presence, the only bait.

A tough cookie. A rampant livewire. A self-centered, yet self-sacrificing enigma. He's most likely had a difficult childhood, but chalks it all up to hard luck. He's big on causes, but causes sadness to you. (Don't let him.)

When he settles down, it can be for good. If he doesn't get wriggly in his chair like a second-grader the last day of school, he may just be okay.

> Sex is as important as eating or drinking and we ought to allow the one appetite to be satisfied with as little restraint or false modesty as the other.
>
> MARQUIS DE SADE

Dangle a lollipop in front of his face. Licking has magical powers and he can be controlled with it. (Wink.)

BOYFRIEND POTENTIAL RATING: High if he gets to his social position slowly and with hard work—not just on his dazzling smile and family connections. Higher if he gets the excessive need for chickadees out of his system. These guys can be womanizers till they settle down (yeah, we're talking to you, Colin Farrell). Extremely low if he can't get over his I-Am-God complex.

CELEBRITY CORRESPONDENTS WITH
GEMINI SUN, VENUS IN GEMINI

John Fitzgerald Kennedy, a.k.a. J.F.K. (May 29, 1917) Known for cheating on Jackie, but stayed married to her.

Bob Dylan (May 24, 1941)

Colin Farrell (May 31, 1976) All over the map, bud.

Johnny Nash (June 13, 1928)

Liam Neeson (June 7, 1952) Used to be well-known ladies' man before marrying Natasha Richardson.

John Goodman (June 20, 1952) Married since 1989.

Paul Gauguin (June 7, 1848)

Tom Berenger (May 31, 1949) Married three times; last one, since 1998.

Dean Martin (June 7, 1917)

Greg Kinnear (June 17, 1963) Married since 1999; one child.

Scott Wolf (June 4, 1968)

Marvin Hamlisch (June 2, 1944) Married since 1989.

Ralph Bellamy (June 17, 1904)

Gemini Sun, Venus in Cancer

"... Because I am a bad girl, people always automatically think that I am a bad girl. Or that I carry a dark secret with me or that I'm obsessed with death. The truth is that I am probably the least morbid person one can meet. If I think more about death than some other people, it is probably because I love life more than they do."

Who said this? It's Angelina Jolie waxing poetic, as opposed to waxing her legs—or injecting collagen into her already beautiful, though insanely large lips. But she also happens to be Gemini Sun, Venus in Cancer . . . and she couldn't have defined this sign combo better.

Remember the Peter Pan complex? Yeah. The creed here is: life is too short. He who has the most toys in the end wins.

Strangely enough, this Gemini guy also likes to help the world—always has a worthy cause greater than he. He's good at seeing the big picture, but his mate may get lost in the shuffle in the meantime. He's a free spirit. And will rebel like a socialist in a third-world sweatshop if his political or sexual agendas are squashed or stifled.

He needs to express himself like a child who talks on and on without taking a breath. Eventually, if you stop him from venting and sharing, he'll respond as violently as if you just asked him to walk into a pharmacy to inquire which tampons are the most absorbent. In other words, you've just cut off his balls.

> The horror of wedlock, the most appalling, the most loathsome of all the bonds humankind has devised for its own discomfort and degradation.
>
> MARQUIS DE SADE

That's a no-no.

Again, there's always that fear of getting old sitting on this guy's shoulder—and his eternal toddler within is irresistible to the rest of us. Damn appealing. He's like a wicked little imp with a devilish smile. His allure is almost tangible. Twinkly eyes, mischievous grin.

And, truth is, unless he's crossed over to ultimate jerk, he can be like a cat climbing up a fish tank. We forgive him 'cause we know it's in his nature. His "didn't mean to do it" mewing after the bowl tips over . . . breaks our hearts. We let him crawl into our laps five minutes later.

Here's the goody bag: he does love life. And sees the benefits of collecting things he adores. However, this doesn't always have to be about monetary gain. Sometimes he surprises you and finds The One early on—and that's the only thing he'll care about.

Forever.

See. He can be committed . . . and not in an icky mental hospital sort of way.

> Kids are at my level. I like goofing around with them.
>
> JOHN GOODMAN

It just depends on what makes him tick. If he's looking for a partner in life, he may just be regarded like a tied tennis game—Love, love. For you. *You* make the call.

BOYFRIEND POTENTIAL RATING: High if he's true to his heart, not his wallet—and chooses well (not just based on looks). Very low if you get too involved in his business. He'll want a wife. Not a business partner. Doesn't like to mix the two.

It's like who-put-this-peanut-butter-in-my-chocolate? To him, chocolate is chocolate and peanut butter is used to make peanut butter sandwiches.

No jelly. Focus, people.

CELEBRITY CORRESPONDENTS
WITH GEMINI SUN, VENUS IN CANCER

Donald Trump (June 14, 1946) Wanna know what went wrong with Ivana? Ivana got too involved in Donald's business (for The Donald). When it comes to business, Melania is smart: she makes like a huge ice cream sundae—and splits. On fourth marriage, but he can afford it.

Gene Wilder (June 11, 1933) Married four times (to Gilda Radner for five years, until her death); current marriage since 1991.

Lionel Richie (June 20, 1949)

Errol Flynn (June 20, 1909)

Tom Jones (June 7, 1940) Married since 1957 . . . Though he had several well-known affairs, including with Elvira, who was apparently a virgin before he got to her, he remained with the woman he married at sixteen.

Clint Eastwood (May 31, 1930)

Ian Fleming (May 28, 1908)

George H. W. Bush (July 12, 1924)

Lenny Kravitz (May 26, 1964) Married Lisa Bonet in 1987. He cheated. They divorced.

Shane West (June 10, 1978)

Marquis de Sade (June 2, 1740) Most of his writing was done from jail. The word "sadism" comes from his name. He tortured prostitutes, usually with the help of his wife. Was sentenced to death but appealed successfully.

Joseph Fiennes (May 27, 1970)

Salvatore Ferragamo (June 5, 1898)

Beau Brummel (June 7, 1778)

Bob Hope (May 29, 1903)

Mario Cuomo (June 15, 1932)

James Belushi (June 15, 1954)

Notorious B.I.G. (May 21, 1972)

Danny Aiello (June 20, 1933)

Sam Mack (May 26, 1970)

Chick Corea (June 12, 1941)

Joe Namath (May 31, 1943) A playboy. The epitome of cool in the '60s and '70s. Settled down at forty-one. His wife and kids left when he was fifty-five.

Colin Quinn (June 6, 1959)

Gemini Sun, Venus in Leo

"She isn't young enough or pretty enough to be the President's wife."

—NEWT GINGRICH, on why he left his first wife.

(Gemini Sun, Venus in Leo)

Someone gong this guy. Don't let him talk for more than three seconds. The boos are deafening. So . . . You're not gonna like this list of Gemini/Leo guys: Prince Ali Khan, international playboy. Rock star Dave Navarro: married three times before he hit thirty-five. Joe Piscopo: left wife and married his kids' babysitter!!! Newt Gingrich: divorced wife while she was on her *deathbed*!!!!!

The roster reads like a Who's Who of While You Were Sleeping, he was getting *some* Sleeplessness in Seattle.

It all boils down to confidence. Or lack of. This guy puts on a good show. Though he eventually can't help announcing his weaknesses to the world. And he *seemed* so squeaky clean.

He loves a standing ovation—but does so standing on one foot. And can't keep his balance. He's like a kid on a pogo stick, blindfolded: it's hard for him to control where he's going. He's like a horny hetero guy on Viagra . . . in an all-male jail cell.

Anxiety runs deep in him. It's like how Felix Unger would feel were you to put him in a messy room with no vacuum or cleaning products. Confused. Frustrated. Damned near helpless. It's all that air (Gemini) and fire (Leo). It's what happens when you light a match near an open flame and blow on it: He's combustible.

Unfortunately, superficiality plays a serious part here. He doesn't want to drown (in his feelings), so he stays close to the surface, where he can breathe. He's also needy and dramatic, but has no patience for it if you are.

So here's my advice. Do yourself a favor. Check out his Mars, Moon, and maybe even his rising sign (you can find this stuff on the Net). If he has some earth in him (Virgo or Taurus—not Capricorn, that'll just make him wanna cheat with a super-model), he could be okay. If he finds ways to quiet his insecurities, and you can keep him on his toes but still let him know He Da Man, good.

Just don't let him trick you. In the beginning he's a full-on romantic who gives a settled-in feeling right away. When you two get cozy by the fire, however, he may just go off for some marshmallows and never come back. He'll steal your heart's treasure . . . and go looking for other, ahem, booty.

BOYFRIEND POTENTIAL RATING: Extremely low, period. High if you're a glamour queen, and keep some worthy prospectives around you at all times. That should keep him on his toes, even if he sucks at pointe. Just don't make him wear a tutu. His real fear is that someone other than he will wear the pants in the family. He begins to suspect that if *he* does, he'll just have to return them anyway—'cause he only got 'em on loan.

CELEBRITY CORRESPONDENTS WITH GEMINI SUN, VENUS IN LEO
Prince Ali Khan (June 13, 1911) Married Rita Hayworth.
Dave Navarro (June 7, 1967) Married three times; last one, to Carmen Electra.
Barry Manilow (June 17, 1943) Married for one year. Annulled.
Newt Gingrich (June 17, 1943) On third marriage.
Paul Lynde (June 13, 1927)
Joe Piscopo (June 17, 1951)

GEMINI DIC*-TIONARY

MAGNETIC <MAG-NEH-TICK> He's got "it."

Translation for potential girlfriend: Attracting anyone with a Y chromosome within hundreds of miles.

HORNY <WHORE-NEE> Nymphomaniac.

Translation for potential girlfriend: Ironically, it may not even have to do with a big, huge, um, libido. He's got doubts. Lots of 'em. And if he's smitten, he'll be *into you* (and out of you, and into you, and, well, you get it) every hour just to make sure you're still into him.

GENEROUS <GEN-UHR-US> Gives to both worthy and unworthy causes.

Translation for potential girlfriend: He vacillates between blowing money on a horse race with 100–1 odds to not spending a dime to fix a flat tire on a car that won't run without it. Also, he's known for occasionally giving more to charity than he'll invest in a relationship. Well, the former makes him feel good about himself. *That's* important.

CHARMING <SHARRR-MING> He can lead any horse to water *and* make it drink.

Translation for potential girlfriend: Who else but a Gemini could break love goddess Marilyn Monroe's heart? John F. Kennedy. (While she was busy breaking everyone else's heart . . . they were *both* Geminis.)

STUD <STUH-UD> A male animal utilized to spread his seed in order to impregnate females.

Translation for potential girlfriend: Perfectly explicit definition above.

CHAPTER 4

Cancer, Ex or Next
(the Crab, June 21–July 22)

CANCER RUDE-IMENTS

 Bermuda Triangle. Ever hear the myth? It's supernatural. A mystery. It reels you in and you disappear without a trace.

See where I'm going here? This is Cancer. If you're not careful, you can get caught in his web. He's the spider. You're the Purina Spider Chow. He'll leave you there, dangling, dangling. Waiting, waiting. Then he'll eat you alive.

Okay. This is getting disturbing.

Cancer must have what he wants: namely, you—if you're the object of his desire at the moment. (But he'll settle for a nice condo in Aspen.) In fact, he doesn't just want your mind, body, soul. He wants to control the outcome of every conversation, every thought in your brain, every utterance you make. That's right. This guy wants to master you. Own you. Finance you (if you come with a good return). (We'll talk about his weird obsession with money, power, and you in a moment.)

First, here's the problem. He does this psyche tweaking so subtly, you may not even notice. One morning you'll wake up wearing a geisha getup and wonder where it came from. (Don't throw it away. Save it for Halloween. It's your color. Honest.) You *can* lose yourself in him. He's a power vampire. His ideal mate is a genie in a bottle that he can take out, *rub,* and make wishes upon. (And she wears that sexy little harem-pants number. You know, like Barbara Eden wore in *I Dream of Jeannie.*) Call him Master sometime. He loves that.

> Any idiot can get laid when they're famous. That's easy. It's getting laid when you're not famous that takes some talent.
>
> **KEVIN BACON**

He wants a woman who's easy to get along with. A round hole for his, ah, peg. She doesn't irk him or call him on his faults. She stands by him through thick and thin, in sickness and in, well, psychoness. She can withstand his moods—and gets how incredibly *deep* he *thinks* he is. *Poor me. No one understands me.* (Translation: No one gets how utterly f*cked up I am.)

However, when the subject changes to keeping you, not just getting you, it can be good. This guy's got stamina and a few moves. He can do, in life, what Ahhhrnold can do with a machine gun and black sunglasses: terminate. He's the king of networking. Hottie impressive. He can create something out of nothing. And he knows that 1 percent talent, 99 percent perspiration (and inspiration) will get him through the front door. (By the way, ever hear of back door? Pardon. Pardon.) Well, needless to say, this guy has a few fetishes he may never let you in on. If he does, you're in. If he lets you enter into his psychedelic, kaleidoscopic Pink Floyd fantasy life, it's a good Peace sign. And if he confides in you about his childhood, he may be looking for something more serious with you.

> There's a difference between solitude and loneliness. I can understand the concept of being a monk for a while.
>
> **TOM HANKS**

Unfortunately, if his go-getter charismatic ways are suppressed, he gets lazy, depressed. He goes into a self-pitying coma and won't even respond to shock treatment. *I'm having the child of the alien who kidnapped me,* you tell him. No response. Nil. Brain-dead. Duhhh.

I do not read advertisements. I would spend all of my time wanting things.

FRANK KAFKA

Yeah. They say that Gemini guy has two sides. Like I mentioned before: not true. He's got many and changes his mind constantly. Gemini is too flit-y and fly-y to only have two. Instead, Cancer guy *does. He* has two sides. Entirely factual: It's *Cancer* who has the dual nature. One moment he's remarkably cheery, warm, friendly. Sweet.

Then he turns to stone. He hides. He's frighteningly cold and withdrawn. He huffs, puffs, and gives you the big, pouty-sad lip like Arnold Jackson gave Willis on *Diff'rent Strokes*. He can be nasty. Or just ignore you completely. (Don't fall for this. Leave him alone and let him come out of it. He'll find you when he does. Again, remember: Bermuda Triangle. Don't suck up to him—and get sucked in.)

His sense of humor is *muy importante* to him. He always thinks he's the funniest, cleverest guy in the room. Sometimes he is. Mostly he is. Sometimes he's not. His jokes can get as grating and offensive as Liza Minnelli's (bad) taste in men. He'll only stay with someone who can banter with him, match his adept turn of phrase. But if you have a different perspective than he does, he'll be off like the worst amateur comedian on no-drink-minimum night.

He won't tell you either. He'll just stop calling.

Here the term "object of his affection" really means what it says. You're an object to him. To him, people aren't necessarily people. (Harsh, right?) He collects things, and he needs certain specimens for his collection. This person, good for work contact. Check. This person, good for snuggling and making me hot. Check.

A few juicy traumas early in life and he can be one step away from psychotic. He'll have to work out his childhood and family problems through you. Just remember that if you disappear for a while (and he really wants you), he'll pull out all the stops and go get Lassie to help him locate you down the well. He'll make a big, dramatic scene of it. He'll pretend he's Romeo and purchase the poison just in case he doesn't get to you in time. *Oh, woe is me. I can't live without her.*

My "fear" is my substance, and probably the best part of me.

FRANZ KAFKA

Just make sure he doesn't change his mind and give *you* the vial. (Just to see what happens.)

CANCER TONGUE LASHING

"Pumpkin." "Sweetheart." "Cupcake." He'll call your mom and quiz her on your favorite pet name so that he knows exactly how to push your buttons. Tug heart strings. He's the ultimate ladies' man because he really does identify with Mom. And he'll *attempt* to treat you in accordance. (He does a good job of it. To understand him truly, though, ignore his impeccable, chivalrous manners and get to the heart of how he *thinks.*)

Two thousand years ago, we lived in a world of Gods and Goddesses. Today, we live in a world solely of Gods. Women in most cultures have been stripped of their spiritual power.

DAN BROWN

However, when an evening doesn't go right, he'll blame it on you. "I was just trying to make you happy," he'll mumble. And he'll infer that *that's* obviously impossible because *you're* so difficult. Yeah, r-i-i-i-ght.

When Cancer guy is "on," however, he radiates confidence, charisma, and charm like no other. He glows like a night-light. Lights up the room like a lava lamp. *Nobody Does It Better* blares from the speakers in his groovy bachelor pad. (Meanwhile, there's a Pussy Galore waiting in the wings for you to drop the ball. Yeah. They all want him. And he knows it. Don't worry, though. He's a serial monogamist. He can only handle one Pussy at a time.) He can be so sweet, you fear becoming a diabetic.

Know this, though. His sexy verbal foreplay is meant to woo you into *his* world—not done so that he can enter *yours*. (He doesn't see outside himself. It's what you bring to the table *for him*—in bed, in life, any situation. Period.)

They say he's sensual. Yet there's something a little contrived about his tactics. Oddly, he's sexual, not sensual. His technique is good, but it's less slow and methodical, more burning-passion-that-smolders-to-ash if he's not totally in the moment. And in love. That's how you'll know if he's *not* into you: It doesn't reach your gut. He'll seem removed enough that you'll sense he needs a threesome before he settles down. Or before breakfast. Whichever comes first.

Last thing: He may talk love and marriage—but probably only because you don't mention it first. Do ya? Don'tcha? Yeah, you know how to handle this one. It's called *withholding*—and I'm not talking about any payroll tax, either, ladies.

> I love to be alone. I never found the companion that was so companionable as solitude.
>
> **HENRY DAVID THOREAU**

CANCER: IS HE *INTO* YOU?

Here's the good news. When Cancer is into you—when he's in love—he can be the most romantic of all the signs. Sounds good, right?

Only thing is, he runs so hot and cold—in bed and in life— you'll be tempted to call the landlord to ask if something can be done about that.

Oh. And it can't.

C'mon, sistah. He's Cancer. He loves women. (Yeah, yeah, we'll get to the mom thing. You picked up *this* book. Stop projecting.) He can also be generous when he's courting you. Very gallant, with impeccable manners.

> I would rather sit on a pumpkin and have it all to myself, than be crowded on a velvet cushion.
>
> HENRY DAVID THOREAU

One thing you need to be careful of: This guy hates confrontation. Especially with lovers. If you get into the thick of it, he'll say "Let's talk later" and dodge you like the fat girl avoiding gym class. He'll go to the nurse, cry yellow-fever (yeah, he's scared—the pun's there for a reason), and run off to play hooky with his bestest buddies.

Speaking of buddies: This guy has a weird relationship with them. How shall I put this? Hmm. Well, there's nary a Cancer man who doesn't have a few, um, oddly effeminate or not-so-hetero affects. It's strange. Cancer *is* a feminine sign (even though he's still blazing hot). And this plays out with his male friends. He treats them like he does girlfriends. He lives for them. He's close to them. He pushes and pulls and manipulates them like he does you. So don't feel so bad.

> As a rule, men worry more about what they can't see than about what they can.
>
> JULIUS CAESAR

You'll know when this guy is into you when he speaks in We. *We* love that. *We* should invite them over for dinner. *We* get along so well. *We* can do that. *We. We. We.*

That's SO *us*. (Right, there's the *us* there, too.)

When Cancer's not interested, he curls up into a ball and rolls away. That's how you'll know. He won't kick you to the curb. He'll hint, hint like Alex Trebek when he favors a contestant. He'll throw you a fastball—and pray you bat *him* out of the field.

Speaking of balls. Um, baseball. He spends his money on stupid things. Anything sports-related: soccer, hockey memorabilia. A motorcycle. A "dope" car. Power tools. (All the things that prove his studly ultra-hetero (again, hmmm . . .) nature. BUT. If he's into you—and only you—he will want to capture the stars and bring them down for you. He'll buy you anything you want, and label you Worth It.

If worse comes to worst and the relationship isn't going right, pull out all your contacts. You can fall into his work category: Access Hollywood. And, if you play the game right, dropping names without sounding too much like Paris Hilton's stolen cell phone address book, you'll make his top ten work-user buddy list. At least.

Thanks for sharing.

ADVICE TO THE FUTURE MRS. CANCER

Here's a story. This one tops it.

Emily, *we'll call her Emily*. Emily has a thing for Cancer guy. He has a thing for her—back. He's her college T.A. (teacher's assistant). She's his, um, "student." After she graduates, they have a few dates. He blows her off and starts dating someone else. Then, oops, he offs and *marries* another girl.

But—and here's the big *but*—he keeps in touch with Emily and wants to be friends. She consents. Plays it cool. (By the way, she never slept with him. Cancer will look for elegance, class. This was a huge plus in her favor.)

Two years later, he separates from new wifey because he doesn't trust her (she's depleting his bank account without being honest about it. Cancer can never be happy if he can't trust her). His friend Em is still there. Fun. Interesting. Has her own life. Not pining after him (though in secret,

I became very famous, as a teenager, and my name and photo were splashed in all the media. They made me larger than life, so I wanted to live larger than life, and the only way to do that was to be intoxicated.

YUSEF ISLAM, FORMERLY CAT STEVENS

she is). Has a great sense of humor that matches his. Coy, perhaps. Intoxicating. Financially stable, too.

I like drama. I love being in a drama where I get to be the funny guy. That's what I really love the most.

JOHN LEGUIZAMO

Three weeks after the divorce goes through, he calls her and wants to date. They do. For one year.

Then he gets cold feet. Again.

Emily runs away to a cottage with no phone. No cell. No Internet. For seven days (not longer—Cancer man will give up if it's too much). He goes nuts. Doesn't like feeling abandoned. Doesn't go over well with him.

Yet, does.

End of story: He wants her back. Gets her. They have a beautiful little girl and live happily ever after.

Bottom line: Cancer guy is like a flounder. Fish, in general. If *you* move too fast, *they* swim away. *Don't scare the fish.* Don't be too aggressive. You have to remain stationary. Calm. Motionless. Fixed. Immobile. At a standstill. Static. Inert.

Don't contact him. Let him find you.

Under the bottom line: He's got issues. Cancer is a feminine sign. He wants to have control of the situation, wants to be Da

I am a target.

O. J. SIMPSON

Man. This dictates his role with women. He runs away at breakneck speed, and the only thing you can do to get him back is to *run the other way,* like salmon going upstream.

Last note: Cancer guy will first go for the woman he can "save." He loves tending to women with psychological issues, financial issues—with a woman much older than him who he feels he must rescue from advanced maturity without a Friday-night date. But then he'll wind up with someone who's got her act together, whatever age. He needs that kind of security like Linus, Charlie Brown. It's *his* trusty woobie blanket.

ADVICE TO THE EX MS. CANCER

This is tough, tough, TOUGH. Here's why: Cancer guy, when he's not ready, *will* push you away. But there's absolutely nothing you can do to combat this except remain stationary (see above).

It's impossible. If you contact him, he knows you want him. He'll feel *omnipotent*. If you don't, he's on to the next game. Double-edged sword. Damned if you do, damned if you don't.

So here it is: there's only one way to get him.

Be his friend. Don't encourage, don't discourage. Always be the first to bow out of the conversation (in person, on the phone, live-bait, etc.).

Oh. This is so tough. If you have a picture with you and a new boyfriend—no, no, don't send it. BUT—if you have a photo of you with someone important, harmless, but good baiting prowess (like a celeb—*Oh, gee, just met this person*), it's perfect. Send it to him with a casual "hey." He's incredibly intuitive, so your amateur make-jealous, makeshift tactics won't work on him. But if you can find a way to incite his emotions, to play with him without looking like you're trying to push-pull, you've got him.

I didn't beat her. I just pushed her out of bed.

O. J. SIMPSON

If he invites you over for S.E.X., don't go the first time. Pooh-pooh him. Just be friendly-like. Mysterious. Cancer lives for a good puzzle—*New York Times* crossword-style but twenty times harder.

He's *not* gonna come right out and proclaim his affection for you. It has to be slow. But, if he keeps pursuing you in his subtle hint-hint way, you can eventually say, Um, maybe. You'll *maybe* come to the big bash he's throwing.

Go. Don't get all starry-eyed over him. Treat him like a good buddy. He'll fall into line.

Here's the trick: Cancer always feels a little uncomfortable around himself. If he can feel sure and steady, comfortable and good

around you, he'll stay. This is where the mommy thing plays out.
He's looking for someone who'll give him unconditional love. But
who, not unlike his mother, will put him in his place
with a loving tap to the tushy. Everyone tiptoes
around him. Don't you. You have to be like a macrobiotic vegan in a room full of carnivores. He's
looking for earth mother, grounded. Michelle Pfeiffer in *A Midsummer Night's Dream*. Fantasy-like.

Just make certain you're not harsh with him.
You have to ease it out of him—like gently apply-
ing a little WD40 to a creaky door. Slow simmer
on a low flame.

You can get him if your glass is always half full,
your mysterious bank is always three-quarters full,
and his ego is 125 percent full, replete. Done.

My job in this
life is to give
people spiritual
ecstasy through
music. In my
concerts people
cry, laugh, dance.
If they climaxed
spiritually, I did
my job. I did it
decently and
honestly.

CARLOS
SANTANA

SUN/VENUS COMBINATIONS:
THE TRUE LOVE POTENTIAL TEST

Cancer Sun, Venus in Taurus

Ve-ry in-te-res-ting, this guy. When he finds his mermaid, he'll dive
into rocky waters and give up everything to go live
with her under the sea. Daryl Hannah and Tom
Hanks—*Splash*. He longs for peace, tranquillity,
real love. It's a crapshoot with fixed dice, though.
Destiny with an ironic sense of humor—because
he knows what he wants, but he's not good at recognizing it or choosing right.

Happiness in
intelligent
people is the
rarest thing I
know.

ERNEST
HEMINGWAY

If fate gives him a break, and he catches a
woman he respects and adores, he'll never leave. He'll cling like a

barnacle to a sunken ship; like Saran Wrap to a hunk of cheese; like a wet T-shirt to barely legal breasts in *Girls Gone Wild*.

If he marries the wrong one, though, he'll keep trading up, up like you'd do with an automobile. He'll keep the car and go to all the dealerships looking for something faster and shinier. (He'll never get rid of the old car first. He's too practical—and he needs it for safety measures, this guy. How else will he get to and from work?) When he finds the right car, he'll do the trade-in and expect a good investment.

Speaking of moola, a Cancer/Taurus combination will want luxurious, beautiful things. He's a bit of a low-key show-off: He won't brag about his new Porsche, but he'll leave it in the driveway every day and polish it, so that everyone can see how cool and successful he is. Ask him about it. (That way he doesn't have to let on to how freakin' insecure about his status he is.)

> Never go on trips with anyone you do not love.
>
> **ERNEST HEMINGWAY**

This guy analyzes the human mind and implements the psychology of it even in his work. He's able to blaze new trails in whatever type of business he's involved in. Actually, his real victory will come when he combines creativity with his job. Then he's unstoppable with Greased-Lightning motif to boot. His flair for the dramatic and over-the-top flair definitely works in his favor.

Sometimes he seems like an incredible cynic—the way he mocks and judges things and people around him. In reality, it's just his armored truck protecting the loot inside. He's susceptible. Touchy. Perhaps gives the impression of being impervious to catcalls and comments, but in truth, he's as thin-skinned as a Pinot Noir grape at harvest.

BOYFRIEND POTENTIAL RATING: High if good fortune is smiling upon him—and you. If he gets it right the first time, you have yourself a great husband: one who's odd, a bit neurotic, but will cater to your every whim. Low if you rely on him too much or suppress his childlike fascination for the world. He'll be sneaky, sneaky, and try pulling the wool over your eyes. Using 100 percent polyester.

Not saying he's good at it.

CELEBRITY CORRESPONDENTS
WITH CANCER SUN, VENUS IN TAURUS

Prince William (June 21, 1982) A Cancer, like his mum.

Mel Brooks (June 28, 1926) Married for a decade before he was married to Anne Bancroft from 1964 until her death in 2005.

Tom Stoppard (July 3, 1937)

Gilberto Gil (June 26, 1942)

Ned Beatty (July 6, 1937)

Michael Blake (July 5, 1945)

Donald Faison (June 22, 1974)

Cancer Sun, Venus in Gemini

People are drawn to him like flies to manure. Don't worry. You're the fly. He's the dung.

Seriously, this guy gives out sexy and magnetic—but when you get close, he's incredibly humble and self-effacing. How does he do it? How can one man be so charming, yet have the power to seem so grounded, sweet, and—dare I say it—shy? It's a heady love potion number 9. You'll be reeled in like a celebrity to the Dalai Lama (a Cancer, by the way).

I love sleep. My life has the tendency to fall apart when I'm awake, you know?

ERNEST HEMINGWAY

He doesn't usually show his goofy thufferin-thuckotash side, but when he reveals it to you, you'll sink like you're in quicksand—fast. Thing is, he knows his appeal to the ladies. But he doubts himself. His midlife crisis looms (even when he's in his twenties), and he wants to fit in all the good stuff now. He dreads Viagra on the shelf, reading glasses on the night-table, and a middle-aged wife who looks more like his mother than the hot-to-trot sexpot/saint he married.

However, if you're amusing, grounded, upbeat, never lecturing, overly analytical, or literal, you can be his piña colada lady. (The song, remember? He got sick of her, then realized she was the one he'd been looking for—come with me and escape . . . and they lived happily ever after. Uh, after.)

This guy is loving and intelligent. Translation: potent. His sense of timing is excellent in life—comic, dramatic . . . He can use this to woo you or confuse you. It's a landmine trying to outfox this guy. It's hard to outrun him, and even when you walk away slowly, *kapow!*

> There is no lonelier man in death, except the suicide, than that man who has lived many years with a good wife and then outlived her. If two people love each other there can be no happy end to it.
>
> **ERNEST HEMINGWAY**

Just make sure you stand up to him. If he can control you as much as he tries to, he'll respect you about as much as critics do Jessica Simpson's acting skills.

This guy will crave attention like a waitress/actress craves tips. But be warned: Much of what he does is for show. You have to be spontaneous, fun, get close to him, but also have a life of your own. Otherwise, he'll ruin you like a husband to his bride in southern Italy: He'll do it behind closed doors . . . then hold up the sheet in public for all to see.

BOYFRIEND POTENTIAL RATING: Extremely high if you're mentally agile and can stand your ground. Keep in shape, too. He loves that. Quite a few good guys here can make it for the long haul (see celebs below). Low, if he just got successful or better looking and hasn't been all these years. Lower, if his reaction to a weekend together and holding hands gives him hives. When he's in love, you'll know it. If not, you're like luggage without wheels. He'll take you out only when he has nothing else—then label you difficult to steer . . . and put you back in his closet until he needs more baggage. (And P.S.: Who does??)

CELEBRITY CORRESPONDENTS WITH
CANCER SUN, VENUS IN GEMINI

Harrison Ford (July 13, 1942) Married twice; once for eighteen years.

Tom Hanks (July 9, 1956) Married twice; happily, to Rita Wilson since '88; also was married before from '78–'87.

George Michael (June 25, 1963)

Chris Isaak (June 26, 1956)

David Spade (July 22, 1964)

Richard Lewis (June 29, 1947)

Ringo Starr (July 7, 1940)

Julius Caesar (July 12, 101 B.C.)

Nelson Mandela (July 18, 1918)

Cat Stevens a.k.a. Yusef Islam (July 21, 1948)

Franz Kafka (July 3, 1883) Suffered from madonna/whore complex. Sex repulsed him. Was not able to do it with someone he liked or respected.

Kevin Bacon (July 8, 1958) Still married to Kyra Sedgwick (Cancer/Leo): great couple.

Giorgio Armani (July 11, 1934)

John Cusack (June 28, 1966)

Dan Brown (June 22, 1964) Still married to the same woman.

Henry David Thoreau (July 12, 1817)

Kris Kristofferson (June 22, 1936)

Peter Weller (June 24, 1947)

Milo Ventimiglia (July 8, 1977)

Michael Rosenbaum (July 11, 1972)

Chace Crawford (July 18, 1985)

Gustav Klimt (July 14, 1862)

Gerald Ford (July 14, 1913)

Patrick Stewart (July 13, 1940)

James Brolin (July 18, 1940) Married three times, currently to Barbra Streisand.

Scott Foley (July 15, 1972)

Forest Whitaker (July 15, 1961) Married since '96.

Norman Jewison (July 21, 1926)

Doug Savant (June 21, 1964) Married twice, currently to (*Melrose Place*) Laura Leighton; they have one son, one daughter together.

Huey Lewis (July 5, 1950) Married with one son, one daughter.

Jamie Farr (July 1, 1934) Married since '63 with one son, one daughter.

John Leguizamo (July 22, 1964) Also married with one son, one daughter.

(Uh. Getting freaky . . . Moving on.)

Cancer Sun, Venus in Cancer

Okay. This one may be hard to catch, but when you do, he's yours for life. And I do mean life. I mean, he'll never fall in love with anyone else ever again. Cancer/Cancer, when he falls, he falls over a cliff. A big one. Remember the cliff that Coyote falls over when he chases the Roadrunner? Yeah, that kind of cliff.

Also, remember the mama thing with Cancer? Okay, this one will actually want you to order him around. He wants to be whipped. Hard. 'Cause when he's not in love, he can flit, float, and fly from woman to woman. But he's most comfortable in a long-term thing.

Don't ever leave him. He'll follow you—or, um, stalk you. If you don't want him. Scary, he is. He's so in love. Jealous, he can be, too. (O.J., we're not talking about you.)

Know this, though. He can be as insecure and unsure of himself as a freshman coed doing the sorority walk of shame down fraternity row in a chiffon dress.

Also, this is what he appreciates best: a woman who says whatever comes to her mind. Do not edit. I mean it. Go crazy. Just blab. Just don't try too hard. Talk and talk and say whatever. *What-ev-er.* He's yours. For good.

This one's a keeper, though. Just make sure you go to the back of this book and see that your Venus is in a water sign, too (Cancer, Pisces, or Scorpio), or you'll be so sick of this softie after a few years that *you'll* want to jump over a cliff, too. A real one.

BOYFRIEND POTENTIAL RATING: Very low if you get pregnant before you're married or before the relationship is rock solid. He should be in his thirties, at least. This guy's a big baby sometimes. Wipe his nose, please. The rest of us aren't interested in his politically incorrect boogers. Extremely high if he picks you. Just make sure you're really in love with him 'cause he's gonna stick around forever. And so will his mother because he's talked about you so highly, she thinks you're his wife already.

CELEBRITY CORRESPONDENTS WITH
CANCER SUN, VENUS IN CANCER

Willem Dafoe (July 22, 1955)

O. J. Simpson (July 9, 1947) No comment.

Fred Savage (July 9, 1976)

50 Cent (July 6, 1976)

Yul Brynner (July 11, 1920)

Donald Rumsfeld (July 9, 1932)

Ernest Hemingway (July 21, 1899) Married four times; killed himself.

Antoine de Saint-Exupéry (June 29, 1900)

Carlos Santana (July 20, 1947) After excessive drug use and casual sex, became "spiritual" and married health-food-shop owner in San Francisco, 1973; still married with three children.

Nelson Rockefeller (July 8, 1908)

Dan Aykroyd (July 1, 1952) Happily married since 1983 to Donna Dixon (pretty blonde from *Bosom Buddies,* remember?).

Calvin Coolidge (July 4, 1872)

Albert Brooks (July 22, 1947)

Derek Forbes, of Simple Minds (June 22, 1956)

Carson Daly (June 22, 1973)

Milton Berle (July 12, 1908)

Danny Glover (July 22, 1947)

John Bradshaw (June 29, 1933)

Jimmy Smits (July 9, 1955)

Billy Crudup (July 8, 1968) Left girlfriend Mary-Louise Parker for Claire Danes when she was seven months pregnant.

Don Henley (July 22, 1947)

Paul Young (July 3, 1944)

Art Linkletter (July 17, 1912)

Jean-Baptiste Dumas (July 15, 1800)

Woody Guthrie (July 14, 1912)

Pat Morita (June 28, 1932)

Arlo Guthrie (July 10, 1947)

Cancer Sun, Venus in Leo

This guy can be a nightmare. He's like that boogeyman you always feared was hiding in your closet. Or under your bed. Actually, he becomes your night-light. You get addicted to it. Can't sleep without it. Without *him*. He's magnetic. Sexy. Charming. Radiant. Flamboyant. Yet reserved.

Devious. Yes, it's true.

This guy, at his worst, will use you and everyone else around him to climb up the social ladder. Appearances are very important, and unless he's at the top of his game in whatever Chutes and Ladders thing he's playing, he'll get very board. (Board game. Get it? Moving on.)

He is also so authoritative, so headstrong, and has such a larger-than-life personality. His other half risks becoming just like him—literally, his life mate. (Ever see what happens to twins born conjoined at the head? Sadly, one is the stronger of the two. One must use the other to survive.)

Being happy is something you have to learn. I often surprise myself by saying "Wow, this is it. I guess I'm happy. I got a home I love. A career that I love. I'm even feeling more and more at peace with myself." If there's something else to happiness, let me know. I'm ambitious for that, too.

HARRISON FORD

Unfortunately, at his best, he's so passionate, playful, convincing, sweet, and oh-so-chivalrous, you keep expecting the white horse to appear out of nowhere. He mounts it gracefully, sweeps you up in one fluid motion (you go, girl), and bounds off with you into the sunset. (He might even joke around with you to put this into your head.)

Right. Here's the other thing. This guy knows his audience. He "gets you." Knows what to say, when to say it. His insight is keen; his sense of humor, sharp. He knows exactly how to woo you. Play you. Push your buttons. If you like the sound of a foreign language, he'll learn a few phrases—perfectly. You like chocolate? He'll buy up Godiva. Like theater? He'll snatch up the hottest tickets in town. He even likes women who have a little meat on them. (Olsen twins, stop crying.) So he's not averse to voluptuous. Ness.

He loves spontaneity and appears to be incredibly so. But, guaranteed: Every step he takes, every move he makes, every breath he takes, and every cake he bakes, is planned.

It's designed like a pirate treasure map, then studied, analyzed, and implemented in order to win the booty.

That's why he's so successful in business.

He also wants things to be easy. He knows he can be moody and volatile—and searches to keep it in harbor, away from the big motorboats (that cause annoying waves). He needs you to be his anchor.

Keep in mind, it's tough to keep this guy true to you—unless you're the ultimate package. He talks passion, passion. And when he falls in love, it's over the edge. Plunging down, down, without a net.

It takes him a while to decide on you. He tosses it around in his head like a Cobb salad. You have to be inert while he's mixing in the creamy dressing. When he's ready to serve, though, it'll be a five-star presentation worthy of Emeril.

Now: If you don't help his career (by pure contacts, just looking good on his arm, or at least feeding him with good ideas), he can be as dangerous as a rowboat in rough seas. With a hole in it. And no oars. Made of lead. Also, he can be as faithful as a stud horse in a corral with ten pretty mares. Unless he's in love. Then he's yours.

Having kids is important to him—so if it doesn't happen, it'll affect him in life and with you. He'll freak. He might agree to adopt, but it'll filter into his neuroses and the way he sees you. Be forewarned. He'll want to pass on his royal blood lines.

Jealousy doesn't work on him, ladies. Mystery does. And Janet Jackson sings: *Con-tro-ol*. Now I've got a life.

BOYFRIEND POTENTIAL RATING: Potentially high if you can figure this guy out—it's like navigating cobblestone streets in Rome with six-inch heels. Don't be too pushy. *He* must make all the moves. From start to finish. You can get him *only* this way. Low if you don't like to be controlled, manipulated, bandied about like a puppet, and dragged around like a three-year-old's favorite teddy bear.

CELEBRITY CORRESPONDENTS WITH CANCER SUN, VENUS IN LEO

Geraldo Rivera (July 4, 1943)

Tom Cruise (July 3, 1962) Katie Holmes is a Sagittarius: fire. Fire and water (Tom Cruise, Cancer) are both emotional. This combination can work better than water and air (Nicole Kidman, Gemini) or water and earth (Penelope Cruz, Taurus).

George W. Bush (July 6, 1946)

Sylvester Stallone (July 6, 1946)

Dalai Lama (July 6, 1935)

Tobey Maguire (June 27, 1975)

David Hasselhoff (July 21, 1952)

George Orwell (June 25, 1903)

Freddie Prinze, Sr. (June 22, 1954) Father of Freddie Prinz, Jr.; had drug problem; killed himself at age twenty-two.

Vincent D'Onofrio (June 30, 1959)

Stewart Copeland, of the Police (July 16, 1952)

Bob Fosse (June 23, 1927) Was romantically linked with Ann Reinking and Jessica Lange while he was still married to Gwen Verdon.

Merv Griffin (July 6, 1925)

Chris O'Donnell (June 26, 1970)

Antonio Gaudi (June 25, 1852)

George Steinbrenner (July 4, 1930)

Ross Perot (June 27, 1927)

Bill Blass (June 22, 1922)

Brian Dennehy (July 9, 1938) Married fifteen years to first wife; since 1988 to second.

Gil Bellows (June 28, 1967)

Nathaniel Hawthorne (July 4, 1804)

Neil Simon (July 4, 1927) On his fifth marriage; married twice to Diane Lander; once to Marsha Mason, for four years; first marriage lasted twenty.

Cancer Sun, Venus in Virgo

This Cancer guy is remarkably creative, but all done with a serious edge. There's a warmth to him. A logic to his actions. A depth to his scope (bad breath, huh?). He's known for his quirky sense of humor, his intellectual turn of phrase.

He has an intense desire to save the world from itself. Yes, it's true. Charitable, charitable—wants to make a difference but has a tough time reaching into his wallet—his arm's too short. It's not that he's stingy—on the contrary. It's just that he wants—needs—the refuge of money in the bank. Without it, he feels lost. Like Pippi Longstocking, without her freedom to sail the High Seas. George without his curious side. Paris without her vapid smile and small, rodent-like dog in her arms.

If he's dangerous, it's because his personality is constantly growing and changing. It's not that he falls out of love with you. He becomes a different guy. He's continuously searching for answers and tweaking his perception of things that go with it. He sheds his skin in the process. Like a snake. Or a Mexican Bearded Lizard (the truly venomous kind).

Again, it's the intellectuality combined with vulnerability. He's able to leap pronouns with a single bound, then melt like a snowflake into a lover's arms. He's a dominant man with a soft side. A Brillo pad on one side with three-ply silk toilet tissue on the the other. It's hellfire, torture, without satellite television to fall back on when you've nothing else to do.

Only thing is, he keeps much to himself. His natural desire to be seen as a role model good-guy plays out, even with you.

Here's the advice: Keep at him. Don't let him cop out like a mom who promises to pick out a really pretty prom dress—and then shows up with a frilly-crepe godawful excuse of one. (Three minutes before you have to get dressed and you've finally snagged a date with the captain of the football team.)

Get him drunk and malleable. I know, awful. But you've got to make him open up. If he confides his fears to you and still talks to you in months to come, you've got good coming. He'll feel like he just got away with an unpaid bill . . . if it's done calmly. The proprietor messed up, according to him. And it's not a mom-and-pop shop so he'll feel free and clear—'cause his conscience won't ride him like an amateur on a mechanical bull in a seedy bar.

BOYFRIEND POTENTIAL RATING: Very high if you can get him to open up, confide in you, and consider you family. (This works with most Cancers.) Low if he's too analytical and gets off by confusing others and engaging in some kind of sick mental masturbation. He internalizes too much. Get it out of him so his train won't switch tracks, collide head-on with the goddamned gas station on the other side of the road . . . and blow up.

Last word on all Cancers, but especially Cancer/Virgo: Again, get him to open up like a clam in bouillabaisse. Now you're the sauce. He's the shellfish. So, according to him, you two fit perfectly together.

CELEBRITY CORRESPONDENTS
WITH CANCER SUN, VENUS IN VIRGO

Anthony Edwards (July 19, 1962)

Vin Diesel (July 18, 1967)

Robin Williams (July 21, 1951) Was married twice—the second time to his kids' nanny.

Josh Hartnett (July 21, 1978)

Marc Chagall (July 7, 1887)

Marcel Proust (July 10, 1871)

Confucius (July 28, 551 B.C.)

Donald Sutherland (July 17, 1935)

Adolphus Busch (July 10, 1839)

Cheech Marin (July 13, 1946) Married twice.

Edgar Degas (July 19, 1834) Was straight but never married.

Jim Kerr, of Simple Minds (July 9, 1959) Married and divorced twice; first marriage to Chrissie Hynde.

Richie Sambora (July 11, 1959) Heather Locklear filed for divorce in 2006.

Terence Stamp (July 22, 1938)

Arthur Ashe (July 10, 1943)

John Quincy Adams (July 11, 1767)

Hume Cronyn (July 18, 1911)

Kenneth Starr (July 21, 1946)

CANCER DIC*-TIONARY

FEMINIST <FEH-MEEN-IST> Someone who loves women and is on their side.

Translation for potential girlfriend: He still remembers feeling safe and protected in the womb. So much so, ladies, that he spends his entire life trying to get back *in. As often as possible.*

PLAYFUL <PLAYY-FULL> Likes to kid and tease, even if costs *your* self-esteem dearly.

Translation for potential girlfriend: Playboy of the worst kind, because he passes himself off as a nice, good mama's boy from the first.

DEFENDING <DEH-FEND-ING> Will protect you and shelter you. Meaning: Defensive. He needs to protect himself, which is why he's so keen on protecting you.

Translation for potential girlfriend: He loves being called on his tricks, but insult him or hurt his feelings, and you're out like Pee-Wee Herman in a male-porno theater.

SELF-AWARE <SELF-AHH-WEAR> Knows what's going on around him because everything always relates back to him.

Translation for potential girlfriend: He can be so self-absorbed, they wanted to name a paper towel after him. (Is his name Scott?)

MYSTERIOUS <MISS-STEER-EE-US> Hard to tell what he's up to, which is how he lures you in. Being with him is like riding a roller coaster for the first time: thrilling, exciting, anxiety-causing, but makes you throw up your cotton candy.

Translation for potential girlfriend: Manipulative. Sneaky. Like Mom when you were a teen. She let you go to that "sleepover at your friend's house" (a.k.a. fiesta keg party), then waited at the door when you came home to smell your breath.

CHAPTER 5

Leo, Ex or Next

(the Lion, July 23–August 22)

LEO RUDE-iments

Leo guy wants his ass kicked by a woman. That's right. He just doesn't know it yet. But he will. *You* have to wear the pants in the family . . . secretly. Don't let him know you're doing it. Women's lib, baby. Culottes circa 1977. Cool beans. It's the only way he'll fall in love. Trust this. And that it's as hard as his abs.

But read on. Here's something you didn't know. Leo man plays it off, but he's sensitive. Or *was*. The narcissistic cocky side you're seeing is a full-on product of his family criticizing him (or rejecting him) when he was a wee-boy, growing

Love is the only gold.

ALFRED, LORD TENNYSON

up. He needed to compensate. It's a lot like a guy with a small hmm-hmm who buys a Ferrari. With Leo, his job, friends, and status are actually all a direct extension of his manhood.

When he finds the right milieu, though, Leo throws himself into his work. He takes the temperature of his career every five minutes. He can do any kind of work, but if he's not having success with it, he'll resemble a moody, up-down, depressed Cancer more than his happy Leo self. Whatever he does, he has to be the best at it. Handstand down.

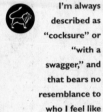

I'm always described as "cocksure" or "with a swagger," and that bears no resemblance to who I feel like inside. I feel plagued by insecurity.

BEN AFFLECK

He wants his special brand of Hollywood Walk of Fame to mark every endeavor and project he takes on—including you. He needs to be proud to have you on his arm. See, Leo guy, at first, will go for the superficial hottie-pants woman, but then he'll wind up with a gal whom he respects and trusts—not necessarily the supermodel (though looks will always be important to this guy). In fact, Leo's worst fear is to marry someone who's capable of hurting him or leaving him. *That's his job.*

Here's where astrology gets really nifty. Aries is the baby of the zodiac. He doesn't think his way through; he feels. Tells it like it is, even though his version is usually *wrong*. Then, Taurus is just Aries, but a bit more "grounded." Yeah, right. He's still immature, also amoral, sensitive (and insensitive), yet pulls off a more "logical" persona. Then comes Gemini. He's still got the complexes of Aries and Taurus combined, but adds in that mental agility; that fun, free-lovin' aspect to it. A neurotic mess, sometimes vengeful, a little spoiled, but plays the cool card well. Until someone trumps him. Instead, Cancer takes the three previous to another level by discovering that the world is even more interesting *with him in it*. He's just figured that if you cry long enough, Mommy gives you that candy you want. (Or he taunts and plays the push-pull game until she throws her hands in the air and just gives up.)

I'm not the type of guy who enjoys one-night stands. It leaves me feeling very empty and cynical. It's not even fun sexually. I need to feel something for the woman and entertain the vain hope that it may lead to a relationship.

BEN AFFLECK

Instead, Leo is a wild card. He's still not so trustworthy (forget the loyal thing you heard about Leo—that mostly works with his good friends—unless he's truly in love). He's kind of the turning point when it comes to maturity, but he still has all those ridiculously immature traits lurking just beneath the surface. Push the wrong button and you're like the girl in *Willy Wonka and the Chocolate Factory* who's labeled "bad egg" and gets tossed.

> Sometimes it's Britney Spears and sometimes it's Carrie Fisher. I can't tell if I've got a Lolita complex or an Oedipus complex.
>
> **BEN AFFLECK**

Leo's an idealist and wants the best. He believes there's a right way and a wrong way but isn't above cheating a little to get it. (More on this. His ability to be faithful ties in to his maturity level and how important you are to him.)

He has many sides: serious Leo, creative Leo, sunny and sweet Leo, dramatic Leo, dashing Leo, fun Leo, moralistic Leo, bold Leo, argumentative Leo, bully Leo, womanizing-in-secret Leo, then in-love-and-over-the-moon Leo. It'll be interesting to see which Jekyll or Hyde you bring out of him.

So, back to why Leo needs his ass kicked. Well, not kicked. Just forced into the box. Leo guy needs boundaries like a recovering sex addict locked up in a brothel would. If you don't set these up, he'll push the envelope to see what he can get away with. He's like a James Dean rebel.

> I have a love interest in every one of my films—a gun.
>
> **ARNOLD SCHWARZENEGGER**

Right. Without a cause.

See, Leo's the kid on the swings you tell to not swing so high, he'll hurt himself; then he swings higher. A self-destructive edge earns him attention, and he'd almost rather get it by putting himself in danger than others. Well, that's nice—at least he's out scraping his knees, not making you bow down to him, making you scrape yours.

That's it: Leo knows he's his own worst enemy. Like the guy who sleepwalks off a high-wire tightrope. He hasn't quite moved into the guilt aspect of Virgo yet, but he senses he's on his way.

And he's capable of doing bad things. Like the Mother Goose "girl with the little curl right in the middle of her forehead": When she was good, she was very, very good. And when she was bad, she was horrid.

He has a strict code of how people should comport themselves. They say Leo is proud and cocky. True. But believe it or not, Leo guy is seriously humble, too. Chances are, Leo is so fair, he's likely to blame himself for mishaps and things gone wrong before he blames you. He'll be happy to wear the dunce cap, sit in the corner, or write "I will not talk in class" a hundred times on the blackboard—if he agrees he's wrong (which happens a lot, once he thinks about it). His conscience scares him like the Sleestack in *The Land of the Lost*, when you were a kid.

When it comes to his moralistic side, he can be as determined as Jim Bakker on crack, spewing "truth," on his own goddamn preacher show. He'll go over to the dark side, though, if he doesn't think he's being taken seriously. Like a chameleon, he'll change his color into whatever you've labeled him as.

He's also got a few obsessive tendencies that lurk around in the *Buffy the Vampire Slayer* tomb of his mind. Deep down, he thinks he's got a big *S* on his shirt—he prays it stands for Superman—not Shithead. Or, even worse for Leo guy—Stupid. God forbid. See, it's his mission in life to show the rest of the world the way things *should* be, *and* prove how smart he is.

> The best activities for your health are pumping and humping.
>
> **ARNOLD SCHWARZENEGGER**

> I am sometimes a fox and sometimes a lion. The whole secret of government lies in knowing when to be the one or the other.
>
> **NAPOLEON BONAPARTE**

But he also wants a woman to call *him* on *his* crap. She must adore him, appreciate him, think he's the cat's meow—yet stand next to him like a schoolteacher with a ruler, ready to crack him one if he's naughty. She won't put up with it.

> Never interrupt your enemy when he is making a mistake.
>
> NAPOLEON BONAPARTE

That turns him on. He thinks it's sexy. He imagines her with some lacy Victoria's Secret confection under her gingham skirt. (Incidentally, the schoolmarm fantasy works with Virgo man, too. See chapter 6. And get out those sexy porn-star librarian glasses.)

Leo man is looking for a woman who's grounded, never dramatic (as he can be), and strong—who's willing to walk away from him if he treats her the way real journalists treat Kelly Ripa. For reference, water signs such as Cancers, Scorpios, and some Pisces women are excellent beavers for Leo.

Um, beavers—in the way they can thump, thump, pat down problems before the dam breaks, explodes, and floods the rest of us. These signs know how to navigate rocky waters: how to steer Leo's leaky boat safely to shore. (They never let him get swept out to sea before he loses his Lucky Charms.)

> Don't have sex, man. It leads to kissing and pretty soon you have to start talking to them.
>
> STEVE MARTIN

Even the worst kind of Leo playboys can be incredible husbands. When they're really in love, they're pussycats. They just need to be tamed.

Lion tamers have to hone their skills, too. Walk softly. And carry a big whip. Ah, stick. (Teddy Roosevelt, Scorpio.)

LEO TONGUE LASHING

If you're not used to noble, sexy stillness, Leo is likely to scare you with his intensity. There's a depth and goodness about him. He's intuitive, so he'll get it if you like him from the first.

Leo doesn't ask if he can kiss you. He just does it. His boldness is legendary. Like a cat, he waits for the right time, then pounces.

"Dump that guy" Leo insists. "He's all wrong for you."

"I will not!" you answer. "He's my boyfriend."

"Yeah. But he's kinda a moron, don't you think?" Then he mumbles, just loud enough so that you hear him, "He's not good enough for you." And he proudly struts away as you watch him go. Hubba, hubba.

> I believe that sex is one of the most beautiful, natural, wholesome things that money can buy.
>
> **STEVE MARTIN**

You sense that Leo guy will work on you softly about it. You're right. He'll convince you slowly and surely—instinctively. And when he's done (tactfully) wooing you by showing you that you deserve the best—namely, him—he'll cut out the strong, silent-type thing; take you in his arms, and kiss you so thoroughly, you'd swear you just leapt onto the pages of a Gothic romance novel. He's the fair-haired Viking. You're the maiden in distress. Your knees will shake and threaten to give out. Lions, and tigers, and bears. Oh my.

> There is one thing I would break up over, and that is if she caught me with another woman. I won't stand for that.
>
> **STEVE MARTIN**

Let's face it, Leo guy is irresistible. He's graceful. Masculine. He gets what he wants through actions, not necessarily words. He's sensitive, smart, intuitive, playful, dark, deep, and mostly ironic. His sense of humor borders on sarcastic—but without the biting, mean edge. It's like dark chocolate—yummy and sweet, but bold and rich. You get a toothache—not from the candy, but from smiling so much that your teeth ache.

But can he be trusted?

Well, do pigs fly?

LEO: IS HE *INTO* YOU?

He's magnanimous. Generous. Possesses boundless energy to leap tall buildings when he's in love. (Then he needs to retreat into his cave to get recharged—Leo knows he can't be *on* all the time, and would much rather take ten steps back than show you his not-so-perfect side early on.)

> I love the idea of "the one," but I actually believe that there isn't a Miss Right. There are twelve thousand Miss Rights out there, and it's all timing.
>
> MATTHEW PERRY

Here's the finger tip: Leo hates the fine details. He despises going over things again and again. And pettiness is his absolute top pet peeve. It's like a miniature pup to him, yip, yip, yipping at his heels. If you're petty, he'll swat you away like a bug. He needs things to be fluid and languorous—a long, romantic lovemaking session. That's how he'll want to see you handle life. You should be earthy, sensuous, stable, and passionate, about everything you do. That's all. Then you'll get him.

This man likes people who talk only when they have something to say. He doesn't mind the silences in between. You can be gregarious, outgoing, and tell interesting, funny stories, but don't talk just to make conversation and fill in the blanks.

> I used to be a real Prince Charming if I went on a date with a girl. But then I'd get to where I was likely to have a stroke from the stress of keeping up my act. I've since learned the key to a good date is to pay attention to her.
>
> MATTHEW PERRY

When Leo guy's into you, he gives, gives, gives, and keeps on giving. He's like that maxiroll of toilet paper you get at the dollar store—the one with the fifteen thousand sheets. He'll do everything for you. He'll let you have whatever you want, whenever you want it. Especially if he's in a good mood. And especially especially if it's in bed. Only problem is—(yawn). Wait a moment. I'll get around to it. A moment. Just . . . (yawn)—

all that fire and yet he's so goddamn *lazy*. How can he be so generous and yet so lazy? How did that happen? It's like a weird time-warp *Rocky Horror Picture Show* thing. Slow motion. Here's why: It's not exactly *lazy*. It's typical cat ate the canary. Leo just licked the bowl and grins back at you with that smug, satisfied *I've got you* look. This suits him just fine. He doesn't want to work too hard, 'cause—here it is: *If it doesn't work out, he's wasted his time.* There's nothing Leo hates more, except having a low limit on his Visa card.

> I like the idea of being alone. I like the idea of often being alone in all aspects of my life. I like to feel lonely. I like to need things.
>
> ROBERT PLANT

Also: Leo guy doesn't want to admit it, but he's a perfectionist when it comes to love. He wants lightning bolts to strike. Romance from an Audrey Hepburn movie (like Cancer). A deep, dark tango that lands with him surprise-dipping you to where you're nearly touching the floor, trembling and crying for him until he assaults your bod. That's what fascinates him: passion, baby.

> If you have this enormous talent, it's got you by the balls, it's a demon. You can't be a family man and a husband and a caring person and be that animal. Dickens wasn't that nice a guy.
>
> DUSTIN HOFFMAN

He'll still want you once he gets you, but you have to play rough with him—like you'd do with a big dog. He's part of the pack. Discipline him and he'll feel loved. In fact, the only way he'll fall is if he senses he's conquered an impossibly tough cookie. Something freshly baked—and still hot. Not a spoon-in-uncooked-chocolate-chip-cookie-dough, though. Trix are for kids.

He loves winning against the odds. That's why you have to be strong. Rock solid. Unbreakable. Dynamo girl. Wonder twin powers, activate.

There's a downside. Even though he's done so much to woo you, at some point in the relationship he'll probably balk like a bull who's forced to mate with the same cow. Ouch. He'll slow down to a snail's pace. He'll mess up so that he can test you—and himself. He's like that pathetic loser you overhear in the bar, sobbing into his whisky over how he lost the love of his life—and it's all his fault. Do we feel sorry for him? Nope.

Leo goes by his gut and doesn't take one step forward until he's totally geared up to go, like suburban girls with scrunchies and matching shoes. Ick. And that's usually when he's already faced the idea of losing you—and has decided you're the woman he wants for good. And plenty.

> A particularly beautiful woman is a source of terror. As a rule, a beautiful woman is a terrible disappointment.
>
> **CARL G JUNG**

Well, you may just have to guide him where you want, in bed and in life, 'cause he's waiting for you to service him first. He just wants to *seem* like you can do no wrong, but in truth, he's waiting for you to give up, f*ck up, and *do all the work*. (Then he can call you a weak, pathetic yes-girl, determine he was right, and walk away with a good conscience.)

Don't let him get away with it. Slap him psychologically a few times. Be brutal. That's the only way to keep him faithful. He'll be the Bogey to your Bacall. Aw. Give this guy a minute of your time. If you like.

> An intellectual is a person who's found one thing that's more interesting than sex.
>
> **ALDOUS HUXLEY**

Just be sure you're not too hooked 'cause it's tough keeping him around till he's 100 percent ready. You'll know he's there when you meet his entire family. He keeps his girlfriends hidden till it's real 'cause he hates hearing opinions about you that aren't his.

ADVICE TO THE FUTURE MRS. LEO

Here's a tale that's not tall. A woman, Karen, had a fiancé of nine years. They were finally nearing marriage. Then she met Leo guy.

Though he never admitted it to himself, Leo guy was attracted to the fact that she was safely tucked in the warm embrace of another. Slowly, surely, he playfully hinted. Then seduced her one night.

> Beauty is worse than wine; it intoxicates both the holder and beholder.
>
> ALDOUS HUXLEY

After, he pulled away, but gave the impression that he was still interested—just giving her space. See, he never played it slick or acted like it was a one-night thing. He showed her he was true but not her puppet. That worked. The sincere thing is attractive to any girl. He won her. That was the plan.

Fast-forward to two years later. They're incredibly happy. Leo freaks out and cheats. She finds out, of course.

I told you, Leo guy is self-destructive. Because he believes in the power of true love, he'll subconsciously mess things up by pushing you away, cheating, et cetera, before he makes the final commitment.

So, she does the right thing. Leaves him. *Adiós.* Refuses to listen.

> Men do not shape destiny. Destiny produces the man for the hour.
>
> FIDEL CASTRO

He does everything to get her back. For weeks. Meanwhile, they have a vacation coming up. The tickets were confirmed before all of this happened. *Well, hell*, she thinks. *This is for me.* (See, that's the thing with Leo. If you do what you think will get to him, it won't work. Instead, if you do what you want to do, he'll absolutely respect that.)

Long story short—they went away together. He slowly, surely seduced her back. After her putting her foot down for some time, he finally realized she was The One. They've been married ten years now and have a baby. He is a loving, wonderful husband.

But during that rocky time in the beginning, she shoved a *Marriage and Communication with Your Partner* book into his hand, made him discuss it like in eighth-grade social studies, and told him how she needed to be treated—or else. Again, Leo man needs serious guidelines. If he pulls away, you're not going to *show* him you're right for him by calling or stalking him. If it gets to the point where he comes for you, resist. He'll do everything in the world to get you back.

> I think that a man should not live beyond the age when he begins to deteriorate, when the flame that lighted the brightest moment of his life has weakened.
>
> **FIDEL CASTRO**

Bottom line: He's looking for someone who's strong enough to leave him. He can't stand weakness because he desperately fears it in himself. Instead, if you're brave and powerful, he'll sense it'll rub off on him—and he'll be worthy, too, by association. If he doesn't respect you, he'll torture you the way he tortures himself.

Under the bottom line: Leo wants the best. Know what you're worth. Be imported fresh mozzarella in a caprese salad, not Cheez Whiz.

ADVICE TO THE EX MS. LEO

Got to be honest here. Leo man is like Aries. If you chase after him, he'll dump you like Adriana and Pussy, in *The Sopranos,* after they snitched. See, it's not even about calling and saying "the right thing." There is no right thing. Any attempt at getting him back will be seen as a sign of weakness. (If you're gonna do it, at least be clever about it.)

After a breakup, Leo is looking for serious space. But here are other important things to know:

1. Again, don't ever be petty. Leo will run like an American tourist caught by accident in Pamplona during the bull run. Here's what "petty" really means: If you call Leo guy and tell him off—that he's a bastard, jerk, guy-with-a-big-L-on-his forehead, it will just make him *never consider you again*. In other words, if you tell him you're fed up and he's not worth your time—and you mean it—fine. Just don't be nasty.

2. Be nice and let him know you're sorry it came to this but you just won't have it. That shows you have *control*. Instead, if you tell him—again, petty—things like he sucked in bed or that his Oscar Meyer (wiener) was really small, or something else cruel, you're as history as the two-dollar bill.

3. You have to be a lady about it. And grounded. (See above.)

4. A lady does not mean a sucker. Don't be nice to him if he doesn't deserve it. Just don't attack him.

5. Calling him to get your sweatshirt or disposable razor back will not work. (Again, he'll see it as petty. He'll think you're trying to trick him. Which, let's face it, you are.)

6. If he wants to sleep with you, don't do it right away. Work it, like Missy Elliot. But afterward, leave. And show him you're still grounded—not trying to get him back. Yeah, you have feelings. But, you've got to go—you have work tomorrow. Show him he's not the end of your universe.

7. Blow off his calls for a while. Let them be like heat coming off a steaming tarmac in the dead of summer.

SUN/VENUS COMBINATIONS:
THE TRUE LOVE POTENTIAL TEST

Leo Sun, Venus in Gemini

This guy can be a nightmare if he's not totally in love. How do you know he's in love? Easy. It's not the flirting, the playful banter, the little remarks that make you think he *might* be jealous. When this guy is in love, it's all-out *American Bandstand* style. You'll know it. Lookie here. It's not *maybe*. It's definitely. It's: I need you. I want you. I don't want anyone else but you and I want a full-on commitment. Full stop.

It can be as scary as your seriously overweight friend borrowing a pair of your favorite jeans—or as tranquil as a cat stretching out on a warm windowsill. Again, it's either/or. It's not difficult to discern which.

This guy is looking for a strong woman: Abby from *Eight Is Enough*. Carol Brady, without the seventies-style 'do.

And here's what strong means: NOT someone who complains about everything. In fact, don't. Just someone who's totally, unbelievably honest about all she thinks. And lucky you if those things actually: make sense.

What it all comes down to is someone whose neuroses match yours. This guy's got a lot of them. But he wants someone who's going to *get him*. And not take away from his "me" time by being self-centered. More than he is.

True, he can be a double agent. 007, without Q and all the neat gadgets to back him up. He's good at keeping things hidden until he wants to

> This is the epitaph I want on my tomb: "Here lies one of the most intelligent animals who ever appeared on the face of the earth."
>
> BENITO MUSSOLINI

> You do not merely want to be considered just the best of the best. You want to be considered the only ones who do what you do.
>
> JERRY GARCIA

reveal them. He's more Antonio Banderas in *Spy Kids,* though, than Sean Connery as James Bond. You'll get it out of him if you want to. He can't keep secrets for long from people he loves. His eyes are a dead giveaway. He's see-through—like a shady porn photographer's changing curtain.

> When did I realize I was God? Well, I was praying and I suddenly realized I was talking to myself.
>
> PETER O'TOOLE

Here's one good thing: When he finally "gets himself" (and that usually takes some time), he'll pick the right one and stay in love. Deep down, he's a romantic—and he'll stick to you like a mouse on a glue trap.

Romantic, right?

BOYFRIEND POTENTIAL RATING: Super high, if you make him suffer long and hard like a pup waiting for a little boy's ice cream to fall off the cone. (It keeps dripping on him, but you never cave as he whimpers and whines and flashes you cute, sad puppy eyes at your feet.) You've got to be tough with this guy. Low, if you let him get away with anything. He'll crush your heart like Grandma's generations-old locket you accidentally stepped on with your Jimmy Choos.

> I am a deeply superficial person.
>
> ANDY WARHOL

CELEBRITY CORRESPONDENTS
WITH LEO SUN, VENUS IN GEMINI

Jean Reno (July 30, 1948)

Sir Alexander Fleming, inventor of penicillin (August 6, 1881)

Edward Furlong (August 2, 1977)

Alfred, Lord Tennyson (August 6, 1809)

Laurence Fishburne (July 30, 1961) On second marriage.

Marlon Wayans (July 23, 1972) Has two children with his girlfriend.

Richard William Wright, of Pink Floyd (July 28, 1945)
Martin Gore, of Depeche Mode (July 23, 1961)
Gus Van Sant (July 24, 1953)

Leo Sun, Venus in Cancer

There's something maniacal about this guy. He needs to be a star, even if it's behind the scenes. He's dictatorial, controlling. He lives for respect and freaks out if you don't give it to him. Don't ever patronize him. He might stay with you long enough to "win" your respect, but he'll resent you for thinking anything less than the best of him. His heart's in the right place, and he'll go nuts if you don't know that his intentions are good.

Deep down, he also lives for love and family and kiddies. He'll live . . . for you. He just doesn't know if he can trust you with that information yet.

Here's the bizarre thing. If he finds the right partner, that is, someone who's incredibly grounded, kind, hard to get, a lot of fun, never boring, yet deeply in love with him, he can be oh-tay Spanky. Berry good. Berry good, like Dracula with the heart-shaped surprises. Indeed, as a love partner.

BUT. If not, he can be ardent, fervent, avid, . . . quick-tempered, easily incensed, hot-blooded, obsessive, possessive . . . Continue? He'll give the *Psycho* shower scene a new look, with a psychedelic wig and an extra-sharp knife. Truly, this combo of signs can be fear-inducing. As well it should. You'll need a warning.

It's like big, black clouds before thunder and lightning come; twice. Don't stick around for the drama. Shakespeare's tragedies don't end well, y'know?

> I have Social Disease. I have to go out every night. If I stay home one night I start spreading rumors to my dogs.
>
> ANDY WARHOL

> I love Los Angeles. I love Hollywood. They're beautiful. Everybody's plastic, but I love plastic. I want to be plastic.
>
> ANDY WARHOL

Here's why this happens. This guy doesn't want to cope with his deep-seated sense of uncertainty—about the world, and about you.

I'd asked around ten or fifteen people for suggestions. Finally one lady friend asked the right question, "Well, what do you love most?" That's how I started painting money.

ANDY
WARHOL

If he's in love, he truly feels like a worm on a hook—he doesn't know which will do him in first: drowning in water or the fish about to swallow him. Truth is, he doesn't want to put himself out there. He thinks he does, but he's in denial. And when he does step forward, he's nervous about it. He's more anxious than the gym coach in a carnival dunking booth—with his star athlete throwing, the day after he's been docked from a game.

He's always at odds. *Allegedly* like Michael Jackson in a room full of young boys.

He isn't sure you'll fit into his strange, complex, fantasy world.

Truth is, he's a philosopher, a poet, a romantic, an idealist. And a sweet, loving, sincere guy—if only he can find the right gal to cherish him the way he fantasizes and daydreams about.

When I got my first television set, I stopped caring so much about having close relationships.

ANDY
WARHOL

If not—and she shows a certain diffidence about the union when he's decided it's right—he scarily morphs into a female black widow spider: She mates only once but bites the male's head off when she's done. (That must hurt. Not easy to recover from without it.)

Don't worry, though. He feels guilty about it. Afterward.

BOYFRIEND POTENTIAL RATING: High if he's got balance and can be honest about his sensitivity. Low if he names the children you're going to have together—the first week you're dating. And admires Glenn Close and her impressive cooking talents in *Fatal Attrac-*

tion. One last note. This Sun/Venus combo produced real winning guys: Fidel Castro, Benito Mussolini, and Napoleon Bonaparte. But you can also have a good guy if you pick right.

CELEBRITY CORRESPONDENTS WITH
LEO SUN, VENUS IN CANCER

Ben Affleck (August 15, 1972)

Robert Redford (August 18, 1937) Was married for twenty-seven years; divorced.

Arnold Schwarzenegger (July 30, 1947) Married since 1986; four children.

Martin Sheen (August 3, 1940) Married to wife, Janet, since 1961.

Napoleon Bonaparte (August 15, 1769) Married Josephine, a widow with two children; married again in 1810 and had a son.

Edward Norton (August 18, 1969)

Steve Martin (August 14, 1945) Was married to Victoria Tennant for eight years; divorced. Remarried in 2007.

Christian Slater (August 18, 1969) Married in 2000; divorced.

Matthew Perry (August 19, 1969)

Dustin Hoffman (August 8, 1937) Married to second wife since 1980; has six children—two from first marriage.

Carl Gustav Jung (July 26, 1875)

Aldous Huxley (July 26, 1894)

Fidel Castro (August 13, 1926)

Benito Mussolini (July 29, 1883) Committed both wife and son to an insane asylum because he thought they were a threat to his power. They both died early deaths there.

Tony Bennett (August 3, 1926)

Sydney Omarr (August 5, 1926)

Dean Cain (July 31, 1966)

Jerry Garcia (August 1, 1942)
Peter O'Toole (August 2, 1932) Married for twenty years; divorced.
Peter Bogdanovich (July 30, 1939)
Robert Plant (August 20, 1948) Married for fourteen years; divorced.
Bert Convy (July 23, 1934)

Leo Sun, Venus in Leo

Oh. This guy is so dangerous. He can be number one, numero uno, in passion, love, romance, and lovemaking. But it's like that sweet, nice guy in high school you never thought could turn into a bastard.

Though he could. And did.

This guy is the last man left standing to part the Red Sea. He has special powers. Boredom, to him, is death. Drama. Drama. He needs it. It has to just about drown him.

Here's why. He's more than special. He's Adonis, with a tan. Achilles, without the problem heel. Midas, with an extra-golden touch (that will touch you *in all the right places*).

BUT. BUT. You're *not* the only one who thinks so—and he knows it.

Here's the deal. No joke. You must *torture* this man—not just to have him, to keep him. All through life. He craves one life-changing scenario after another; this is what makes him feel his love for you. Otherwise, he retreats into a fantasy world to get his rocks off. He creates spies, an underworld, and paranoid afflictions until you don the Inspector Clouseau persona and call him on it.

Sometimes love is stronger than a man's convictions.

ISAAC BASHEVIS SINGER

For our anniversary, I had a certificate drawn up that states I can never leave Angelina for eternity. It has the seal of the great state of Louisiana on it. I signed it in my own blood with a paintbrush.

BILLY BOB THORNTON

You'll never understand his capacity for true strangeness until you've lived through it.

One day, you may realize that you wasted your time with a totally romantic, completely f*cked-up, weird, creative, incredibly lethal freak-weirdo. If you can make this guy feel special—at the same time showing him you're not dying for him, or too much in love (*he* must be the one to woo *you*)—he'll be a rock-solid partner when he senses that his brand of once-young, hot Elvis, now freakishly bloated older Elvis, has left the building.

> I believe in running through the rain and crashing into the person you love and having your lips bleed on each other.
>
> **BILLY BOB THORNTON**

BOYFRIEND POTENTIAL RATING: High if you can crush his spirit like an Atkins dieter in a donut factory. He'll crave you more. This guy can go the good-guy route, but he can also be evil. Make sure you know which before you get embroiled like the *Diff'rent Strokes* kids (in criminal activity for the remainder of their lives). Low if you're his first (or second) wife . . . Unless you can work the drama like a Jerry Springer guest.

CELEBRITY CORRESPONDENTS WITH LEO SUN, VENUS IN LEO

Pete Sampras (August 12, 1971)

Andy Warhol (August 6, 1928)

John Holmes (August 8, 1944)

Alfred Hitchcock (August 13, 1899) Married once, from 1926 until his death in 1980.

Stanley Kubrick (July 26, 1928) Married three times; the last time for forty-one years, till his death.

Yves Saint-Laurent (August 1, 1936)

Claude Debussy (August 22, 1862)

Coolio (August 1, 1963)

Julian McMahon (July 27, 1968) *Nip/Tuck* dude's dad was the former prime minister of Australia. Divorced twice; second wife was Brooke Burns: they had one child together.

Billy Bob Thornton (August 4, 1955) Married and divorced five times; last marriage was to Angelina Jolie.

Mike Douglas (August 11, 1920)

George Hamilton (August 12, 1939) Married once for five years. Perpetual tan.

Eddie Fisher (August 10, 1928) Married five times; wives included Connie Stevens, Debbie Reynolds, and Elizabeth Taylor.

John Glover (August 7, 1944)

Isaac Bashevis Singer (July 24, 1904)

Leo Sun, Venus in Virgo

Just be his twin: in woman form. Monkey see, monkey do. Think like he thinks. Mirror his actions. Have some opinions, but make sure they match his. This man wants his other half—literally. He's in it for deep, soul-kinda-love. But it's not easy. He wants a woman who's rational and practical in public yet sexy, even vampy, in private. Madonna/whore. Madonna/whore. Madonna/whore. Get it? Then you'll get him. Be like weed: bio-organic, down to earth, but used for wicked things, too. This guy's macho. He's got balls. There's a mysterious, sensual air about him.

He's also a master of physical expression. You know *that look*? The one your dad gave you across the dinner table, telling you to shut up? Yeah, *the* look. This guy can tell you 101 different things without one goddamn word. He's quiet, yet larger than life. In fact, you may have to stop yourself from blurting out, "What? Are you talking to me? Are you talking to ME?"

> It's important not to indicate. People don't try to show their feelings, they try to hide them.
>
> ROBERT DE NIRO

> It's all right letting yourself go, as long as you can get yourself back.
>
> MICK JAGGER

Oh, but he can be sweet too. A charmer, this one. Full stop. He's got a twinkle in his eye. He's special. In fact, be careful not to worship him—it's easy to do. But you'll just be banished to the nosebleed seats in the back of the stadium with all the other screaming fans.

I like to believe that love is a reciprocal thing, that it can't really be felt, truly, by one.

SEAN PENN

And by the way, it's okay to be one of these obsessed South Beach–diet people. Counting calories and talking about how many carbs you've had today is like foreplay for this weight-control weirdo. (Note: This only works with Venus in Virgo. DO NOT try this with the other men—see specific sign combos.)

When he falls in love, he does it truly. If he's looking over your shoulder at other women, dump him like last year's designer shoulder bag. He's already halfway out the door. He'll tell you, though. Eventually. Leo/Virgo can't fake it when he's not in love; he's as successful at keeping feelings hidden as gossip columnist Liz Smith is when she's got the goods.

That on a romantic level, if you feel it about somebody and it's pure, it means that they do too.

SEAN PENN

BOYFRIEND POTENTIAL RATING: Medium high if you're his type. Super-high if you're a descendant of some noble family. Or a rock star. Or blond. Even higher if you're a supermodel. Low if he hasn't attained some success and is still reaching for the piece of dark chocolate hidden on the top shelf. Marriage for life if you don't quake in his presence like everyone else does.

Normal love isn't interesting. I assure you that it's incredibly boring.

ROMAN POLANSKI

CELEBRITY CORRESPONDENTS WITH LEO SUN, VENUS IN VIRGO
Antonio Banderas (August 10, 1960) Currently married to second wife, Melanie Griffith.

Mick Jagger (July 26, 1943)

Robert De Niro (August 17, 1943)

Sean Penn (August 17, 1960) Ex, Madonna, is a Leo, too. Married Robin Wright in 1996.

> I admired Melanie before I loved her.
>
> ANTONIO BANDERAS

Roman Polanski (August 18, 1933)

Mark Knopfler, of Dire Straits (August 12, 1949)

Neil Armstrong (August 5, 1930)

Patrick Swayze (August 18, 1952) Married since 1975.

Louis Armstrong (August 4, 1901) Married four times; first time, when he was just sixteen years old.

Matt Leblanc (July 25, 1967)

Herve Vilard (July 24, 1946)

Casey Affleck (August 12, 1975)

> I got started dancing because I knew it was one way to meet girls.
>
> GENE KELLY

Kevin Spacey (July 26, 1959)

Robert Mitchum (August 6, 1917)

Henry Ford (July 30, 1863)

Ray Bradbury (August 22, 1920)

Peter Jennings (July 29, 1938) Married four times.

Louis Vuitton (August 4, 1821)

Wilt Chamberlain (August 21, 1936)

Herbert Hoover (August 10, 1874)

David Crosby (August 14, 1941)

Wesley Snipes (July 31, 1962)

Magic Johnson (August 14, 1959) After marrying in 1988, announced in 1991 that he was HIV-positive.

Kid Creole (August 12, 1951)

Denis Leary (August 18, 1957)

Timothy Hutton (August 16, 1960) Married to Debra Winger for four years; to a French children's book illustrator since 2000.

Danny Bonaduce (August 13, 1959)
Eriq La Salle (July 23, 1962)
Dom DeLuise (August 1, 1933)
Oscar Peterson (August 15, 1925)
Peter Weir (August 21, 1944)
Jason Robards (July 26, 1922)
John Eisenhower (August 3, 1922)
Max Factor, Jr. (August 18, 1904)

> Good-looking people turn me off. Myself included.
>
> **PATRICK SWAYZE**

Leo Sun, Venus in Libra

Remember the guy in high school who was such a stud, he dated every hot girl on the planet? *They all knew* he was a serious womanizer, but they still wanted a piece of him anyway? That's right. He's Leo, Venus in Libra.

Here's why. He's bright. Disarming. Charming. Alarming. So powerful—he's the one your eyes move to in a room. He's still. Intuitive. Can sense what turns you on; what'll make you want him. Convince you to parachute without a spare for backup. A staaaah.

Listen, he can be the worst kind of playboy. He can also be abusive—both physically and mentally—depending on how over-the-edge he is. You have to examine his morals and scruples. Is he more Andy Griffith or Andy Dick?

He has an addictive personality. He gets addicted to things. You get addicted to him. He's simply addicted to love, like Robert Palmer.

The worst problem: You don't care. He's charismatic. He lights up your life like Debbie Boone. Yet smothers your dreams of happily-ever-after like Kenny G did to real jazz. Power, success, and diligence come naturally to

> Women do not win formula-one races, because they simply are not strong enough to resist the G-forces. In the boardroom, it is different. I believe women are better able to marshal their thoughts than men, and because they are less egotistical they make fewer assumptions.
>
> **HENRY FORD**

this guy. He's usually very bright and will expound on any subject. Nah. He'll actually steer the subject to what he knows about 'cause he loves hearing himself talk. If he's not center stage, he'll complain like a drunk in church.

> The worst moment from all of this was driving from that doctor's office, to tell my wife that I was HIV-positive.
>
> MAGIC JOHNSON

This guy will gravitate toward elegance and beauty. He's more interested in Madonna, the Mother of God, than, say, Madonna, the Material Girl. (Though a woman with money and status will attract him like fruit flies to a bowl of overripe peaches.)

He's his own brand of celebrity. And he'll brand you *his* if he knows he can trust you to never reveal what special kind of jerk he can really be. He would absolutely freak if his fans knew the truth. He's looking for the girl who'll let him cheat off her in algebra—then never tattle about it. He cheats. You suffer.

> There we were in the middle of a sexual revolution wearing clothes that guaranteed we wouldn't get laid.
>
> DENIS LEARY

And that's okay by him.

By the way, did you know that Kenny Rogers was married five times? So damned unassuming . . .

BOYFRIEND POTENTIAL RATING: High if you put up with all his crap. He's like the most angelic-looking, gorgeous child who smiles prettily as he throws your priceless antique vase down the garbage chute. Low if you can't stand the heartache and angst of wondering who he's charming the pants off now. Literally.

CELEBRITY CORRESPONDENTS
WITH LEO SUN, VENUS IN LIBRA

Bill Clinton (August 19, 1946) Note on Bill and Hillary: She's Scorpio, Venus in Scorpio. Their suns match. Venuses don't. Water and air? Ouch. Plus, Venus in Scorpio can be jealous. (For good reason.)

James Cameron (August 16, 1954) On his fifth marriage.

Fred Durst (August 20, 1970)

Sultan Aga Khan (August 15, 1898) Notorious playboy.

Davy Crockett (August 17, 1786)

Malcolm-Jamal Warner (August 18, 1970)

Ted Hughes (August 17, 1930) Was married to Sylvia Plath until she killed herself; married eighteen years to second wife, until his death. He was said to be an abuser and an incorrigible cheater.

Kenny Rogers (August 21, 1938) Married five times.

Don Ho (August 13, 1930)

James Marsters (August 20, 1962)

Joe Jackson (August 11, 1954)

Orville Wright (August 19, 1871)

Frank Gifford (August 16, 1930) Married three times, currently to Kathie Lee. Had an affair with flight attendant.

Frank Perry (August 21, 1930)

Kevin Dillon (August 19, 1965)

Steve Carell (August 16, 1962)

LEO DIC*-TIONARY

SEXUAL <SECKS-SHOO-ALL> In. And out. And under. And over . . . Translation for potential girlfriend: Likes doing it a lot—which is good for you. Especially when he's not doing it with *others*, at the moment.

ROMANTIC <ROW-MAN-TICK> Thinks he's Rudolph Valentino.
Translation for potential girlfriend: *Isn't* Rudolph Valentino (who was allegedly arrested for prostituting himself; at least he was paid for it).

POWERFUL <POW-URR-FULL> Able to light up and control a room.
Translation for potential girlfriend: May also have the ability to control you.

MAGNANIMOUS <MAG-NAH-NI-MUSS> Gives, gives, and keeps on giving.
Translation for potential girlfriend: Only when he feels like it.

CLEVER (WITH WORDS) <CLEH-VURR> Knows the right thing to say and when to say it.
Translation for potential girlfriend: This can be confusing. You want to call him on his dartboard shot—but it was right on the mark (even though it hit below the belt *and still hurts*).

CHAPTER 6

Virgo, Ex or Next
(the Virgin; August 23–September 22)

VIRGO RUDE-IMENTS

 Listen up, cutie pies. There's something very *wrong* with the way we've been thinking about our fair Virgin. Know why?

'Cause Virgo's really about as virginal as Drew Barrymore—at twelve (with her drug problem). As virginal as Britney Spears when she was with Justin Timberlake—and went on every media show *claiming* it. As virginal as Madonna on her *Like a Virgin* world tour. Ahem.

See, something's been misconstrued here. Virgo's difficult. Yes. You sense this. Ridiculously systematic. And guarded, like the actual hiding place of Jimmy Hoffa's body. Dark, like when someone dies in a Harry Potter book. (You don't expect it.)

Yet there's something else. What? Is it? Gasp! Virgo is actually one of the sexiest, most intelligent guys around. He's got sometin' special, mon. Yeah, mon. Peace out. Yup, he's Indiana Jones and James Bond and Richard Gere (Virgo) and Sean Connery (Virgo) and Hugh Grant (Virgo) combined. Ooga, ooga.

Bet you didn't know. He's also damned charming. Eccentric. Made him and threw away the mold. Has odd habits (but he'd rather you didn't know that yet). His comic timing is genius. He's a great storyteller. Does impersonations you wouldn't believe. He's generous with his time and always puts others before himself. A perfectionist. Romantic (in his own way). A true poet with a gift for language. Presence.

> On a good night, I get underwear, bras, and hotel-room keys thrown onstage. . . . You start to think that you're Tom Jones.
>
> KEANU REEVES

Problem is, where is all that yowza directed? He's so goddamn contained. He *seems* so open, yet he always leaves something in reserve—like that extra tip of a condom *in use*.

Hey, kids. There's a part of him hidden from the rest of the world. Well. He's not aware of it. If you ask him, he's an open book. (Yeah. Read him and weep.) In reality, though, he's as closed as a Puritan's eyes on Forty-second Street.

Here's the thing. Virgo is strangely intuitive and senses who truly likes him and who doesn't. But when it comes to sussing out his own current love predicament, he's completely lost. Because he just doesn't see things the way you or I do. He's too analytical to let karma, energy, and his natural-born intuition *ruin the facts*. Strangely enough, something has to be proven for him to believe it, even though he's the consummate idealist. So he's at war with himself.

> Any jackass can kick down a barn, but it takes a good carpenter to build one.
>
> LYNDON B. JOHNSON

Subconsciously, too, he doesn't want to be "discovered." He's his own worst critic. In fact, admitting his "faults" would be like proclaiming himself a witch in the 1500s—in Salem, Massachusetts. He's overtly, yet covertly afraid he'll be burned at the stake. He hates putting himself out there, so he analyzes everything to death to prevent it. It's a control thing.

He's insecure, touchy, paranoid like Scooby-Doo, with an extra toke of the "Mystery Machine" herb stuff. (Yeah, y~~

that van had dark, tinted windows and Scooby and~~

had the munchies? Uh-huh. Riiight.)

The scariest thing for Virgo is to be embar-
rassed **in public**. Yet he's drawn to scandal like
Jennifer Lopez is to marriage. (She's a Leo, Venus
in Virgo. Instead of simply sleeping with guys, she
let her guilt complex get to her and *married them:*
Um, Virgo influence.) Don't believe me? Check

Actually, I'm an
overnight
success, but it
took twenty
years.

MONTY HALL

this out. Virgos: Hugh Grant (sex with a prostitute in public);
Charlie Sheen (numerous scandals with prostitutes); Fred Durst
(sex-tape scandal); Kobe Bryant (rape scandal); Bill O'Reilly (accused of employee sexual harassment/taped phone sex); Michael
Jackson (accused of pedophilia); Robert Blake (accused and acquitted of killing his wife of six months); Leo Tolstoy (wrote about
sexual addiction; had sex with his serfs and kept diaries); Ivan
the Terrible (raped many women, also buried them alive, hanged,
and mutilated them); Caligula (alleged incest with his sisters);
William Kennedy Smith (alleged rape); David Copperfield (alleged rape sex scandal). All Virgos. Uh. That's a pretty long list.

Here's the ironic thing. Virgo has a more-than-odd relationship
with sex. He's a sex symbol, yet doesn't necessarily want to be regarded as such. (River Phoenix, a Virgo who died of a drug overdose, for example, hated being revered in this way.) He has fetishes
that he doesn't want anyone to know about. *Even you.*

But here's the real problem: He's not even aware of it. He
thinks—is *convinced*—that he wants love for forever and ever. Yet
he does everything—everything, folks—to f*ck it up. Want to
know why?

Virgo is a closet masochist.

That's right. He likes to suffer but doesn't know it. He's the
Marquis de Sade of the astrological *Wayne's World. Wayne's World,*

'cause he's got a strange sense of humor but he's the only one allowed to laugh (especially if the joke's on him).

Humiliation is a dirty, rotten scoundrel game for him, and he gets off on being murky, ruining his reputation, then making a comeback and showing us all he's not necessarily the good little boy we thought he was—but can still walk around among us clean folk (and get away with it). He plays the victim card all too well. He needs his dirty laundry aired so that he can be punished for it, get it off his conscience, then go back to being the noble prince.

> No self-respecting gay guy would have ever made some of the hair and clothing choices I am still trying to live down.
>
> DAVID COPPERFIELD

One more thing. Virgo guy's so bright, it's hard to understand why he does *such stupid things*. Especially in love. In his work life, he's the poster child for good business sense. He's organized and brilliant.

This one's a keeper, though, and can be faithful when he's in love (after the decades it takes him to finally decide on you). Just make sure you talk things through with him—in and out of bed—or he'll secretly construct a scenario where the heroine (you) gets it in the end. And doesn't get the guy.

> A little nonsense now and then is relished by the wisest men.
>
> ROALD DAHL

Well, obviously. 'Cause she's dead in his mind.

His drama is hidden like a murder weapon in a Latin soap opera.

But it's there.

Oh, it's there.

VIRGO TONGUE LASHING

"You're a naughty little girl and you want me to punish you for it," Virgo whispers in your ear.

"Hmm? What?" you reply.

Virgo pretends he never said it.

If you react (and play along), Virgo guy will embroil you in an intense schoolteacher little-Catholic-girl-school-uniform role-play-foreplay sex talk. (It's his way of distancing himself yet getting the goods.) Doooooo behave! Like Austin Powers, he loves to be naughty. Though he keeps it contained, like Renée Zellweger . . . and her faux–Bridget Jones accent. (Which was pretty good, by the way.) "Why are you so spoiled?" Virgo will ask you, changing the mood entirely. He'll kid about it. Grin and wink. Hug and pat you like he's burping a baby (right, where's the intimacy?). The damage, however, is done. It's obvious that he's being as real as Tara Reid's rack.

> I just don't think I'm that interesting. I don't think what I have to say is that interesting. To hear me go blah, blah, blah, blah, blah. I mean, who . . . cares?
>
> JAMES GANDOLFINI

Leo guy, by contrast, turns and tosses in bed, hoping and praying that what he did today was right. However, he works it out for himself. Virgo, on the other hand, takes it one giant leap further. He can't help but criticize and find fault with *your* life. He'll blame you for the way you, ah, *dance* through it. "Where's your reliability?!" he chides. Yet he cha-chas, sambas, rumbas, tangos, salsas, waltzes, and breakdances through *his* life (and gets a 2 from the judges—out of 10).

He's more critical of himself than he is of you, though. Know this: He doesn't want to tap-dance his way out of *accountability*. *Responsibility*. That's some serious stuff for Virgo. He feels responsible for the state of the world at large. Again, serious.

It's hard to break that barrier or label him anything but "good-guy." He's self-effacing, modest in a charming way. Humble. He'll listen to you. Help you with your problems. Be the rock you can lean on. Give you great advice. Things need to be focused on him, though. He's a martyr sometimes, but only because it lets him be the center of attention. He needs to be appreciated for his efforts. It's like if Leo were cornflakes, he'd be the same brand, but with a harsh, grainy-nut side. He's like an Oprah guest ranting and raving about how no one's paying attention to the poor, starving children in Africa—but doesn't leave the stage before he flashes his new book and a winning smile.

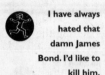

I have always hated that damn James Bond. I'd like to kill him.

SEAN
CONNERY

Want to know what gets him fired up? Besides being "forced" to have hot, covert sex in a public bathroom?

Read on.

VIRGO: IS HE *INTO* YOU?

He can be generous, this guy. Just make sure that necklace you want isn't near his accountant's office. It'll remind him that he owes the guy money.

Seriously, though. If he's got the money to spend, he'll spend it. It's just that he doesn't want to go overboard and *show his emotions*, so you might just get a Diet Coke with a bendy straw for your first anniversary, instead. Just sayin'.

However, if you give a hint that you want those new surround-sound speakers or an extra computer for your home office, he won't balk at getting it for you. Actually, he's more likely to spend his money on you (and on electronics or cookware) than he is on himself. He's probably very methodical about money. This can take on many Silly Putty color forms. Shrinky Dinks. Money, to him, is security and status, and he likes having a few projects going at the same time. Not saying he's wealthy or anything—though he usually has a few coins put away. Sometimes, however, he lets his perfectionist side interfere with his moola-making. For instance, he probably stays up nights wondering why they put George Washington on the one-dollar bill, since he lied about the cherry tree and everything. (Lying, to him, is unforgivable. Again, trust, for this guy, is HUGE.)

However, Virgo guy definitely has a kind demeanor. He'll care about helping you and your state of affairs: that's Virgo. He's got a hyper-intelligent mind that makes him think too much, so he tries to steer it away from *his* emotions . . . but he's perfectly willing to help you with yours.

Obsessing about work stuff and holding emotions in is normal for this guy. It's a little scary when he finally does open up to you and spill the beans on what's been bothering him. He's calm, calm. He'll smile and pat the couch next to him for you to sit down. Then he'll erupt like a thundering volcano that hasn't exploded since Mount Vesuvius.

You've got to get him to open up. Easy, though. He has to learn to confide in you. Secretly, he's a real gossip hound. And he worries that his public image will be shot if he lets on about anything—even to you. When he does let go, though (especially in bed), he's the best mix of sensuality and slick moves—with good aim.

Pull away so that he can win you. Like a professional gambler, he'll only bet on you when he's sure of the odds.

> Oh, that. I just do that for the extra money, and to satisfy my male need to kill and win.
>
> **CHARLIE SHEEN**

ADVICE TO THE FUTURE MRS. VIRGO

Virgo guy is a serial monogamist. He believes in one gal at a time. Typical Virgo will definitely feel more if his woman doesn't hop into his bed right away. He's slow on the draw because he likes to study and analyze his partner's moves—so that he can use that information to his advantage in the future.

He's really lazy about finding someone who's perfect for him 'cause in a way he doesn't truly believe she's out there. That's why he'll usually stick around for awhile with one girl—till he finds the next.

> I don't want to die in a car accident. When I die it'll be a glorious day. It'll probably be a waterfall.
>
> RIVER PHOENIX

Virgo is the most difficult of signs to drag to the altar. I say "drag," because that's just what you might have to do to get him there. It's gonna take years of being sure . . . Virgo guy's not likely to go to Las Vegas with you, drink bottles of champagne till he's blotto, and wind up in Elvis's "little love shack of marriage" in front of a priest.

Come to think of it, that's not a bad idea . . .

Listen. There *is* something very pure and idealistic about the way Virgo sees love. He's practical about it—and understated. Yet there's something romantic in that, too. Know this: If you manage to secure a Virgo guy, he'll likely make a very good husband—plus, he'll wipe your nose and take care of you when you're sickly with the flu. His love will be dependable, like good absorbent undergarments for bladder control. And randy—like a teenage boy in his hot ex-babysitter's presence.

> What I'm doing right now, I'm chasing perfection.
>
> KOBE BRYANT

Physical affection out of bed? Nah. You don't need it. It's just like the movie *Titanic*—overrated.

ADVICE TO THE EX MS. VIRGO

Really want to hear the truth? Listen up.

Virgo guy, if he's left you, has probably mulled it around in his brain a million times. He's not likely to make rash decisions, like your sloshed friend who leaves drunk, idiotic messages on her ex-boyfriend's answering machine. (Yeah, that'll work: telling *him* not to call *her* anymore.)

Good news: Virgo guy is maybe the only one in the zodiac to tell it to you straight. (Most guys just disappear like Casper.)

If you're calm, rational, grounded, and you ask Virgo guy to talk it out with you, he may take the smelly fish bait. And be stand-up. You can work it from there. Seriously, though, he's about as likely to change his mind about you as Coca-Cola and Pepsi are to join forces, form a deal, and unite.

> There is no me. I do not exist. There used to be a me, but I had it surgically removed.
>
> PETER SELLERS

Do NOT play the trampy sex card. He might go for it, but he'll respect you about as much as the TV repair-man he had over last Thursday—who didn't fix the set, damn it. Also, because Virgo is so contained, he can do abstinence like an executive in a midlife crisis does his secretary. (Or like I-am-God-therefore-I-can-do-what-I-want celebrities do their kids' babysitters: witness Steven Segal, Jude Law, Joe Piscopo.)

Better just wait and see what happens. If Virgo wants you, he'll hunt you down like the noble professor did Clarice (with a picnic basket full of fava beans and a nice Chianti—very elegant and finesse-y, y'know).

But it won't be spooky and he won't eat your brain (yeah, the gory sequel, *Hannibal*). He'll need that mental part of you so he can fall in love with you all over again.

Aw.

SUN/VENUS COMBINATIONS:
THE TRUE LOVE POTENTIAL TEST

Virgo Sun, Venus in Cancer

This guy can't shake the nice-guy image . . .'cause he is one. Truth is, he does care about how he affects other people's lives. He's as generous with his time as groupies are to giving it away to rock stars.

Actually, there's something odd about his selflessness. He's seriously manic about showing he likes "keeping it real." It's like "Jenny from the Block," though—sporting a flawless ten-carat diamond and wearing Juicy sweats. He does like the simple things. A Spartan life. He'll trek into the wilderness (and drag you with him) just to prove his case. See? Why does he need to show everyone he's able to give up creature comforts? It's hypocritical and weird—'cause we know he's got enough in the bank to own a piece of it.

He's a good joke teller, but his sense of humor is offbeat, strange, sometimes dark. He'll gravitate toward the one at the dinner table who laughs the hardest at his jokes. His optimism is legendary—but when things go wrong, he retreats into a cave and tries to work things out by himself.

Don't go after him. The bear behind him might not attack you, but it's possible Virgo guy won't be so nice about it. Just let him know you're there for him when he wants to talk. That, he'll respect.

Speaking of respect, all Virgos—and this one in particular—have an odd pseudo-relationship/love affair with it. He'll use this as his excuse for everything. If he's having a tryst with a married

> When I was in first grade, everyone made fun of my name, of course. I think it's kind of a big name to hold up when you're nine years old. It seemed goofy. I used to tell people I wanted to change the world, and they used to think, "This kid's really weird."
>
> RIVER PHOENIX

woman, for example, he'll say that her husband's a maggot anyway, he doesn't respect *him*. If he cheats on you, that's where it'll
come from. A woman's got to meet his standards in order for him
to give her an A+ in "respect" on her report card
(y'know, the one he keeps handy in that sacred
chest Grandpa gave him, next to his bed). This
guy will want to settle down more than the other
Virgos. Just make sure that you have a deep, dark
past—and you've now turned things partway
around. He attracts hardship like rock stars, hot women.

> The words
> walked right out
> of my mouth.
>
> **JAMES BRADY**

BOYFRIEND POTENTIAL RATING: High if you play the damsel in distress. Warning, though: this guy's luck is about as bad as Murphy's
(of Murphy's law: What goes wrong can always go wronger).
Pretty dern faithful, though. Solid. Good choice. Just make sure
you don't catch the bad luck (aimed at him). It searches him
out like teenagers flock to arcade galleries at tacky suburban
malls.

CELEBRITY CORRESPONDENTS
WITH VIRGO SUN, VENUS IN CANCER

Keanu Reeves (September 2, 1964) Had a string of tragedies—
  accidental deaths of young people close to him: first, River
  Phoenix, then his estranged girlfriend.
Macaulay Culkin (August 26, 1980)
Lyndon B. Johnson (August 27, 1908)
Billy Ray Cyrus (August 25, 1961)
Chris Tucker (August 31, 1972)
Monty Hall (August 25, 1921) He's been married to the same
  woman for years and has two daughters (including Joanna
  Gleason) and one son.
Muhammad (August 30, 570)

Blair Underwood (August 25, 1964) He married actress Desiree
DaCosta in 1994 and they have three children.
Maxwell (August 26, 1956)
Caligula (August 31, 12)

Virgo Sun, Venus in Leo

I'm just like anyone. I cut and I bleed. And I embarrass easily.

MICHAEL JACKSON

I am not a dark person and I don't consider myself dark.

TIM BURTON

I always knew I'd accomplish something very special—like
robbing a bank perhaps.

MICKEY ROURKE

Anyone who has a continuous smile on his face conceals a
toughness that is frightening.

GRETA GARBO

Here's the weird thing about Virgo/Leo. He's got serious *proble-
mos*, but you may not pick up on it. He truly wants to stand out
and make his birthmark, Cindy Crawford–style.
This feeds his Venus/Leo counterpart, yet that
Virgo Sun sign holds him back from being, um,
normal—'cause the two signs *clash* big-time.
He's a juxtaposition, of sorts—like your Has-
sidic friend who's just become a staunch Republican.

> I've had a few arguments with people, but I never carry a grudge. You know why? While you're carrying a grudge, they're out dancing.
>
> BUDDY HACKETT

He's methodical about the way he does things
and, for that reason, hits work stuff out of the
park. However, he's an idealist and a purity freak;
he wants to retain his innocence—so much so that

when he gets into his upper thirties, it may start to seem a little creepy.

People actually overlook his strangeness because he's so god-damn fascinating (like in a rubbernecking car-accident way).

These men, Virgo/Venus in Leo, need to be different and stand out. Yet their proclivity for the bizarre and false ranks higher than the "off" factor of Pamela Anderson's breasts on her 108-pound body. However, he gets away with it. There's hardly an audience he doesn't jibe with. And that's what truly makes him happy: putting smiles on others' faces.

He carves out his niche like a good skirt steak, becoming the best at what he does. Yet—a closer examination of the object in question indicates that he's not quite in his right mind while doing it. Well, actually . . . he always lets his on-the-mark instinct take over. There's something *genius* about this guy.

> You loan your friend money. You see them again, they don't say nothin' 'bout the money. "Hi, how ya doin'? How's ya mama doing?" Man, how's my money doin'?
>
> **CHRIS TUCKER**

That's the good news. Here's the bad. Though there's a certain kind of integrity to his work vision, he has serious issues in his relations with real *people*. Again, it's the conflict of the earth (Virgo) and fire (Leo). Because both signs have scary perfectionist traits, this guy becomes either really, really good at what he does or really, really addicted to *something bad* in order to squash all his worrying and cope with it—or both.

It's not that he doesn't love you. He's just so wrapped up in tormenting himself that he can't see you standing there—in back of the one-way police-lockup questioning-room mirror.

BOYFRIEND POTENTIAL RATING: High if he needs you to solve his problems in some way. (And if you have the patience of a sugary sweet substitute teacher the first day of detention.) Realize, too, that if this guy settles down, it's probably to have the security he needs to pursue his work dreams. Low, if his eternal-child within freaks you out like a middle-aged Harrison Ford with an earring.

CELEBRITY CORRESPONDENTS
WITH VIRGO SUN, VENUS IN LEO

Check out the "cut the mold and threw it away" factor.

Michael Jackson (August 29, 1958)

David Copperfield (September 16, 1956) He was engaged to model Claudia Schiffer and, in 2007, was involved in a huge alleged-rape sex scandal.

Paulo Coehlo (August 24, 1947)

Jeremy Irons (September 19, 1948)

Mickey Rourke (September 16, 1953)

Van Morrison (August 31, 1945)

Brian De Palma (September 11, 1940)

Leo Tolstoy (September 9, 1828) Had thirteen children and later his marriage was described as one of the worst. He had sexual relations with his serfs and kept diaries of it.

Tim Burton (August 25, 1958) He married once, dated Lisa Marie Smith, and is currently engaged to Helena Bonham Carter, with whom he has two children.

Leonard Bernstein (August 25, 1918)

Miguel de Cervantes (September 8, 1547)

Dweezil Zappa (September 5, 1969) Married since 2005; has dated Katie Wagner (Robert's daughter), Sharon Stone, and Lisa Loeb.

Ferruccio Ferragamo (September 9, 1945)

Alain Ducasse (September 13, 1956)

O. Henry (September 11, 1862) He eloped when he was seventeen. After her death, he married his childhood sweetheart.

Roald Dahl (September 13, 1916) He was married for thirty years to actress Patricia Neal. His dark sense of humor in children's fiction is legendary (but he was also thought to be an anti-Semite). In 1983, he married his ex-wife's best friend.

James Gandolfini (September 18, 1961)

Dan Cortese (September 14, 1967)

Andy Roddick (August 30, 1982)

Bob Newhart (September 5, 1929)

William Howard Taft (September 15, 1857)

Bobby Short (September 15, 1924)

Terry Bradshaw (September 2, 1948) He's been married three times. Jokes incessantly about his divorces.

Ludacris (September 11, 1977)

John Ritter (September 17, 1948)

Arnold Palmer (September 20, 1929)

Jesse Owens (September 12, 1913)

Jerry Bruckheimer (September 21, 1945)

Phil McGraw, aka Dr. Phil (September 1, 1950) Was married once for three years before current wife since 1976.

Harry Connick, Jr. (September 11, 1967)

Itzhak Perlman (August 31, 1945) Still married to the same woman.

Steve Guttenberg (August 24, 1958)

Virgo Sun, Venus in Virgo

Okay. You could be on the right track with this one. See, here's the thing. This guy also has the infant-within thing goin' on, but in a more refined, Virgo kinda way. He has a deep, deep sense of responsibility to family and those around him—which actually makes him a decent potential lovah guy for you.

The absolute funniest, most ironic (albeit strange) men live under this fortress of a sign (trying to break through is tough,

tough—but, once you're in, it's preeeetty). Hey, he's got his defenses up, so he's not gonna woo you by clinking champagne glasses by the fire—he's more likely to do it by blowing champagne through his nose. His M.O. is to make you laugh, then move in for the kill.

When this guy gets married, he wants to do it right the first time. He actually knows he's as sensitive as a baby's butt, and likes to test the product for a while (um: you) to see whether or not he has an allergic reaction to your special brand of baby powder.

(Here's interesting: Our *Friends* friend Courteney Cox must be attracted to a good guffaw—she had a six-year relationship with Michael Keaton—Virgo/Virgo before she married David Arquette—also Virgo/Virgo. Both guys with the same sign combos.)

Michael Jackson and I talk all the time. I think we understand each other in a way that most people can't understand either of us.

MACAULAY CULKIN

Though this guy is hold-your-pee-in hilarious, it's not your typical garden-like variety. His humor is odd, strangely low-key—not necessarily in your face. And it's used to protect him like a power shield. He's quick to mock himself, and has a certain humility to the way he actually sees himself. In fact, his insecurity can be as pronounced as Jennifer Grey's original shnoz—but you may not recognize it. It's bound to take form in a few peculiar habits. He can give OCD a new name. Like, does he only let you shoot his pic from a certain angle? Does he wash his hands first thing every time he gets home?

Listen. You can live with the weird stuff. He more than makes up for it in the love department. He might not be an all-out romantic with words, but he'll show ya he loves ya by being dependable and reliable. And refreshing—like a cold brewski on a hot summer day. With lime.

BOYFRIEND POTENTIAL RATING: High if you like men who always seem, well, ahem, high. Higher if you can take some of the worry burden off their shoulders—'cause they think that they're the Atlas guy, holding up the world. Low if you don't have that clean Audrey Hepburn good-girl vibe—and don't laugh at their jokes. They'll cast you off like an Olympic athlete's jockstrap after practice.

CELEBRITY CORRESPONDENTS
WITH VIRGO SUN, VENUS IN VIRGO

Bill Murray (September 21, 1950)

Adam Sandler (September 9, 1966) Married to model Jackie Titone since 2003.

David Arquette (September 8, 1971) Married Courteney Cox in 1999.

Jimmy Fallon (September 19, 1974)

Michael Keaton (September 5, 1951)

Peter Falk (September 16, 1927)

Chris Columbus (September 10, 1958)

Gene Kelly (August 23, 1912) He was married three times; his shortest marriage was six years.

Mark Harmon (September 2, 1951) Longtime married to actress Pam Dawber.

Rocky Marciano (September 1, 1923)

James Coburn (August 31, 1928)

Andrea Bocelli (September 22, 1958)

Ryan Phillippe (September 10, 1974) Was married to Reese Witherspoon in 1999. She filed for divorce in 2006.

Jimmy Connors (September 2, 1952)

John Cage (September 4, 1912)

Joe Perry (September 10, 1950)

Hank Williams (September 17, 1923) He had a problem with alcohol and painkillers, which destroyed his first marriage. Married twice.

Upton Sinclair (September 20, 1878)

William Golding (September 19, 1911)

Frankie Avalon (September 18, 1939) He married in 1962 and the couple have eight children.

Cal Ripken (August 24, 1960)

Peter Lawford (September 7, 1923)

Dick York (September 4, 1928)

Richard Marx (September 16, 1963) He's been married to actress Cynthia Rhodes since 1989.

Charlie Parker (August 29, 1920)

Travis Knight (September 13, 1974)

Virgo Sun, Venus in Libra

Love may not make the world go round, but I must admit that it makes the ride worthwhile.

SEAN CONNERY

This one's like chocolate truffles when you're PMSing: irresistible. It's devastating. He has enough charisma and hotness to wipe the skankiness from Courtney Love's public persona. (Not easy.) The charisma to subdue Madonna's aggressiveness. (Impossible.) The sex appeal to make Jennifer Love Hewitt's boobs grow between episodes 36 and 37 in *Party of Five*. (Yeah, like Mohammad, um, moving the mountain.)

Now, if you haven't already noticed, any guy who's got Venus in Libra is bound to be sex-appeal legendary. Though with each Sun sign it takes on different forms. For example: Sun Leo, Venus in Libra: Bill Clinton—out-there sexy, who uses it to his advantage—and, uh, sometimes cheats. Sun Libra, Venus in Libra: Christopher Reeve, Will Smith—gorgeous and hunky but modest, and very good hubbies. Sun Virgo, Venus in Libra—what we's talkin' 'bout here: Richard Gere, Sean Connery, Hugh Grant, Charlie Sheen, River Phoenix, Colin Firth . . . the list goes on. Dang.

Here's the deal. This guy reeks of sex like a booty call at one in the morning. However, he's as closed as Church Lady, from *Saturday Night Live*, without the sense of humor.

Yeah, he gets himself. True. He knows that *not admitting to anything* equals fans. He can be as vague as Ross Perot in his presidential campaign—he doesn't get to the heart of the matter.

Even if you're with him for decades.

This guy is waiting for a wake-up call. And he will not settle down with one person unless he gets one. Sometimes this alarm clock takes on the form of recognizing and battling some form of addiction, combined with a car accident or a near-death experience; a sickness; losing someone close to him; almost losing you, et cetera—and it's sad he has to go this way 'cause his partner usually kicks him to the curb by then.

If men knew how women pass the time when they are alone, they'd never marry.

O. HENRY

Until he's had this "enlightening" experience, though, he's bound to treat you like the Lego set he had when he was five: He'll take you out to play when he feels like it, then see his sister's Barbie in the corner and pick her up out of curiosity. Ahem.

It all comes back to a sense of entitlement. Deep down, this guy knows he's scorching hot. He has urges—as strong as a guy who's just downed a pitcher of beer (without a toilet in sight). He can take what he wants without worrying about the consequences (think of alleged sex-scandal offenders Hugh Grant, Kobe Bryant, Charlie Sheen, William Kennedy Smith). He feels a little unconquerable and likes to tempt fate *just to see what happens*. He's also scared of real love and of being discovered—

like a female celebrity buying a pregnancy test at a public pharmacy.

This guy also has such a keen mind that he can talk his way out of anything. His charm is polished; his smile, little-boy cute. Because he always seems reserved, it's hard to imagine that he can open himself up to anyone—else. Oh, but he's a Pandora's box. No one can resist trying to lift that lid, and they get a really bum cereal surprise when they empty out the carton to see what's there.

BOYFRIEND POTENTIAL RATING: High if he's had some transformative experience and has "seen the light." (Chances are, it'll be the flashlight you shine on him in the back bushes, with your neighbor. Ouch.) Low if you let him get away with things. He'll twist the truth around like the high school captain of the football team giving the class geek a wedgie.

CELEBRITY CORRESPONDENTS WITH
VIRGO SUN, VENUS IN LIBRA

Richard Gere (August 31, 1949) A Buddhist, Gere was married to Cindy Crawford from '91 to '95. He remarried in 2002.

Sean Connery (August 25, 1930)

Hugh Grant (September 9, 1960) Couldn't stay out of the tabloids. Cheated on Elizabeth Hurley with a prostitute. They broke up a few years later. Was involved with British heiress Jemima Kahn.

Charlie Sheen (September 3, 1965) Can't stay out of the tabloids. He married Denise Richards in 2002. She filed for divorce while pregnant with their second child. Sheen has been named on Heidi Fleiss's list for hiring many high-class prostitutes.

Guy Ritchie (September 10, 1968) Married to Madonna.

River Phoenix (August 23, 1970) Died from a drug overdose.

Colin Firth (September 10, 1960) He had a child with Meg Tilly before marrying an Italian filmmaker in 1997.

Lance Armstrong (September 18, 1971) He was married from 1998 to 2003. Public courtship of Sheryl Crow in 2005 ended in 2006.

Mike Piazza (September 4, 1968)

Marc Anthony (September 16, 1968)

Kobe Bryant (August 23, 1978) Huge alleged rape case.

William Kennedy Smith (September 4, 1960) Huge alleged rape case.

Rick Springfield (August 23, 1949)

Peter Sellers (September 8, 1925) Rumored to be abusive. Was married four times.

Chad Michael Murray (August 24, 1981) Separated from Sophia Bush after five months of marriage. Rumored that he cheated on her with Paris Hilton and his childhood sweetheart.

Maurice Chevalier (September 12, 1888)

Freddie Mercury, of Queen (September 4, 1946)

Prince Harry of England (September 15, 1984) Constantly in the news for small scandals: dressing up as a Nazi for a party; attending strip clubs.

Barry Gibb (September 1, 1946)

Larry Hagman (September 21, 1931)

Moby (September 11, 1965)

Buddy Holly (September 7, 1936)

Jay Mohr (August 23, 1970) He has one son from his six-year marriage to former model Nicole Chamberlain. Married Nikki Cox in 2006.

D. H. Lawrence (September 11, 1885) The woman he spent his life with was already married with three children. They eloped.

Damon Wayans (September 4, 1960)

Tom Felton (September 22, 1987)

Stephen King (September 21, 1947)

Otis Redding (September 9, 1941)

Gengis Khan (September 14, 1186)

Elvis Costello (August 25, 1954)

Ivan the Terrible (August 25, 1530) Tortured and ordered thousands to be killed. Married seven times, sometimes divorcing after just days.

Stephen Jay Gould (September 10, 1941)

Donald O'Connor (August 25, 1925)

Ben Gazzara (August 28, 1930)

Conway Twitty (September 1, 1933)

Tom Skerritt (August 25, 1933)

Geoffrey Beene (August 30, 1925)

Rex Smith (September 19, 1955)

Stephen Fry (August 24, 1957) Kept his homosexuality a secret by maintaining a celibate lifestyle for sixteen years.

Adam West (September 19, 1928)

Barry White (September 12, 1944) Was jailed at seventeen for four months for theft. (He was in a gang.) He married the lead singer of the Supremes. They divorced fifteen years later.

Virgo Sun, Venus in Scorpio

These guys like to make people smile. They actually reveal the fantastic in the ordinary. In fact, if he doesn't seem to be paying attention to you, give him a good whack. Chances are, he's too caught up in watching people around him. Yeah. This guy is obsessed with *other people's lives*.

Not good news for you.

He's got the genius to discover bizarre eccentricities in people's normal, everyday behavior. This can take the form of a one-year-old with lots of fun keys dangled in front of him.

Actually, his humble charm is probably intriguing to you—like

Reese's Pieces to E.T. Though more alien. You'll want to figure him out.

Don't try. He's as elusive as Carmen Electra's bikini line in re-runs of *Baywatch.*

Let's go deep here. Virgo/Venus in Scorpio is, oh, just a tad obsessed with death and war. He probably talks about it, scorns it, hates it—yet always has a comment on hand about it, like Joan Rivers about celebrities' fashion choices on the red carpet.

Make no mistake, though. This guy has a wild streak he keeps hidden like Sylvester Stallone's porn movies.

You may just play second fiddle to his work life. He's like a Lab digging in the ground where he knows his bone is: He won't give up till he succeeds (and even then he'll go off and chew on it—ignoring you).

Speaking of chewing, Virgo/Scorpio may have an odd relationship with food. It's different for each of these guys, but it could be: vegetarian or macrobiotic, always watching everything he puts in his mouth; he could have strange food allergies . . . whatever. It's totally as kooky as Michael Jackson putting oxygen masks on his children. Wow. Okay. But not quite as strange and sad.

This guy is probably very independent, too—except when there's a beautiful woman in the room. He's attracted to beauty, whatever that means *to him.*

Look. Virgo/Scorpio usually has relationships that last a while—before he divorces and moves on to the next wife. He takes love seriously, but unless you're his ultimate dream Fantathy Island Love-boat, he'll probably commit to you about as much as an eighteen-year-old with ADD hunkering down to study for the SAT or ACT.

His dry wit and wonderful gift for language make him interest-

It is said that love makes the world go round. The announcement lacks verification. It's wind from the dinner horn that does it.

O. HENRY

ing. Just beware that he might someday give you the boot—like the geographical layout of Italy on a map. Without two weeks' notice. Like macho bad boy Eddie Murphy cavorting with a transvestite, he hates being discovered. Unless your past is dark, really dark, he'll tune you out like a horny teenage boy whose girlfriend just told him she's saving herself for marriage.

BOYFRIEND POTENTIAL RATING: High if you can enter his weird, bizzaro world and *fit in*. Like ten midgets getting into a clown car. If he doesn't make you cry like an old AT&T commercial when your hormones are out of whack, you may just be okay. Especially if he's already had a devastating relationship, has learned from it, and doesn't try to cover it up like fat girls, with sarongs, on the beach. Low if your dream is to be a beautiful, elegant princess— who isn't cheated on by the prince (with an uglier version of you).

CELEBRITY CORRESPONDENTS
WITH VIRGO SUN, VENUS IN SCORPIO

Oliver Stone (September 15, 1946) Married and divorced twice.

Ethan Coen (September 21, 1957)

Robert Blake (September 18, 1933) He was married for nearly twenty years before meeting Bonnie Lee Bakley. When they married, it was his second marriage, her ninth. They lived in separate houses until she was murdered in 2001. Blake spent a year in jail until the trial, when he was acquitted.

Tommy Lee Jones (September 15, 1946) On his third marriage.

Corbin Bernsen (September 7, 1954)

Ed Begley, Jr. (September 16, 1949) On second marriage, with Rachelle Carson, since 2000.

Sid Caesar (September 8, 1922) Had problems with alcoholism and drugs but kicked it. Married to the same woman since 1943.

Allen Funt (September 16, 1914)
Karl Lagerfeld (September 10, 1938)
B. B. King (September 16, 1925)

VIRGO DIC*-TIONARY

DEVOTED <DEH-VOE-TED> Attached when he's truly hooked.
Translation for potential girlfriend: Incredibly vengeful if it doesn't work out.

QUICK <QWIK> Intelligent. Clever. Bright. Great in business.
Translation for potential girlfriend: Retarded when it comes to choosing a mate who's good for him.

CAPABLE <CAY-PAH-BULL> Extremely detail-oriented; always gets the job done.
Translation for potential girlfriend: In love, though, getting him to see the big picture is like asking a color-blind person to help you decide between a red skirt and a pink one.

SERVICING <SUR-VAH-SING> Which can translate as: good in bed.
Translation for potential girlfriend: Sexual, not sensual. And can be as repressed as a die-hard Yankees fan sitting on the "wrong" side of the bleachers with Red Sox fanatics.

DEPENDABLE <DEH-PEN-DAH-BULL> All-around good guy; there when you need him.
Translation for potential girlfriend: Has such a precious ego that, if you don't take his advice, he discounts you like women's underwear in a flea-market bin.

CHAPTER 7

Libra, Ex or Next
(the Scales, September 23–October 22)

LIBRA RUDE-IMENTS

Remember the Botticelli painting of Venus, the goddess, on the shell? That's how he'll see you if he's in love. He wants a woman so ultra-feminine, it'll counterbalance his not-so-masculine traits. Not saying he's not white-hot. This guy can light fire to a snowbank. Sell a chastity belt to a nymphomaniac. Get a grunge dude to wear yuppie suspenders. Charm thing: Libra. You know the drill.

It's the adoring push-pull thing that makes him seem so sensitive. Like the tip of his ding-dong: poised and ready, it needs no guidance. Yowza. Okay. Well. He *gets* suffering. He's done it all his life. *And wants to avoid it at all costs.*

Because Libra guy does seek equilibrium, he'll want to keep his emotions at a distance—like a football team after practice in the showers. Until he really falls, he'll see dating a woman the way Fred sees the fake ghost at the end of a Scooby-Doo episode: annoying but—well, okay, it was inevitable.

Speaking of sense and sensibility, this guy will tilt a picture until it's dead center on the wall. (Right. In some places, they call that OCD—Overly Caring of Decor.)

Libra is concerned with the beauty around him. You probably knew that. But here's why: It's like yin-yang. Ebony and ivory (go together in perfect yada-yada). Truth is, he doesn't want his world shaken up *because he just can't handle it.*

I know what you're thinking: That Libra guy is really deep. Uh, no. It ain't necessarily so. Most Librans tend to keep things on the surface where they can watch for impending chaos or disaster. Like a guy in a lighthouse waiting for boats about to crash.

Libra guys like to be in control. But they're more like the eyes of a storm. They start a heated debate, then watch it explode around them. And tear out before someone drags them into it. The study of character, action, and human behavior makes them feel powerful and prepared. They use the insight they gain in their quest for *their* holy grail: tranquillity.

I never had a good year.

JASON ALEXANDER

The worst thing a Libra guy can do is go for the younger, weaker target. He's drawn to it like pubescent boys to Pamela Anderson's rack. However, he's better off with an older woman or at least someone who can call him on his low-grade tequila shots (and make him eat the worm if he's bad).

If you're happy-go-lucky, but grounded, sociable but not too social, have a personality, but also go well as arm-candy . . . motherly but not nagging; feminine but not too flirty—Libra guy may be right for you. But it's like asking for French fries and a double cheeseburger without the fat: A tall order.

This guy, though he's a Libra—and can catfight as well as a coked-up supermodel backstage at a Dolce & Gabbana show—

does NOT like con-fron-ta-tion (sotto voce, like it's a disease). Or arguing. Pull away and let him come after you.

Advice, dahhhling. Use it or lose him.

Libra Tongue Lashing

Tease him. Be playful.

He'll get there. When he finally stops grilling you like a hot dog on the Fourth of July (and gets the answers he's looking for), you can relax.

Fatal attraction, 'cause he's sexy but with a sweet vulnerability. Hypnotic. But is he sensual? That's a good question. In reality, he's a lot of talk. Or, rather, he talks in a different ice cream à la mode.

"Come hither" definitely works best with his dreamy bedroom eyes. (Think Hugh Jackman, Libra.) He knows it. So will you.

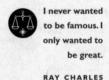

I never wanted to be famous. I only wanted to be great.

RAY CHARLES

Here's the thing. Status is so important to this guy, he's bound to notice what designer clothing or expensive watch you have on; who you know; what you represent; who your friends are; what your position in society is and how it'll make him look. Libra is very conscious of the way other people see him.

"What do you mean?" is bound to be part of the verbal foreplay with this guy. He's the original Keanu Reeves devil's advocate. (Notice how they picked someone so bland to play opposite Al Pacino? The contrast worked.) See? You're Al Pacino in your relationship with Libra guy. *He* wants to remain quiet, fair, unassuming—and make you do all the devil's work. It's like Olivia Newton-John (Libra) to John Travolta, in *Grease*. Like Fergie (Libra), to the British Royal Family. Like Barbara Walters (Libra) to every shnook, world criminal, and messed-up celebrity she interviews.

Libra guy is like George (Jason Alexander: Libra) in *Seinfeld*. He's too wimpy to break up with Susan—is miserable with her, but submits, anyway (because the alternative, to him, is Scary Spice).

An extreme real-life example would be good, funny-guy Phil Hartman (Libra) who couldn't leave his psychotic, abusive wife; (she eventually murdered him when he threatened to leave her).

Wow. That's terribly sad. Moving on.

LIBRA: IS HE *INTO* YOU?

This is gonna sound weird.

Libra guy, when he's into you, will make you laugh in bed.

And that quiet, charismatic thing always seems to work (with any specimen of the other sex around; even the gay guys, too—that's the problem).

Yet, he's almost got too many moves. Too many moves—like the marathon Olympics—with this guy. *Put your leg here. Put your arm here. Now switch. Roll over.* Pant, pant. You feel like Fido, only without the treat. What's going on here?

Libra is like liquid ice. Yeah, how does this work, anyway? He's hot, yet cold. Out there and "open," yet mysterious.

> I have often wanted to drown my troubles, but I can't get my wife to go swimming.
>
> JIMMY CARTER

So do this. When he's really yours, after *he* has sufficiently wooed you—and I'm saying he should be worshipping the ground you walk on—tell him to make love to you. Use those words. *"Make love to me."* Whisper it. He'll stop the freestyle and start the synchronized swimming. And you'll like it.

He'll spend, if he deems the things (and you) worthy, by the way.

When he settles down, it's usually for good. Especially if you're his second wife. (Don't get discouraged, though. He can also be as committed as a beauty-pageant contestant is to convincing the judges she's all about world peace—really *really* committed.) It all depends on his timeline. Yes, it's timing. Like a cooked egg before it cracks when it's been cooked too long. Bleaching hair and taking out the foils before it turns green. Knowing when to hold 'em, fold 'em. Walk away.

Rituals are important. Nowadays it's hip not to be married. I'm not interested in being hip.

JOHN LENNON

Run.

Libra guy knows when he's ready to settle down. And you will, too. Just be patient. Like Heinz ketchup: It's sloooow good.

ADVICE TO THE FUTURE MRS. LIBRA

Just tell him you're a virgin already. Or close to it. But you've been trained by professional strippers. And your boyfriend is waiting for you "back home." You've just *never had the chance* to put your new skills to the test, 'cause you haven't found "someone you really trust."

Then wait six months before you do the deed. He's yours.

No, seriously. Libra guy wants to see purity in the woman he marries. But he'll likely follow you to the ends of the earth once the ring-around-the-collar is on his finger. Libra takes commitment seriously. It's like the guy who's dragged to the opera and is suffering through it—but he's in the first row so he's guilted into staying.

In fact, at worst, you may see Libra get a little some-some on the side, but even then, he usually won't divorce. (Marcello Mastroianni had a well-known on- offscreen affair with Catherine Deneuve but never left his wife.) Okay. Not saying it's pretty, but it's pretty common. Libra can, however, remain faithful when he's got a woman he respects.

Libra guy is like Play-Doh. He can be molded and shaped to fit any creature you want. He'll go for either the virgin or the mother; those are his two types. One doesn't threaten him in any way (she's malleable, changeable, his Ms. Potato Head)—and the other makes all the decisions for him, like the stern head counselor at sleep-away camp. Just make sure to bundle up. It can get miiiighty cold out there without sufficient emotional warmth. Bring an, um, rum toddy, hot apple cider, and/or a down comforter. Protect yourself from below-freezing temperatures.

ADVICE TO THE EX MS. LIBRA

Running after a Libra man is the surest way to say *adiós* to his spicy burrito taco buns. He's looking for the easy paper route—again, someone who takes care of things for him, or someone *he* can take care of and pamper like an infant with diaper rash. Chances are, he'll always wind up with a strong wife—whether she's older or younger—who will subtly tweak and maneuver him. He'll never, ever go for the ball breaker. She intimidates him too much—like newbies in real estate trying to make a deal with money mogul Donald Trump.

I exist in a state of almost perpetual hysteria.

STING

If you're the ex and he still has *any* interest in you, he'll monitor you from a distance like high-security prisons with armed guards in the tower. Here's the thing. If you try to make him jealous (or are seen with any men) he will absolutely, resolutely discount you from his search like a Net date who's got a ten-year-old photo up *when she used to be hot*. But if you leave early from a party together, and play the good girl like the '50s characters in *Pleasantville* (before the movie turned Technicolor), he may just want you back. You have to be lovely, enchanting. Cinderella who leaves her glass slipper and disappears.

Nevertheless, it's not up to you.

One hint: If you see an article that would help him with his work—or if you've just reached celebrity status or you have access to them, send him a note saying "Thought you might like this." He'll be curious, but he won't necessarily pick up the phone or write back. He'll wait for you to call him. He suspects you will. Knows it's inevitable, like cheesy reality shows and "lays" at Mardi Gras.

> I'm not cynical about marriage or romance. I enjoyed being married. And although being single was fun for a while, there was always the risk of dating someone who'd owned a lunch box with my picture on it.
>
> SHAUN CASSIDY

Wait a few weeks. Call as a friend. Ask how he is. Appear to be concerned. If you have mutual friends, ask if he'd like to come along. Make it light like whipped cream, reduced fat. If you can get him to engage in person, you may just have a chance. *Don't talk about him to friends.* If word gets back to him that you're as weak and pathetic as a plastic-wrapped glass jar of food in a paper bag, it won't work.

You'll be as over for him as guys who still listen to Milli Vanilli on their ghetto blasters.

SUN/VENUS COMBINATIONS:
THE TRUE LOVE POTENTIAL TEST

Libra Sun, Venus in Leo

This guy is most likely mild-mannered. Passive. Emotionally elusive—which is odd for someone with all that moonshine firebrand of Venus in Leo.

Here's why.

Thomas Wolfe (Libra/Leo), the great twentieth-century writer, had an affair with a woman twenty years his senior. Only mentioning this 'cause you should check out Libra/Venus in Libra—but it applies to many Libras. Libra guy likes being with a woman who has more power in the relationship. Or way, way less. Simply put: Libra guy, when pressed, prefers to let his woman make all the decisions. He can be as lazy and as unwilling to move as a Lab getting his belly scratched. And as ineffective as a failing student copying off the class moron.

Libra wants to give the hard jobs to you. It's only when he chooses a partner who's controlling and manipulative that he gets into trouble. He's easily pushed around. A more manipulative Libra girlfriend can put a bun in her oven; then ask him for some dough. Scary. So Libra guy needs to be careful.

He gives her what she wants because he finds it hard to say no. This guy can be sweet. But if he feels threatened, he can be passive-aggressive. When he starts pulling away and distancing himself, you should confront him. He won't like it. He'll try to run away. But you can get him if you're like a bird in the hand, rather than two birds *beating around* the bush. Be assertive, mature. Not aggressive.

> It's difficult for me to meet women because my crowd is much older. I know that for some of the young women I do meet, a relationship with me can be envisioned as a benefit to their career.
>
> MICHAEL DOUGLAS

BOYFRIEND POTENTIAL RATING: Low if you let him have control in the relationship. High if you don't. He'll worship you. You can have the balls in the family: Throw him a few fast ones. Like a Lab with tennis balls, he'll run, fetch 'em, and bring them back to you. Every time.

CELEBRITY CORRESPONDENTS WITH LIBRA SUN, VENUS IN LEO
Jason Alexander (September 23, 1959)
Truman Capote (September 30, 1924)
Jimmy Carter (October 1, 1924)

Clive Owen (October 3, 1964)

Marcello Mastroianni (September 26, 1924)

Charlemagne (September 24, 768)

Heinrich Himmler (October 7, 1900)

Maurizio Gucci (September 26, 1948)

Phil Hartman (September 24, 1948) Was murdered by his wife.

Sir Peter Blake (October 1, 1948)

Ivan Petrovich Pavlov (September 26, 1849)

William Faulkner (September 25, 1897)

Thomas Wolfe (October 3, 1900)

William Rehnquist (October 1, 1924) Married to the same woman from 1953 until his death.

Libra Sun, Venus in Virgo

The world is his for the taking, as he's well aware. This Libra is shrewder than the others. For this reason, people tend to label him "difficult." He deserves it. He is. He's as critical as a heart condition. As demanding as a diva with requests for specific noshes in her dressing room. As snobby as the thickest Royal Family British accent (served up with tea and crumpets).

> I'm the only man in the world with a marriage license made out: to whom it may concern.
>
> MICKEY ROONEY

You'd never suspect it. He comes off as pleasant enough.

This guy, though, is looking for his equal. His match. Nay, his superior, if he can find her. He may *seem* insecure, but, deep down, he's as sure of his ability to capture hearts as Bill Clinton is in a room full of single Democratic women voters.

Anyway, it's a done deal once he gets over his fear of success. He wants it as badly as a teenage boy with blue balls. Though he's not completely convinced he can make the commitment, *afterward.*

What he wants is soul-love that stems from beauty—inside and out. That Venus in Virgo gives him a philosophical, poetic bent; he needs to express his feelings and beliefs about how the world should be. If you're his muse, he'll never leave you.

That's who he'll marry. Someone who'll inspire him to climb *Sound of Music* mountains . . . ford every stream. The passion comes when you leave him in peace to find himself. He needs serenity, even when he's with you, because his mind is always in turmoil. Like a nymphomaniac on a desert island with the ugliest man on earth, he needs time to resign himself to the situation. (Ever see *Blue Lagoon*? Yeah, being stuck on a deserted Caribbean island with a sixteen-year-old Brooke Shields. Tough.)

> I was married to Heather for seven years, Pamela five. Lot of years of marriage. I am just enjoying just trippin' out by myself.
>
> **TOMMY LEE**

This Libra guy can get seriously focused and narrow-minded. He works best when he's in a calm, cool relationship—and can trust his partner to be his Dwayne Johnson Rock.

Oh. One last thing. Lewd, vulgar, or loud noises scare this guy away. Tread softly. Hide the big stick for later.

BOYFRIEND POTENTIAL RATING: High if you crave peace like Lindsay Lohan craves media attention. Low, unless you can be as grounded as a 747 during a blizzard.

CELEBRITY CORRESPONDENTS
WITH LIBRA SUN, VENUS IN VIRGO

(Check out all the singers.)

John Lennon (October 9, 1940)

Eminem (October 17, 1972) Married the same woman twice—1999–2001, 2006–present.

Sting (October 2, 1951)

Friedrich Nietzsche (October 15, 1944)

Roger Moore (October 14, 1927) Currently married to fourth wife.

Luciano Pavarotti (October 12, 1935)

Julio Iglesias (September 23, 1943)

Bryan Ferry (September 26, 1945)

Yves Montand (October 13, 1921)

Ashley Hamilton (September 30, 1974) Married and divorced twice. For a year to Shannen Doherty. Then for a year to Angie Everhart.

Sean Lennon (October 9, 1975)

Jerry Lee Lewis (September 29, 1935) Married his thirteen-year-old cousin, Myra Gale Brown.

John Coltrane (September 23, 1926)

Johnny Mathis (September 30, 1935)

Sir Winston Churchill (October 10, 1940)

George Westinghouse (October 6, 1846)

Shaun Cassidy (September 27, 1958)

Guy Pearce (October 5, 1967)

Edward Kennedy (September 26, 1961)

Oliver North (October 7, 1943)

Jack Wagner (October 3, 1959)

George C. Scott (October 18, 1927)

Lee Iacocca (October 15, 1924)

Chevy Chase (October 8, 1943) On third marriage since 1982.

Steve Miller (October 8, 1943)

Emeril Lagasse (October 15, 1959)

Don McLean (October 2, 1945)

Jerry Orbach (October 20, 1935) Had two very long marriages.

Liev Schreiber (October 4, 1967)

Randy Quaid (October 1, 1950)

Ed Sullivan (September 28, 1902)

John Mayer (October 16, 1977)

Eric Stoltz (September 30, 1961) Lived with Bridget Fonda
from 1990 to 1998. And with Jennifer Jason Leigh before that.
Married to Bernadette Moley since 2005.

Tom Bosley (October 1, 1927)

Jackson Browne (October 9, 1948)

Libra Sun, Venus in Libra

Yeah, this guy's intense. Hot. Masculine. Yet candy-heart pretty
boy, too. A metrosexual. Hey, if he tells you to wear the Gucci instead of the Prada, do it. It'll probably look better, hon.

You're probably jealous of his eyelashes. Stop complimenting
him on them. He'll work harder.

In fact, it's not just that this guy is pretty. He's also got a thing
for young girls. Not in the sordid, icky underage Catholic priest sort
of way. Just much younger than he is, in a plaid-
skirt-and-knee-socks way. Or—in a switched-
gender thing—Cher way. Because he senses he can
control them. And that's important to him. Or
maybe he just wants a virgin because she can't
compare how (awful?) he is in bed with others.
But, on the other hand, he can go the opposite direction and fall in love with: Granny. Yup. A woman way older than
him who's gonna whip his effeminate butt into shape.

> I can resist
> everything
> except
> temptation.
>
> OSCAR WILDE

Oh, okay, he's also a romantic, romantic soul, so he's not that
bad. Poetry. Sunsets. Sunrises. Rainbows. Courting, to him, is second nature, so just get out that Regency romance book you've been
hiding behind *War and Peace* and *be* the heroine. Throw down
your hair and let him climb up it. He's a little flaky but kinda sweet,
and you like it. Dontcha?

Aww. Have fun. If you can stand all the flirting with others he
manages to fit into a day, you've got it made. He's faithful, though.

It's only his eyes that wander. It *can* be kind of annoying, though, when he's checking out your eighteen-year-old cousin. Or your great-great-aunt.

BOYFRIEND POTENTIAL RATING: Very, very high if you're a girly-girl or a femme fatale who can snap her fingers in z formation. He needs to respect you, but this guy is gold; he's happiest in a solid relationship. You'll just have to deal with all his neuroses. Low if you like guys with balls who don't need to *captivate* the world just to feel good about themselves. Note to a small portion of Libra/Libra men: Enough with the mysterious, quiet thing; childhood fantasies, and weird age ranges. We've got you figured out.

CELEBRITY CORRESPONDENTS WITH
LIBRA SUN, VENUS IN LIBRA

Michael Douglas (September 25, 1944) Catherine Zeta-Jones is a Libra, too.

Oscar Wilde (October 16, 1854)

Tim Robbins (October 16, 1958) Susan Sarandon is a Libra, too.

Mickey Rooney (September 23, 1920) Married eight times.

F. Scott Fitzgerald (September 24, 1896)

Chuck Berry (October 18, 1926)

Jim Henson (September 24, 1936)

Will Smith (September 25, 1968) Good hubby so far.

Christopher Reeve (September 25, 1952) Was excellent hubby to Dana.

Brandon Routh (October 9, 1979)

(Interesting, huh? That both Supermans, Reeve and Routh, have the same sign combo?)

Aleister Crowley (October 12, 1875) Occult figure fascinated with hedonism and ritual sacrifices. Married twice. Was addicted to heroin and alcohol.

Charlton Heston (October 4, 1923)

Zucchero (September 25, 1955)

Lord Alfred Douglas (October 22, 1870)

Yo-Yo Ma (October 7, 1955)

Paul Hogan (October 8, 1939)

Jeffrey Conaway (October 5, 1950)

E. E. Cummings (October 14, 1894)

Peter Coyote (October 10, 1942)

John Lithgow (October 19, 1945)

Meat Loaf (September 27, 1947) Met and married within a month of meeting his ex-wife. Was married to her for twenty-two years before they divorced in 2001.

Bernie Mac (October 5, 1958)

Gene Autry (September 29, 1907)

Tom Petty (October 20, 1950)

Libra Sun, Venus in Scorpio

Here are the more scorching, defiant Libras when it comes to love and life. They love women, and women adore them right back atcha.

When this guy wants to turn it on, he's got sex appeal and magnetism that will draw in anyone within his line of fire. He does it with finesse, style: he's not slick or unctuous. That's why he's so appealing.

> Women are made to be loved, not understood.
>
> OSCAR WILDE

He can turn it off, too. He's like a sprinkler system with a timer. It exhausts him to be so *on* all the time so he needs to retreat into a cave and recharge. He fears being tied down—though it's his greatest desire. It's all that water (Scorpio), which is so heavy, weighing down his air (Libra). He's a pessimist who cloaks it well with feigned optimism.

He waits for the ominous storm clouds. He's absolutely sure

the rain will come and contribute to his downfall. He's likely to pull away from a situation before it can hurt him so it won't.

He can be the worst sort of cheater if he thinks you Trump him. (Yeah, Ivana got involved in The Donald's business. He didn't like that. Meanwhile, she went off to gross a mint with QVC.)

Also, this man can be drawn toward depression like the late Anna Nicole Smith was to millionaires with one foot in the grave already. And drugs, to compensate. And corruption.

Funny, though. If he finds a way to make a morally just cause heard, he becomes a saint. As good as Toll House cookies Grandma used to make. As fair as a red-haired, freckled Irish lass, in the sun for the first time.

His worst enemy is himself. Which, unfortunately, is what you have to deal with if you want to be with him. He's anxious, like the show-off drunk at a karaoke bar when the words don't come up on the screen. Make sure you give him the script so he has something to read from.

BOYFRIEND POTENTIAL RATING: Low, simply because he's able to detach—nothing personal. He doesn't speak up when something bothers him, so it festers. High if you're a Libra too, and can be impervious to his incorrigible behavior and annoying traits. When a woman makes him feel bad about himself, he stalks off like a lone wolf. And turns to other women to, uh, lick his wounds.

CELEBRITY CORRESPONDENTS WITH
LIBRA SUN, VENUS IN SCORPIO

Jean-Claude Van Damme (October 18, 1960) Notorious with the ladies; currently on his fifth marriage.

Matt Damon (October 8, 1970)

Usher (October 14, 1978) Left his girlfriend and sung about it.

Snoop Doggy Dogg (October 20, 1971)

Sacha Baron Cohen (October 13, 1971)

Zac Efron (October 18, 1987)

Ray Charles (September 23, 1930) Divorced twice; fathered twelve children; had a heroin problem.

Tommy Lee (October 3, 1962) Was on and off with Pammy.

Bruce Springsteen (September 23, 1949)

Hugh Jackman (October 12, 1968)

Eric Benét (October 15, 1970) Who'd cheat on Halle Berry?

Lee Harvey Oswald (October 18, 1939)

Kirk Cameron (October 12, 1970) Married since 1991 with six children. Left mainstream television to teach evangelism.

Gore Vidal (October 3, 1925)

Mahatma Gandhi (October 2, 1869) Said to have slept with virgins to test his celibacy (succeeded).

Silvio Berlusconi (September 29, 1936)

Pope John Paul I (October 17, 1912)

Roy Horn, of Siegfried and Roy (October 3, 1944)

Groucho Marx (October 2, 1890)

Montgomery Clift (October 17, 1920)

George Gershwin (September 26, 1898)

Dmitry Shostakovich (September 25, 1906)

Armand Assante (October 4, 1949)

Jesse Jackson (October 8, 1941)

Eugene O'Neill (October 16, 1888)

Elie Wiesel (September 30, 1928)

Walter Matthau (October 1, 1920)

James Valentine, of Maroon 5 (October 5, 1978)

Mike Judge (October 17, 1962)

Stevie Ray Vaughan (October 3, 1954)

Michael Andretti (October 5, 1962)

Giuseppe Verdi (October 10, 1813)

Chubby Checker (October 3, 1941)

Libra Sun, Venus in Sagittarius

He's got a pleasant, ironic nature. His sarcasm stops you dead in your tracks because it's all delivered with a good-natured smile. The charm just oozes like melted mozzarella on pizza. The biting remarks are the spicy pepperoni.

Also, this guy is willing to try strange things; think outside the box. He may seem normal, but don't be fooled. He's not cut from your classic old-food mold.

In fact, he may have a daredevil side. It's that fire (Sagittarius) added to his air (Libra). Yep, Evel Knievel-like (Libra/Venus in Sag). Reckless.

Here's the thing, though. With women, he wants Emily Post (also a Libra). She was the ultimate authority on everything from elbows on the table to farting in public. Look, it's not that bad. All you need to be is polished, strong, sincere, and sweet. That's all.

Okay. Like Marion Cunningham: Richie's mom, from *Happy Days*. See, here it is. Tom Bosley (a Libra) played Howard Cunningham on the show, the typical Libra. He wants peace. Wants to be happy. Doesn't want any problems and doesn't want to deal with them when they come up. A little old-fashioned. Wants to be mothered and taken care of. Libra. Libra. Libra. Watch how Marion handles him. Seriously. You can get him if you do what she does.

Let him be the one to have all the weird ideas and bounce them off you. Then you can be together for life and they won't have to make a bad spin-off sitcom about you: *Joanie loves Chachi*. Thanks.

BOYFRIEND POTENTIAL RATING: Very low if the going gets tough and he just can't cope. This guy is quick on his feet (in conversations and to run). High if you're his third or fourth serious relationship (or wife). Because of his curiosity about the world, he changes directions as quickly as strippers change pasties.

CELEBRITY CORRESPONDENTS
WITH LIBRA SUN, VENUS IN SAGITTARIUS

Jeff Goldblum (October 22, 1952) Divorced twice; was married to Geena Davis.

Luke Perry (October 11, 1965) Married for ten years, now divorced.

Paul Simon (October 13, 1941) On his third marriage.

Evel Knievel (October 17, 1938)

Deepak Chopra (October 22, 1946) A leader in new age medicine.

Dwight D. Eisenhower (October 14, 1890)

Mario Lopez (October 10, 1973) Married longtime girlfriend Ali Landry. After two weeks the marriage was annulled. It was rumored that he was cheating.

Art Buchwald (October 20, 1925)

Dizzy Gillespie (October 21, 1917)

Billy Zabka (October 20, 1965)

Sean Patrick Flanery (October 11, 1965)

Shaggy (October 22, 1968)

Bela Lugosi (October 20, 1882)

Ty Pennington (October 19, 1965)

LIBRA DIC*-TIONARY

RATIONAL <RAAAAH-SHUN-ALL> Weighs everything out, and in, and up, and down, equally.

Translation for potential girlfriend: Ridiculously indecisive. Makes Puff Daddy's scary name-changing seem normal.

ATTENTIVE <AHHH-TEN-TIVE> To you. And shows you off proudly. Especially if you've got higher status than he does—in beauty or career. Translation for potential girlfriend: Can be, uh, a social climber.

AFFECTIONATE <AH-FEHK-SHUN-IT> Doesn't get hives when he holds hands with you.
Translation for potential girlfriend: Doesn't necessarily stick to holding hands with only you.

CHARISMATIC <CAH-RIZ-MAH-TICK> Devastatingly charming.
Translation for potential girlfriend: A liability, really.

PEACEMAKER <PEEEES-MAY-KER> Nonconfrontational; hates to argue.
Translation for potential girlfriend: Should really learn to fight his own battles instead of running off like a scared little pansy mouse.

CHAPTER 8

Scorpio, Ex or Next

(the Scorpion, October 23–November 21)

SCORPIO RUDE-IMENTS

Sizzle, Sizzle. If he only got off the Prozac, the Vicodin, or the other meds, he'd be even hotter. And scarier. 'Cause he's intense about everything he does. Just glance at his deep, dark *Matrix* side. He's an endless black hole of worry—even when he tries hard not to project it on you. He saves that road rage for his coworkers.

He's hip, even when he's not trying to be. Compassionate—you can talk to him. Savvy and probably dependable—he means what he says. Kissable. Dare I say it? He's also as cool as a seedless cucumber on the surface, yet tormented inside. But wait. He's passionate—whether it's about politics or making his bed. That's good for you. *Or can be.*

Well, okay, call a spade a spade. He's also a perfectionist. He clubs people over the head with it: his ideals, his notions, his power struggles; it's his Bamm-Bamm

> I get a friend to travel with me . . . I need somebody to bring me back to who I am. It's hard to be alone.
>
> LEONARDO DICAPRIO

Rubble motif. Everyone around him suffers . . . but not as much as he does.

His life is usually so tied in with his work that people tend to identify him with it. He can be married to his job (not good news for you)—and if things are going wrong there, his Johnson may not work either. He's like a deer hunter without his (loaded) gun.

> I'm probably not going to get married unless I live with somebody for ten or twenty years. But these people [Romeo and Juliet] took a chance and they did it. We don't have the balls that Romeo did.
>
> LEONARDO DICAPRIO

This guy has a great sense of humor—except about himself. He's all about transformation—him, you, anyone and anything within his vicinity. Take Sean Combs (Scorpio). Right. Maybe you know him better as Puffy. Or what he changed his name to: Puffy Combs. Then Puff Daddy. P. Diddy. Then just Diddy. When Diddy was asked why he changed his name yet again, he responded (with a straight face): "I felt like the *P* was getting between me and my fans, and now we're closer." Just go with it. Aiiiight?

Oh, this man is also what you'd call high-maintenance. To him, there's always a right and a wrong way. He's probably macho, yet has such a polished home. Martha Stewart would be proud.

> With Romeo and Juliet, you're talking about two people who meet one night, and get married the same night. I believe in love at first sight—but it hasn't happened to me yet.
>
> LEONARDO DICAPRIO

Speaking of those who like to hear themselves talk, this guy'll go off on a tangent and stay there until he's dragged away by the nondiplomatic word-fashion police. He's a political firecracker—usually hard-core left wing or right wing. An absolute freak, like the vodka (gone wrong). Don't even get him started. Please. For the sake of the rest of us. Sometimes he's quiet—if he's not off being a diva, a perfectionist, or an educator. When he turns silent, don't talk unless you have to. He wants to affect you, and he can't work his mojo with all that confusion around.

If you're a chatterbox, you're going to turn him off, truly. When he's not ready to talk about something, he won't. When he is, off with the races.

He'll put you down or ask if you're going to wear *that* dress out tonight. That's part of his control-freak M.O. If you're already out, you might as well go home and change. He'll shoot you critical glances all night until you get exasperated and do.

Be afraid. When he gets it into his head to fight, he's a warmonger. He'll bitch-slap you and leave you alone in the jail cell with your pants down. He either loves you or hates you. There's no middle ground. He's never neutral. (He should take lessons from Switzerland.) BUT when he loves you, there's no one more thoughtful or caring.

Incidentally, it should be noted that THE most powerful women in Hollywood (the ones who capitalized and started their own production companies) are all Scorpios. Get this: Demi Moore, Julia Roberts, Sally Field, Goldie Hawn, Roseanne Barr, and Jodie Foster. That's some Fortune 500 list. In the political spectrum, Hillary Clinton, Maria Shriver, Laura Bush, and Indira Gandhi are all Scorpios, too.

> The two most misused words in the entire English vocabulary are *love* and *friendship*. A true friend would die for you, so when you start trying to count them on one hand, you don't need any fingers.
>
> **LARRY FLYNT**

> From the world of darkness I did loose demons and devils in the power of scorpions to torment.
>
> **CHARLES MANSON**

SCORPIO TONGUE LASHING

He's so touchy and sensitive about everything. Translation: totally paranoid. He's wary about any and all comments you make.

By the way, he doesn't *really* have bad hearing. He says "What?" constantly. Truth is, he only hears what he wants to hear.

Just in terms of allocation of time resources, religion is not very efficient. There's a lot more I could be doing on a Sunday morning.

BILL GATES

"Let's just stay in tonight," you tell him.

"What?" he replies. "You think I can't afford it?"

"Huh? No. I just thought we'd relax at your place."

"Why? Do I look like I need to relax?"

Right. It's no-win/no-win.

If you're an earth sign or a fire sign, you'll be completely confused. Then Scorpio will insist that he cook, but resent you for "making him" do it, even though he's a virtual James Beard. And actually revels in cooking.

With Scorpio, the challenge is to find equilibrium. Try.

Success is a lousy teacher. It seduces smart people into thinking they can't lose.

BILL GATES

He's usually earthy, practical, and grounded. For Scorpio guy, there's no middle ground.

He claims he's laid-back, easygoing. Nuh-uh. He's a grenade, ready to explode at any moment. He lets things build up, build up—then lashes out like a dominatrix's whip.

By the way, that myth about how water puts out fire? No myth. His torturous, dangerous side can stifle a sunny, wild, happy nature.

Have fun with this one. Just don't let him pull you down into his harsh, cruel reality. What a world! What a world!

(Hey—ever notice that the Wicked Witch of the West says this when she's melting? Right. Where's the perspective, folks?)

SCORPIO: IS HE *INTO* YOU?

It's no secret when Scorpio is into you. He calls constantly. Wants to include you in decisions he makes. Likes bouncing ideas off you. Then goes the opposite route. And wants to know where you are at all times. If Scorpio guy is really interested, he can call you upward of four times a day. He's not shy. He'll look for you. Here's the thing: You truly are his possession.

> I know a lot of Ninas. My new wife, what's her name now?
>
> **IKE TURNER**

Want to see if Scorpio guy is in love? (Don't say I didn't warn you: This is dangerous.) Start flirting with his friend. Chances are, he'll haul you off and kiss you before your can flip your hair coyly.

Your only questions: Is he into me? Is it for real? Here's the answer: if he stops bringing muffins in the morning to his "friends" at the strip club down the block, maybe. If he stops dating his other girlfriend and his mistress—definitely.

You don't know about it? Well, surprise, surprise. Ask him. He's probably stupid enough to admit it to you.

This guy can go over to the dark side to get his kicks. He's Darth Vader, without the cool voice enhancements; Howard Stern, without the semi-likeable geeky side. He's convinced that no one can get into his head and understand how incredibly profound he is. He wants to be accepted but believes his evil twin must be hidden from the world. He's Kitt's evil-twin car in *Knight Rider*. He hates to be discovered—but it thrills him, too. Open his computer and you'll find oodles of secret files with porn everywhere. He'll have the gall to deny it straight to your face and say they're not his. Okay. Whatever. He'll confess in the end.

> My wife's jealousy is getting ridiculous. The other day she looked at my calendar and wanted to know who May was.
>
> **RODNEY DANGERFIELD**

In truth, he comes off as thoughtful, and he is. But here's the

fresh catch: It always comes around to him. He's flashing the adoring, fiery card *because it serves his purpose.* He can be manipulative, ladies. He's as crafty as a druggie in need of a
fix. It seems effortless, cool and calm. But know
one thing: He's in control—and that's just the way
he likes it.

It's hard for me
to put my
feelings into
words.

JOAQUIN
PHOENIX

Yes, he seems direct. He is. But his brain is
never on cruise control. He plots out his moves
like a therapist who hooks the needy ones into
coming three times a week. Oh, by the way. He'll
spend on fabulous dinners but sucks at giving gifts. Unless you like
Farberware.

ADVICE TO THE FUTURE MRS. SCORPIO

Everyone calls Scorpio sensual. He is.

But sensitive? He's not. Look to Cancer guy for that.

Romantic? Ditto. Scorpio can seem romantic when he's courting you. Make no spelling mistake, though: He knows how to reel
you in. And once he's got you, it's all about him. Think dark,
gloomy. Passionate, yes. If you're the supportive
type, not thin-skinned; if you thrive on ups and
downs—hysterical laughter leading to morbid
pessimism—you've found your lit match with
kerosene, adjacent.

All the
reasonings of
men are not
worth one
sentiment of
women.

VOLTAIRE

You need to be aloof sometimes, and let him
come to you—yet be grounded enough to make
him feel secure when he goes into a rant about
politics, his family, or the goddamn network canceling his favorite
show. Let him write his David Copperfield letter to them, com-
plaining. Don't pooh-pooh him. He'll feel better afterward. A '97

reserve Barolo works best to soothe the savage beast. He's probably a foodie with a palate to rival Emeril's.

Scorpio guy can be a detail-oriented, stressed-out workaholic, yet lazy in the romance and bedroom department. Even though he's talented.

> I hate women because they always know where things are.
>
> VOLTAIRE

Here's how to get him. He'll try the convenience route. Make it impossible. He'll invite you to his house on the beach. Don't go. Let him work harder than any other man. Make him feel like he can't control you fully, and he'll be perplexed. And want you more.

The bottom line: The only way he'll commit to you is *if he says the words*. (Words are important to him.) He's born negative and jaded. If it comes too easily, he'll never, ever appreciate it. Be a born-again virgin. Don't sleep with him till he confesses love. Get your hymen sewn back up.

> I don't tolerate any kind of dishonesty. I bring a lot to the table with my relationships, so I really expect the same.
>
> DAVID SCHWIMMER

Under the bottom line: If not, he'll have so many girlfriends coming and going, you'll wonder who's really *coming*—and how quickly you'll be going.

ADVICE TO THE EX MS. SCORPIO

Scorpio guy needs to go away to realize the ultimate hardship of losing you. It's not likely to happen, but stranger things have. You'll be tempted to call him, or show up where he works wearing crotchless panties (right—you'll miss the sex more than anything). Don't. Sex won't lure him back. *Immediately.* It will only send him into a spiral of guilt, and he'll start avoiding you like the plague.

Here's the other thing. He'll read into everything you do as a way to get him back. *Psycho,* to him, is spelled Y-O-U, and you'll likely turn him off for a while. "A while," meaning this guy is very likely to come back for postbreakup sex, *after* he's convinced you no longer want to bear his children.

He'll test, poke, and prod you until he's sure you're over him. If you're really over him, fine. If not, you're better off with the battery-powered version. It's less torturous, and doesn't have all those problems getting it up because of the Prozac, weed, or other mood stabilizers in his system.

Uh. Get the hint? You may be better off without him.

Scorpio guy is a private soul. If you don't "get" him, and are still trying to figure him out—stop. You never will. He's as much a mystery as Clay Aiken's sexual preference.

> It's a job—someone's gotta kiss Jennifer Aniston. The reality is, Jennifer and I can do our job well because we truly are friends. But when the day's over, she goes home to her boyfriend and I go home to a magazine.
>
> DAVID SCHWIMMER

SUN/VENUS COMBINATIONS: THE TRUE LOVE POTENTIAL TEST

Scorpio Sun, Venus in Virgo

The powers that be did not leave this guy unmarked. His charm far surpasses anyone else's within a ten-mile radius. One hundred, if he's not guarded by a jealous girlfriend.

Right. *Faithful,* to him, is a super-idealistic adjective. "Just Gotta Have Faith" is a song sung by an out-of-the-closet George Michael to hot supermodels: senseless. Scorpio/Virgo has no faith in long-lasting love.

That's it. There's no deep meaning to it, or to life, though he'll convince you otherwise by the way he woos you (as if he's out to win the million-dollar prize on a reality dating show). He'll hang out his Batman sign and flaunt his cape and his latex suit—with big protective cup—to get this party started.

To change the subject—like he does, randomly—this guy can almost have a death wish. He gets himself into truly dangerous situations that make him *feel*.

Here it is. Because of his analytical Virgo mind, he can get so far removed from relationships, it's almost like he's walking through the motions, like the AOL guy on your computer screen. With dial-up.

> A celibate clergy is an especially good idea, because it tends to suppress any hereditary propensity toward fanaticism.
>
> CARL SAGAN

In fact, add in an overprotective mother who tells him his penis is made of gold, and he can become a sociopath (Scott Peterson, for example: Scorpio/Venus in Virgo).

Truly, these men are poet-warriors, and tend to take themselves too seriously. Self-destructiveness takes on a Joni Mitchell/Sylvia Plath ultra-dramatic suicidal tone (both Scorpios/Venus in Virgo, by the way).

On a positive note, if you're an earth sign with a little water in your chart, you may just have found your soul mate. Well, that's the good news. If you

> It's better to burn out than to fade away.
>
> NEIL YOUNG

can deliver the newspaper to his door, where he's got two trained rottweilers waiting for you, mouths foaming, you can wear him down like a hooker's five-inch Payless heels on Hollywood Boulevard.

BOYFRIEND POTENTIAL RATING: High if he doesn't drown in a pool of self-pity before the five-year mark. Seriously: Look to his mother. If he's grown up in an unstable home with deceit, lies, too much criticism, or, on the other hand, too much adulation or idolization, he's a Charles Manson psychopath (yes, also a Scorpio). Low if he's got his therapist's number on speed dial.

CELEBRITY CORRESPONDENTS
WITH SCORPIO SUN, VENUS IN VIRGO

Scott Peterson (October 24, 1972) On death row for killing his wife and unborn child.

Bryan Adams (November 5, 1959)

Weird Al Yankovic (October 23, 1959)

Lou Ferrigno (November 9, 1951)

Jean-Claude Pascal (October 24, 1927)

André Alfred Dumas (November 1, 1908)

Harry Hamlin (October 30, 1951)

Sam Shepard (November 5, 1943) Has been with Jessica Lange since 1982, without the marriage license.

Gavin Rossdale (October 30, 1967) Married Gwen Stefani in 2002.

Keith Urban (October 26, 1967) In 2006, new-wife-at-the-time Nicole Kidman stuck by his side while he was in rehab.

Scorpio Sun, Venus in Libra

Like Scorpio/Venus in Virgo, this guy can be self-destructive. However, usually the Libra factor balances him out—sort of—like a Diet Coke alongside a bacon double cheeseburger. For him, knowledge is the ultimate orgasm. Ultimately: his search for the truth.

> I find it rather easy to portray a businessman. Being bland, rather cruel, and incompetent comes naturally to me.
>
> JOHN CLEESE

There are always neuroses with this guy. He can be a good partner, though, if you let him shine, whine, and dominate the room. Self-deprecation, too, can sound like Jerry Seinfeld on truth serum.

His curiosity about the world gets him going (Christopher Columbus was Scorpio/Virgo), and he will never be swayed by others' opinions. If you're laid-back, supportive, and give him good advice without being too Dr. Phil–analytical about it, you've got him. Gossip about celebrities and the people you know together is like sexual foreplay for this guy. Nothing gets him more riled up.

His sense of humor is exaggeratedly hilarious. A little vulgar, too, when he wants to be Anna Nicole weirdly rubberneckingly out-of-whack strange. Exclamation-pointed.

He's got class, but said in a Fran Drescher–style nasal voice. Elegance, with a hint of dirty to it. It's all done with an edge to get a reaction.

He's like, "Let's bomb Hiroshima to see what happens."

Hah. No. That's *not* funny. And sometimes he isn't either. It's like John F. Kennedy, Jr., failing the bar (three times); "how could he think of flying a plane?" he asks.

No, that wasn't funny, either: We're talking Scorpio. Even when his jokes *are* really funny, there's always a darkness underlying them. Barbed-wire humor. This man will look death in the face for vanity's sake, then go back under the knife after a botched plastic surgery. For fun.

> Being with an insanely jealous person is like being in the room with a dead mammoth.
>
> **MIKE NICHOLS**

> I think there's something incredibly sexy about a woman wearing her boyfriend's T-shirt and underwear.
>
> **CALVIN KLEIN**

BOYFRIEND POTENTIAL RATING: High, actually. This guy knows himself, even if he's *just plain weird*. He commits only to those he can see himself with for the long truckload haul. Be careful, though. His sense of responsibility can outweigh his true desires. Low if he marries for pregnancy, for status, for security reasons, or because the devil made him do it. *So he says.*

> Heard melodies are sweet, but those unheard are sweeter.
>
> **JOHN KEATS**

CELEBRITY CORRESPONDENTS
WITH SCORPIO SUN, VENUS IN LIBRA

Pablo Picasso (October 25, 1881) Married twice and had four children by three different women. Was fascinated by women.

Prince Charles (November 14, 1948) Both Diana and Camilla were Cancers. Extramarital affair with Camilla was well known. They married in 2005.

Matthew McConaughey (November 4, 1969)

Albert Camus (November 7, 1913)

Christopher Columbus (October 24, 1451)

Charles Bronson (November 3, 1921) Was married to Jill Ireland from 1968 until her death in 1990.

Puff Daddy, aka Diddy (November 4, 1969) Classic Scorpio— they're all about transformation and reinventing themselves. How many times has he changed his name *this year*?

Burt Lancaster (November 2, 1913)

Ryan Gosling (November 12, 1980)

Léon Trotsky (November 7, 1879)

Jack Osbourne (November 8, 1985) Reinvented himself by losing the baby fat.

Leif Garrett (November 8, 1961)

Dylan McDermott (October 26, 1961)

Sam Waterston (November 15, 1940)

James Garfield (November 19, 1831)

Henry Winkler (October 30, 1945)

Michael Crichton (October 23, 1942)

Roy Scheider (November 10, 1932)

Walter Cronkite (November 14, 1916) "The most trusted man in America" was married to one woman for sixty-five years, until her death.

Aaron Copland (November 14, 1900)

Bob Hoskins (October 26, 1942)

Josh Duhamel (November 14, 1972)
Dwight Gooden (November 16, 1964)
Glenn Frey, of the Eagles (November 6, 1948)

Scorpio Sun, Venus in Scorpio

Here's an interesting mix. Scorpio Sun, Scorpio Venus . . . tick, tick, tick, tick, BOOM!!! This guy's a chemistry set waiting to explode in the hands of a freckle-faced ten-year-old who just got the stupid thing for Christmas. *What were his parents thinking? What, they thought they'd collect on the fire insurance?*

So, here's the deal. This Scorpio/Scorpio guy has a nasty side. And I don't mean *mean*: I mean dirty, with a collection of porn that could rival Seymore Butt's (King of porn, y'know? . . . Nah, it's better if you don't). Yeah. It's scary. In other words, he's not gonna appreciate you—no, nil, not even a little—if you wear those flannel jammies (with the bunnies on them, you know the ones) to bed. Honey, he's got the video cam out. He's ready. Make the most of it.

Want to know what he likes? He's got "edible panties" written all over him. He looks sweet, but he's *been a bad boy*. Do it. Do the lace-garter-annoying it's-gonna-take-me-twenty-minutes-to-get-this-thing-on. You won't be sorry.

Here's the bad news: Scorpio Sun, Venus in Scorpio can make any girl fall in love with him. He's charming, sexy, and rough-and-tumble fresh—like Ivory soap. He's hot, yet clean. Spiffy, yet slime-free. Scorching, yet charismatic, coolamundo, composed. He might not even be good-

> I have loved eight women in my life. I remember every woman's face.
> **ADAM ANT**

> I didn't lose my virginity until I was eighteen. The first time was a nightmare. Who shows you how to use a condom?
> **ADAM ANT**

> I tell you, we are here on earth to fart around, and don't let anybody tell you different.
> **KURT VONNEGUT**

looking, yet you're drawn to him all the same. Unfortunately, though, so is everyone else. Even the guys. This guy is the opiate of the masses.

For lack of a better term, they've labeled me a sex symbol. It's flattering and it should happen to every bald, overweight guy.

DENNIS FRANZ

When he settles down, it's for good. Trouble is, you'll never be sure 'cause he's got the sneaky, but I'm cool—you're so beautiful, so what are you worried about?—thing down pat. Damn, you'd like to smack him. Or castrate him. Whichever comes first. Unfortunately, he's just, well, let's be honest: He's Fonzie. And you always kinda liked Henry Winkler (Scorpio).

Ayyyyyyyyy.

BOYFRIEND POTENTIAL RATING: High if you're into the sado-masochistic he's-good-in-bed-but-he-may-just-be-boffing-others kind of relationship. Higher if some stripper has

For every Mother Teresa, there's a Jeffrey Dahmer.

JOE MANTEGNA

shown him the way and he's finally figured out that he can't go that route forever. Last thing: You can get him if you're a pretty girl with morals who looks good, but says something intelligent once in a while. Confuse him by talking like a Ring-Ding, in a beauty pageant, about world peace. Then go out and raise a million dollars for it.

Um, yeah. That'll actually work.

CELEBRITY CORRESPONDENTS
WITH SCORPIO SUN, VENUS IN SCORPIO

Leonardo DiCaprio (November 11, 1974)

Ethan Hawke (November 6, 1970) Had a bad divorce from Uma Thurman.

Chris Noth, aka "Mr. Big" (November 13, 1954) Was rumored to be notorious ladies' man in real life, too.

Penn Badgley (November 11, 1986)

Ryan Gosling (November 12, 1980)

Martin Scorsese (November 17, 1942)

Larry Flynt (November 1, 1942) Creator of *Hustler*. Married five times. Longest marriage to fourth wife, Althea, who drowned in a bathtub and was suffering from AIDS.

Charles Manson (November 12, 1934)

Bill Gates (October 28, 1955)

Ike Turner (November 5, 1931) Was abusive to Tina.

Billy Graham (November 7, 1918)

Eros Ramazzotti (October 28, 1963)

Joaquin Phoenix (October 28, 1974)

Pope Benoit XV (November 21, 1854)

Voltaire (November 21, 1694)

Neil Young (November 12, 1945)

David Schwimmer (November 2, 1966)

Kevin Kline (October 24, 1947) Happily married to Phoebe Cates since 1989.

Carl Sagan (November 9, 1934)

Richard Dreyfuss (October 29, 1947)

John Cleese (October 27, 1939)

Gordon Lightfoot (November 17, 1938)

Dan Rather (October 31, 1950)

Ed Asner (November 15, 1929)

Mike Nichols (November 6, 1931)

Calvin Klein (November 19, 1942)

Ron Rifkin (October 31, 1939)

Adam Goldberg (October 25, 1970)

John Keats (October 31, 1795) The English romantic poet never married. Died at age twenty-six.

Adam Ant (November 3, 1954)

D. B. Sweeney (November 14, 1961)

Scorpio Sun, Venus in Sagittarius

At the very least, this guy thinks outside the cardboard box. Has he asked you your star sign yet? He will. Fascination with psychic phenomenon, the paranormal, or simply the unexplained is only one layer of his seven-tier cake. Astrology is the icing.

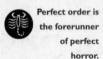

Perfect order is the forerunner of perfect horror.

CARLOS FUENTES

Sure, this guy can be a real ladies' man. Yet he's got such down-to-earth, trustworthy appeal, it's difficult to imagine that he'd ever betray you. That's his game: no game. It's as simple and vanilla as that.

Speak a few languages to impress him. Tell him about your world travels. Mention that child you sponsor in a Third World country. He's seriously attracted to helping the downtrodden. Looks good on his résumé.

There are two dilemmas that rattle the human skull: How do you hang on to someone who won't stay? And how do you get rid of someone who won't go?

DANNY DEVITO

This guy has a genius for self-mocking and can be hilarious as long as he's making the jokes. If he's criticized, however, he's sure to lash out like a hungry snake at a rat.

He's fiercely loyal to friends and family—especially as a daddy. He'll never forget who's been kind to him, and he'll reward them tenfold.

Just don't get on his bad side. It can get Hilary Duff versus Lindsay Lohan scary. (Especially because neither one of them have eaten carbs in a few years.)

Scorpio/Sagittarius can be reflective to the point of depression. If he lets you into his morbid little world, don't feel that honored. He'll actually regale anyone who'll listen to his insights.

Be flattered, though, when he tells you how wonderful or beautiful you are. He means it. This guy is straightfoward. And intense. Staring into his eyes may make you reach for your Ray-Bans.

Passion goes with temper, too, so beware of his explosions.

Know the signs. You may be able to see it coming. He's like a bull before it charges—still, so still, with nostrils flaring. He's out for shock value and clings to his different personalities like a balding, paunchy, middle-aged man clings to his youth.

Speaking of stubborn, he's like Winona Ryder coming out of a store with her pockets bulging, denying she took anything.

BOYFRIEND POTENTIAL RATING: High if you're a paradox: the most difficult woman on earth to get, yet sweet as pie when he finally wins you over a year later. You have to be willing to walk away if he doesn't treat you right. Low if you don't praise everything he does and have a political agenda that doesn't match-game his.

I basically chose this after I read it because I thought it was different and funny and unique and dark—things that I like to do.

DANNY DEVITO

CELEBRITY CORRESPONDENTS
WITH SCORPIO SUN, VENUS IN SAGITTARIUS

Johnny Carson (October 23, 1925) Married four times.

Michael Landon (October 31, 1936) Loved by the public, but had tendency to change wives after they were no longer of childbearing age.

Roberto Benigni (October 27, 1952)

James Cook (November 7, 1728)

Art Garfunkel (November 5, 1941)

Jean-Claude Camus (October 28, 1938)

Theodore Roosevelt (October 27, 1858)

Claude Monet (November 14, 1840)

Erasmus (October 28, 1469)

Michael Dukakis (November 3, 1933)

Ezra Pound (October 30, 1885)

I've wrestled with substance abuse. I smoked cigarettes for almost thirty years, pot for twenty. I went through a period of cocaine abuse. I gave it all up in the mid-eighties.

HAROLD RAMIS

Dylan Walsh (November 17, 1963) On his second marriage since 2004.

Dolph Lundgren (November 3, 1957)

Emilio Pucci (November 21, 1914) This designer was a well-known playboy.

Kurt Vonnegut (November 11, 1922)

Tim Rice (November 10, 1944)

Steve Zahn (November 13, 1968)

Sam Rockwell (November 5, 1968)

Pat Buchanan (November 2, 1938)

Bruce Jenner (October 28, 1949) Was married three times; turned down the lead role of *Superman* (a bit o' trivia).

Michael Collins (October 31, 1930)

Sammy Sosa (November 12, 1968)

Stephen Rea (October 31, 1946)

Dennis Franz (October 28, 1944)

Roy Emerson (November 3, 1936)

Bruno Ducati (November 5, 1904)

Joe Mantegna (November 13, 1947)

Ivan Reitman (October 27, 1946) Married to same woman since 1976.

Charles Berlitz (November 20, 1914)

John Barry (November 3, 1933) The composer married four times.

Boutros Boutros-Ghali (November 14, 1922)

Kevin Pollak (October 30, 1957)

Carlos Fuentes (November 11, 1928)

Scorpio Sun, Venus in Capricorn

Leave it to Scorpio/Venus in Capricorn to pave new ways, yet set up roadblocks that read DANGER: DO NOT ENTER. You want to pass? Well. That makes you either brave or stupid. If you're not getting the respect you deserve, pull out now before he lets his pent-up dam flow. This guy is all about analyzing, experimenting, and implementing. Pity the woman who tries to stop him.

Whether it's creating (Method acting, Lee Strasberg) or forging a new record for the number of times one can marry (Larry King, seven), he likes to be at the top of his game—even if that means being a relentless bastard. He only pursues what he's good at. It depends what's available to him. He instinctively knows what he can get.

Good news: If you're his ultimate woman, you'll never have to read his credit-card statements for afternoon-delight hotel charges. You'll sense if he's true or not. Don't ignore your gut.

Clincal depression can affect this guy. Suicidal thoughts. However, the real problem comes when he denies himself the sadness. He represses it like the American public did with Janet Jackson's exposed boob.

Everything's a process with this guy. He weighs out every aspect, makes a list of what he wants, checks it twice. Marriage can be a chore to him—he sees it as something he's got to do, yet he doesn't necessarily look forward to the nine-to-five part of it. He thinks it's more romantic to stay away, isolate himself, and see you once in a while. He doesn't want to take the bad with the good.

In truth, he treats dating like a science. To him, the bigger, better deal may be just around the corner, so he's not likely to get to the church on time unless he's given an ultimatum. His boots were made for walking.

Don't let him walk all over you.

> I know a man who gave up smoking, drinking, sex, and rich food. He was healthy right up to the day he killed himself.
>
> JOHNNY CARSON

> If variety is the spice of life, marriage is the big can of leftover Spam.
>
> JOHNNY CARSON

> Our relationship is better than it's ever been. We are absolutely not breaking up.
>
> NICK LACHEY, BEFORE THE BREAKUP

BOYFRIEND POTENTIAL RATING: High, actually, if he's done a little soul-searching—and not in the bottom of a vodka bottle. Let him go off on his strange, artistic, attempt-at-making-money tangents. He'll appreciate you for not criticizing him if he falls flat on his face. He's looking for unconditional love. If you give it to him, he'll be as happy as a pig at a trough. Low if he's got access to hotties. He can be as committed to relationships as Madonna is, each decade, to finding new ways to shock us.

CELEBRITY CORRESPONDENTS
WITH SCORPIO SUN, VENUS IN CAPRICORN

Owen Wilson (November 18, 1968)

RuPaul (November 17, 1960)

Richard Burton (November 10, 1925) A heavy drinker. Was married five times—twice to Elizabeth Taylor.

Robert F. Kennedy (November 20, 1925)

Rock Hudson (November 17, 1925) First major American celebrity to die of AIDS; was married for three years—perhaps as an attempt to hide his homosexuality.

Nick Lachey (November 9, 1973)

Fyodor Dostoyevsky (November 11, 1821)

Danny DeVito (November 17, 1944) Married to Rhea Perlman (of *Cheers*) since 1982.

Paul Sorrento (November 17, 1965)

Dick Cavett (November 19, 1936)

Harold Ramis (November 21, 1944) On second marriage since 1989.

Lee Strasberg (November 17, 1901)

Larry King (November 19, 1933) Married seven times.

SCORPIO DIC*-TIONARY

ALLURING <AHH-LURE-ING> Even when he's not all that good-looking.
Translation for potential girlfriend: To all. That's the problem.

AUTHORITATIVE <AW-THOR-IH-TAY-TIVE> Has very powerful beliefs and sticks to them.
Translation for potential girlfriend: Always staunchly something.

CARING <KAA-RING> Can get emotionally involved, which is good for you.
Translation for potential girlfriend: Can smother.

SMOLDERING <SMOHL-DUH-RING> Sexual.
Translation for potential girlfriend: Can't keep it between his legs.

NURTURING <NUR-CHUR-ING> Looks out for you like a loving parent.
Translation for potential girlfriend: Can be as suffocating as a loving parent.

CHAPTER 9

Sagittarius, Ex or Next
(the Archer, November 22–December 21)

SAGITTARIUS RUDE-IMENTS

Sagittarius . . . ohhhh. Did you have to do it? Did you have to fall in love with this guy? Yeah, yeah. I know. He's great in bed. He's funny and smart—yet masterful and sensual. Damn. Okay. Hope you like balance beams. Think walking on eggshells till you get his M.O. You have to learn how to soothe the savage beast. Calm the calamity within him.

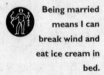

> Being married means I can break wind and eat ice cream in bed.
>
> BRAD PITT

He's modest. Humble. Self-mocking. Sweet. Then scary. Impatient. Mean. Defensive. Violent (in the extreme). He's a double-edged sword. Pick which side to face (I'd pick the blunt side).

Speaking of blunt: Sag missed school the day they taught couching. Seriously. He considers his method of always saying the truth honesty. You'll consider it a liability. He'll tell your country-club friends that your diamond earrings are fake (What's the big deal?). That the two of you are having financial difficulty. How much he makes down to the last dime. Stuff you'd rather not have him say. (Gag him.)

He can't help it. It's his way.

His timing with comments and jokes can be appallingly bad. Then insanely good. He sometimes ruins the punch line in his haste to get to it. Or tells it to the wrong crowd.

His sense of humor is weird, quirky, offbeat. But listen. All he wants is a good audience. If you think he's truly funny and laugh at all his jokes, he will stay with you forever. Like Libra, he goes for an ultra-feminine woman who can stand her ground, yet coo sweetly into his ear. Tell him what a man he is, how talented. And be willing to walk away when he's been bad.

> Is sex dirty?
> Only if it's done
> right.
>
> WOODY
> ALLEN

Sag invented the term "macho." Even if he's a wimp, atypical for this sign, he'll still huff and puff out his chest like a blowfish. His physical presence is overwhelming. He wants to be King of the World. He'll snatch up Kate Winslet and throw Leonardo overboard. Though he may excel at embarrassing you with his poor social skills, lack of dressing sense, or his chronic foot-in-mouth disease—everyone seems to like him because he just doesn't mean it. His naïveté is refreshing. His innocence is humbling. He'll look for truth, justice, and the American way.

> Do you think I
> would speak for
> you? I don't
> even know your
> language.
>
> JUDD NELSON

And for facts, facts. If something cannot be proven, it simply is not true. Does he believe in astrology? Is he very religious? Probably not. A Sag who follows the masses is like good Teflon and public consensus of Bill Clinton—nothing sticks. Sagittarius guy is like an old soul stuffed into a new, pumped-up body. He's got fire like Leo and Aries, but it's more contained. He's still, quiet. He's like that little old lady down the block who's still got some spunk in her. He's strong, and he knows right from wrong, but he can go to that bad place (and I don't mean the joint down the street that serves soggy fried calamari).

Read on. You're just getting to the good part.

SAGITTARIUS TONGUE LASHING

If he's not saying something that shocks, offends, or provokes, he's probably doing his best imitation of a painting at Hogwarts:

Love cannot
save you from
your own fate.

JIM MORRISON

He's still, but the eyes move. He's watching people, studying them. Or he's in his own little world.

Though he may not talk much (or, on the other hand, suffer diarrhea of the mouth; no filtering), his powers of seduction are excellent. He knows how to read his audience and is shockingly intuitive when it comes to winning over those of the opposite sex.

When he says "I love you," he means it. These are words he doesn't mince. Ever.

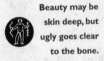

Beauty may be
skin deep, but
ugly goes clear
to the bone.

REDD FOXX

One huge warning: Find out how he feels about women and his mother *before* you get seriously involved. If he's had a rough childhood, and problems with Mom, this guy can be *dangerous.*

It's true. Coinkidinkally enough, in this sign you'll find a number of rapists and serial killers. I'm sorry. The proof's there. Of course, this is the extreme. Just take note: Ted Bundy (rapist/murderer), Lucky Luciano (mob boss/murderer), Edmund Kemper (serial killer), and Billy the Kid.

He may just have weird issues with age and women: Woody Allen, who married his girlfriend's daughter, or Ted Nugent, who adopted a minor just so he could date her. Ick.

Sag man does creepy, tormented soul well. Yet balanced-guy

Sag (who finds the right woman) can be like fine wine: He mellows with age and just gets more delicious.

Make sure to keep him guessing. He's drawn in by secret agents. He likes 99 in *Get Smart*, or Jamie Lee Curtis in *True Lies*. Mystery goes a long way to getting him and keeping him. He likes feminine wiles. Would love to drown in them.

The best woman for Sag guy is someone who can rule the roost but make him think he's still Charles in charge.

> In the past, people were born royal. Nowadays, royalty comes from what you do.
>
> **GIANNI VERSACE**

SAGITTARIUS: IS HE *INTO* YOU?

You gotta know now. This guy can have a fling on a dime. With your sister. And he can justify cheating 'cause it's in his right. That's what he thinks. But look. If you're The One, you're in luck. He will cease and desist all bad behavior. That's right, if he's totally into you, he's yours.

How will you know? Ask him. Remember, he's about as tactful and diplomatic as Rush Limbaugh crashing a secret press meeting. He'll tell you.

By the way, he's generous, this one. Especially if he's trying to get you into the sack. He won't judge you if you sleep with him right away. Just be sure not to say the l-word before he does. You can thank me later.

Here's the thing: Respect and authority are everything to him. If you ask his advice, take it— or he'll think you're not worthy next time. Sagittarius man believes he is always right. If he doesn't know something, he'll admit it.

> I've only been in one fight in my whole life . . . in seventh grade, yet everyone thinks I'm a maniac.
>
> **RAY LIOTTA**

He goes for smart women. An intellectual connection is necessary for him to get emotionally involved. But he's also looking for sweet, kind, and sexy. What he doesn't want is needy. He despises needy. Kill him with kindness, but let him know you've got a million backup plans. He must need you, not the other way around. He'll run faster than Florence Griffith Joyner did (a female Sag) if he senses you're trying to box him in. Give him space, learn a new language, go sailing and vacationing with him. Throw yourself into it. Oh. And cook ethnic food for him. He likes his cuisine the way he likes his women: spicy.

> She still talks to me now, only now she talks to me in my dreams. And I can't wait to go to sleep tonight because we have a lot to talk about.
>
> JAMIE FOXX

ADVICE TO THE FUTURE MRS. SAGITTARIUS

Here's a story. Sag man, after dating for years and years, was convinced that all women were psychotic. No joke. He never realized that he hooked women and ran away—so of course they ran after him. He was just absolutely positive that all women had a screw loose.

> Being a woman is a terribly difficult task, since it consists principally in dealing with men.
>
> JOSEPH CONRAD

So. One smart cookie (a Pisces gal) was cool, calm, collected. She let him run after her. (Remember, macho Sag needs to take the lead.) Once they started dating, she quickly discovered that the silent treatment was the best way to reach him when he was bad. Her quiet glares were the only way to get his attention. After, when he *begged* her to tell him what he'd done, she was direct about it and told him everything. Sag guy is a problem solver. He hates having things carry over till morning. He wants the fight to be finished, done with. If you unplug your phone for one evening, and he can't reach you, he'll run over to your house and throw stones at your window till you come out.

Although he doesn't like to appear so, Sag is just as spoiled as the other fire signs (Leo and Aries) and he'll try to take control of the situation by flaring up and venting, showing his rage. Instead, a fiery response from you will only make him angrier.

> There's a thin line between to laugh with and to laugh at.
>
> **RICHARD PRYOR**

At this point, when you decide to ease the situation, you must coo to him. Fawn sweetly and tell him how utterly masculine and sexy he is. Make your voice breathy like Kate Capshaw's, back in the day. (See? She married a Sag: Steven Spielberg.)

That should work. If it doesn't, get a blowup doll with a permanent smile painted on her face and put it next to him. He won't know the difference.

ADVICE TO THE EX MS. SAGITTARIUS

If you've read the above story, you should already have the picture: DO NOT CHASE SAGITTARIUS MAN.

Sag guy is absolutely convinced that women must have their place—by his side, listening. A woman must be strong, not aggressive. Smart, but not as knowledgeable as he. Again, Sag is all about authority and respect. If you argue with him about facts—and you're wrong—he'll think you're the stupidest woman on the planet.

> Everybody got it wrong. I said I was into porn again, not born again.
>
> **BILLY IDOL**

If you're right, he'll be charmed.

Again, don't ever ask for Sag guy's advice unless you plan to take it.

Here's the real deal: If Sag breaks up with you, chances are that he knows you're not the one for him. If he comes back for a moment, and you lure him to the sack, he may be tempted to change his mind. BUT only because he hates being wrong.

He figures that if he spent all this time with you, there must have been a reason. So he stays. Then, somewhere down the line, he goes away again when the same problems crop up. (Breaking up and making up is common to this bachelor.)

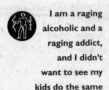

I am a raging alcoholic and a raging addict, and I didn't want to see my kids do the same thing.

OZZY
OSBOURNE

Last word of advice: Let Sag guy decide what he wants. Let him come to you. If you've done something wrong, don't chase and chase. Get him to meet you face-to-face. Tell him you're sorry; ask him to forgive you. Be sweet. State your case, then leave him alone and tell him to come to you when he's ready. Maybe he will.

Instead, if you run after him, he'll make like the Wright Brothers—and fly.

SUN/VENUS COMBINATIONS:
THE TRUE LOVE POTENTIAL TEST

Sagittarius Sun, Venus in Libra

This guy, though he's intensely private, always seems to wind up in the spotlight because of his certain brand of charisma. When he's not act-

Nobody thinks that they're evil or bad. They think that they're doing the right thing.

ANDREW
MCCARTHY

ing like a self-involved only child, he'll go to battle for a cause—especially one of a scientific, radical, cult nature. He needs to feel connected to people and events he deems worthy. And, if he feels it with you, you've got him. He's moralistic and self-righteous, and can go so far as to be revolutionary. Brilliant, but strange; quirky. He is absolutely obsessed by what is taboo. Give him a list of what is not accepted in society, and he'll check them off as he does them (with a shrug, and a rebellious just-try-and-stop-me glimmer in his eye).

What's he looking for? Elegance. A soft soul. Grace Kelly on his arm. He loves to read. Perfection—mentally, physically, spiritually—on his terms. He's like Freud when it comes to analyzing: over the top. To him, women don't just want him—they want to *be* him.

Working with Julie Andrews is like getting hit over the head with a valentine.

CHRISTOPHER PLUMMER

On the upside, he's a true friend and loyal confidant. He loves animals and babies, probably in that order.

BOYFRIEND POTENTIAL RATING: High. Once he's settled, he likes the idea of partnership. Low if he takes the coward's route and opts for a much younger woman who'll yes him to death. Actually, this guy can be a good choice for the long haul—if he doesn't all of a sudden get attracted to your jointly adopted daughter. Lower if you make him feel more insecure than he already does himself.

CELEBRITY CORRESPONDENTS
WITH SAGITTARIUS SUN, VENUS IN LIBRA

Woody Allen (December 1, 1935) Married three times; currently to ex-girlfriend Mia Farrow's adopted daughter.

Claude Levi-Strauss (November 28, 1908)

Pope John XXIII (November 25, 1911)

Charlie Burchill, of Simple Minds (November 27, 1959)

Karl Benz, of Mercedes Benz (November 26, 1844)

Friedrich Engels (November 28, 1820)

Bruce Paltrow (November 26, 1943) Known for his incredible marriage to Blythe Danner from 1969 until his death; daddy to Gwyneth.

Mark Ruffalo (November 22, 1967)

Scott Joplin (November 24, 1868)

Busby Berkeley (November 29, 1895)

Andy Williams (December 3, 1927) Met first wife when he pulled over in Las Vegas to help her with car trouble. She was a dancer. Currently married to Debbie Haas since 1991.

Maxwell Caulfield (November 23, 1959)

Carlo Ponti (November 22, 1948)

Judd Nelson (November 28, 1959) Was linked to Faye Resnick, Kelly Stafford, and Shannon Doherty. Never married.

Sagittarius Sun, Venus in Scorpio

Dark. Dark. Dark. Like blackout shades in hotel rooms in Las Vegas. You know the ones—for those addicts who stay up all night gambling and finally go to sleep at the crack of dawn. Opaque. Creepy. Eerie—like the lake, with an extra e.

If I'm free, it's because I'm always running.

JIMI HENDRIX

He lives to reveal the fantastic in the ordinary. Sees purity in the world and reacts badly when his visions are somehow ruined or shattered. Like a little boy searching, searching for what is wholesome and good . . . which is actually why he can be attracted to the dark side: addiction, drugs, or even murder—if he's not careful.

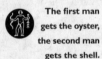

The first man gets the oyster, the second man gets the shell.

ANDREW CARNEGIE

It's the underside of perfectionism. If the world isn't perfect, he might as well fling himself headlong into the corruption himself.

On the other hand, he revels in true love and takes it (and himself) very seriously. If he finds someone he deems truly worthy and special, he will attach himself like paparazzi to Lindsay Lohan. If not, he can be as distant and flighty as Larry King and *all* his marriages.

Oh. He has an odd sense of humor. You must, too, (since you're with him). (Wink.)

Don't fret, though. Save all that energy for determining if he's ripe, juicy, and ready to pick—or, uh, rotten.

BOYFRIEND POTENTIAL RATING: Really high if you like slightly perturbed, strange, masochistic guys. (Kidding. Kinda.) This guy *does* get attached to his mate. Just make sure his code of ethics is good before you subject yourself to king-of-pain suffering. Somehow, it seems like there are self-destructive tendencies here. And he may be obsessed with death. Or just very unlucky.

CELEBRITY CORRESPONDENTS
WITH SAGITTARIUS SUN, VENUS IN SCORPIO

Jim Morrison (December 8, 1943) Speculated to have died of drug overdose at twenty-seven, but not proven. A notorious philanderer and womanizer.

Bruce Lee (November 27, 1940) Died of brain edema at age thirty-two; his son Brandon was killed at age twenty-eight in a freak accident while filming *The Crow*.

Steven Spielberg (December 18, 1946) Films war and bloodshed.

Ted Bundy (November 24, 1946) Notorious serial killer of women.

John Kerry (December 11, 1943) Was married to first wife, who suffered from severe depression, for eighteen years. Second wife is worth $750 million.

Stuart Townsend (December 15, 1972)

Lucky Luciano (November 24, 1897) Mafia.

Keith Richards (December 18, 1943)

Gianni Versace (December 2, 1946) Murdered by serial killer, Andrew Cunanan, in 1997.

Ray Liotta (December 18, 1954)

Jay-Z (December 4, 1970) Married Beyoncé in 2008.

Kirk Douglas (December 9, 1916)

Ozzy Osbourne (December 3, 1948) Had problems with severe substance abuse.

Edmund Kemper (December 18, 1948) Serial killer.

Richard Pryor (December 1, 1940) Substance abuse.

Jamie Foxx (December 13, 1967)

Andrew McCarthy (November 29, 1962)

Rodney Dangerfield (November 22, 1921)

Robert Urich (December 19, 1946)

Bruce Hornsby (November 23, 1954)

Little Richard (December 5, 1932) Spoke out against
homosexuality until he came out himself.

J. Paul Getty (December 15, 1892)

Ridley Scott (November 30, 1937)

Joseph Conrad (December 3, 1857)

E. H. Bailey (November 29, 1876)

Jesse Metcalfe (December 9, 1978)

Ed Koch (December 12, 1924)

Jermaine Jackson (December 11, 1954)

Don Cheadle (November 29, 1964)

Dick Clark (November 30, 1929) On third marriage since 1977.

Chuck Mangione (November 29, 1940)

Phil Donahue (December 21, 1935) On second marriage, to
Marlo Thomas, since 1980.

Robert Guillaume (November 30, 1932)

Redd Foxx (December 9, 1922)

Rich Little (November 26, 1938)

Larry Bird (December 7, 1956)

Clay Aiken (November 30, 1978)

Christopher Plummer (December 13, 1927)

Sagittarius Sun, Venus in Sagittarius

This guy, too, is odd. Intense, but contained—it's always under the
surface, like a crocodile with one eye peering out from the water.
His physical presence is quite compelling. He can look at you and

convey everything he's feeling at the moment with one single glare. Or he can keep his feelings within by coming off as uncaring and unmoved. *He* decides what he wants you to un- understand. (Think John Malkovich.)

There's a lot of power that emanates from him. He can choose to use it wisely. Or corruptly. Depending on his sense of self. He ranges from self-absorbed and self-doubting to narcissistic, cocky, and troubled.

His wiseass, hyperintelligent game keeps him from feeling too much (something he's sure will get him into trouble). His standards are higher for other people to live up to because he doesn't make himself accountable. *Necessarily.*

Unless he's not thoroughly, thoroughly in love, he can make lover-hunting a sport. Duck, duck, goose. You're the goose. He's the gander. He'll wander. He'll wax. You'll wane. If he doesn't fall into his tortured-soul routine, you may just have a chance. Which is why you must torture and control him to make him follow you to the ends of the earth. Forever. It doesn't stop once you get him.

This guy has authority issues. He finds it difficult to respect people; respect to him is *everything*. He cannot perceive you as weak, or he'll step over you as he bolts for the door. You must be able to walk away to hold him. If he feels tricked, boxed in, or tied down, beware of his fear factor. It's legendary.

He runs. You chase. His ego is inflated. Yours disappears.

Beauty, to him, is the mystique that lures him. Brains keep him. He's got to be able to learn something from you—he's always hungry for knowledge.

> Marriage is a wonderful invention, then again, so is a bicycle-repair kit.
>
> **BILLY CONNOLLY**

> Promises and pie-crust are made to be broken.
>
> **JONATHAN SWIFT**

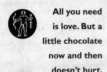

All you need is love. But a little chocolate now and then doesn't hurt.

CHARLES M. SCHULZ

BOYFRIEND POTENTIAL RATING: He frequently makes bad decisions in love. He's as slippery as an oiled-up contestant in a body-building contest. High if he's made his decision and sticks to it. It's *him,* not you—though, obviously, it becomes your problem. Low if he seeks thrills like Tara Reid in a fully stocked bar, filled with hot men.

CELEBRITY CORRESPONDENTS
WITH SAGITTARIUS SUN, VENUS IN SAGITTARIUS

John Malkovich (December 9, 1953)

Jimi Hendrix (November 27, 1942) Found dead with girlfriend Monika Dannemann, after an accidental overdose (or choking from vomit) of sleeping pills and wine. Afterward, Monika took her own life.

Billy the Kid (November 23, 1859)

Ed Harris (November 28, 1950) Has stayed married to Amy Madigan since '83.

Andrew Carnegie (November 25, 1835)

Samuel L. Jackson (December 21, 1948)

Sir Winston Churchill (November 30, 1874)

Jake Gyllenhaal (December 19, 1980)

Frank Zappa (December 21, 1940)

Mark Twain (November 30, 1835)

Billy Connolly (November 24, 1942)

Peter Townshend (November 22, 1914)

Jonathan Swift (December 10, 1667)

Frankie Muniz (December 5, 1985)

Joe DiMaggio (November 25, 1914) It was rumored that DiMaggio was jealous and a bit violent. Marilyn Monroe filed for divorce having not been married a year to him. They got back together after her marriage to Arthur Miller crumbled and it was rumored that they would remarry—but she was found dead before they could.

Bill Pullman (December 17, 1953)

John Laroquette (November 25, 1947) Married to same woman since 1975.

Sam Robards (December 17, 1961)

David Niven (December 15, 1942)

James Thurber (December 8, 1894)

Howie Mandel (November 29, 1955) Married to same woman since 1980.

Charles Schulz (November 26, 1922)

Rick Astley (December 6, 1966)

Shane Black (December 16, 1961)

Fisher Stevens (November 27, 1963)

Sagittarius Sun, Venus in Capricorn

This guy can be a nightmare or an utter saint. True, all men can. But it's more pronounced in this sign.

Good looks are inherent to this man. His charm is infectious because he's so damn down-to-earth and modest. He'll tell you he's not a good dancer, then sweep you off your feet. He'll swear he can't cook, then prepare a sautéed-scallop appetizer, rack of lamb with a Dijon mustard sauce, and buttery mashed potatoes. Flowery words of love are not his style, but you sense that he's a romantic at heart and truly does love you.

When he says he's in love, trust it. He doesn't say it if he doesn't mean it.

Problem is, he's well aware of his place in the world. His moral sense forces him to choose carefully; who to settle down with. In other words,

> If I have any beliefs about immortality, it is that certain dogs I have known will go to heaven, and very, very few persons.
>
> JAMES THURBER

whether he's semifamous, or simply very close to his mother, he'll take others' opinions to heart and it will influence his decision to be with you.

No matter. Once he's made up his mind, he's in it for the long haul. Insecurity, neediness, and distrust on your part are the only things that will make him head for the hills. He wants someone who is kind, together, sensible, sensitive, practical, grounded, and almost regal in bearing. Vulgarity turns him off like lights at curfew in summer camp.

> May you live to be one hundred, and may the last voice you hear be mine.
>
> FRANK SINATRA

Like other Sag combos, he can turn to the dark side if he takes himself too seriously. It's important that he has a sense of humor about himself. If his mother instilled good values in him, you'll never lack for a good mate.

He can be difficult to get along with, though. When something bothers him, he retreats into his shell and it's like pulling teeth to get it out of him—painful, hard, and messy.

Also, he loves children because he tends to identify with purity and innocence. He never loses his sense of awe and curiosity about the world—and is moved by nature and natural beauty; fascinated by human behavior.

> I was the same kind of father as I was a harpist—I played by ear.
>
> HARPO MARX

He honors his commitments; his word is as good as gold. He appreciates those who are loyal to him, and can get mean or belligerent if he feels wronged. Or just distant and cool, if he's mature enough to walk away.

Don't let his optimistic façade fool you. He can be witty and cheerful, then end the conversation with some darkly cynical comment that will really make you think. That's how he reels people in. It's not a trick, though. It's the way his always-pondering mind works.

Because family is so important to them, many of these guys marry a little too young—and come to terms with it later. Even when they have extramarital affairs, they usually don't leave their wives. And they make excellent fathers. Pick your poison wisely.

BOYFRIEND POTENTIAL RATING: He can be a good hubby if you don't piss him off, suffocate him, or ask too much from him emotionally. He'll get there in his own time—like an airline flight during holiday season. Low if you've got too many issues. He can't deal.

CELEBRITY CORRESPONDENTS
WITH SAGITTARIUS SUN, VENUS IN CAPRICORN

Brad Pitt (December 18, 1963)

John F. Kennedy, Jr. (November 25, 1960) Dated Madonna, Daryl Hannah, Cindy Crawford, and Sarah Jessica Parker before marrying Carolyn.

Michael Vartan (November 27, 1968) Was engaged to Shannon Gleason for ten years but never married her.

Frank Sinatra (December 12, 1915) Married his childhood sweetheart but notoriously cheated on her. Affair with Ava Gardner became public. Married Mia Farrow, thirty years his junior. Later married Zeppo Marx's ex.

Kiefer Sutherland (December 21, 1966) Married and divorced twice.

Ludwig Von Beethoven (December 16, 1770)

Pablo Escobar (December 1, 1949)

Walt Disney (December 5, 1901)

Ben Stiller (November 30, 1965)

Brendan Fraser (December 3, 1968)

Adam Brody (December 15, 1979)

Jeff Bridges (December 4, 1949) Married a maid on the set of one of his movies in 1977. Is still married to her.

Peter Facinelli (November 26, 1973) Married Jennie Garth in 2001. They have three daughters together.

David Carradine (December 8, 1936)

Harpo Marx (November 23, 1888)

Giovanni Ribisi (December 17, 1974)

Ira Gershwin (December 6, 1896)

Noël Coward (December 16, 1899) Had one life partner for thirty years.

William F. Buckley (November 24, 1925)

Billy Idol (November 30, 1955)

Dick van Patten (December 9, 1928)

James Galway (December 8, 1939)

Ted Knight (December 7, 1923)

Robert Goulet (November 26, 1933)

Gary Hart (November 28, 1936) Notorious for his scandalous extramarital affair.

Gregg Allman (December 8, 1947)

Paul Shaffer (November 28, 1949) Married to the same woman since 1990. Has four children.

Bob Barker (December 12, 1923) Met his wife at age fourteen and was with her until her death in 1981.

Sagittarius Sun, Venus in Aquarius

With his Venus in Aquarius, Sagittarius guy's dark side gets lightened up with a little air. It's like a balloon with helium in it. Like heavy cream, whipped. It helps. Though he's still intense, this guy is more trustworthy, less creepy. Deadpan is an art form, and he's a master at it. He's not superstitious; it is what it is. In fact, he can see the humor in things—especially in the ups and downs of everyday life. This makes him a good candidate for love. If he does get steamed up about

Women will never be as successful as men because they have no wives to advise them.

DICK VAN DYKE

something, he either blows up about it (getting it out of his system), or pushes it away, pretending it's not there.

This guy is modest, too. Self-deprecating. All he needs is someone strong to be by his side. To support him. He may even like smart women, as long as they are somewhat passive.

Also strange. He's ironic not biting, sarcastic but not mean—a rare feat. He says things as he sees them, sometimes putting his foot in his mouth. Then he backpedals. It's charming to watch—and people just forgive him because it's obvious he didn't know better. Kind of like a puppy dog eating off your plate when you leave the room. (See, okay. Maybe he sort of knows—but he just can't help himself.)

BOYFRIEND POTENTIAL RATING: High if you tease him by dangling Snausages in front of him, then snag 'em away and say, "You'll get them later if you're a good boy." Deal with him like you would a spoiled child. Low if you take him at his word and get frustrated when he does what he wants to do. He'll label you a party pooper and go find some other piñata to bang.

CELEBRITY CORRESPONDENTS
WITH SAGITTARIUS SUN, VENUS IN AQUARIUS

Ray Romano (December 21, 1957)

Flip Wilson (December 8, 1933)

Dick Van Dyke (December 13, 1925) Successfully conquered alcoholism. Married twice.

Andy Dick (December 21, 1965)

Tim Conway (December 15, 1933)

Kenneth Branagh (December 10, 1960) Divorced from Emma Thompson in 1995; remarried.

Casper van Dien (December 18, 1968) On his second marriage, to princess Catherine Oxenberg.

Gustave Flaubert (December 12, 1821)

Donny Osmond (December 9, 1957)

Sammy Davis, Jr. (December 8, 1925) Married three times; last time for twenty years.

Douglas Fairbanks, Jr. (December 9, 1909) Was married to Joan Crawford before he married twice more.

Steve Buscemi (December 13, 1957)

Tom Waits (December 7, 1949)

SAGITTARIUS DIC*-TIONARY

DIRECT <DIE-REKT> Blunt.
Translation for potential girlfriend: Tactless.

HOT <HOTTT> Fiery and Latin-lover-like.
Translation for potential girlfriend: May turn into the Hulk on steroids when he's angry.

HONEST <AHHH-NEST> Tells the truth, always.
Translation for potential girlfriend: Brutally so.

ADVENTUROUS <AD-VEN-TOUR-US> Loves to travel. Fun. Spontaneous.
Translation for potential girlfriend: Unless he's in love, he's all over the map like Magellan.

NAÏVE <NY-EEEV> Refreshingly so. He's kinda pure like that.
Translation for potential girlfriend: Since he can't help himself, he's always sticking his foot in his mouth—which, in turn, can leave a bad taste in yours.

CHAPTER 10

Capricorn, Ex or Next

(the Goat, December 22–January 19)

CAPRICORN RUDE-IMENTS

 Capricorn guy is such a precarious package. You wish you could discount him because he's such a goddamn know-it-all. Yet, he's so freakin' smart, you just can't. Oh, but that's annoying. You jump up and down, do the wave (yourself), and pop champagne when you're right: once a year.

Problem is, he's also emotionally dumb. Handicapped. Compassion-challenged. It's not that he isn't sensitive. He is. He really is. But he can be so stuffed up—like a toilet in a Third World country—that he just can't show himself to you unless he trusts you. Completely.

And getting him to trust you is like offering the president's daughter Halloween candy. She wants to take it, really, she does—and would—if it weren't for the ten bodyguards surrounding her, flexing their muscles Vin Diesel–style. . . . Waiting with Uzis ready-at-hand.

In other words, he wants to believe in you, but he's wary. As he should be. When this guy loses his head, he's *the headless horse-*

man. And he needs his head 'cause his ultra-successful new business venture needs him. Yeah. He's power-hungry and so corporate- and finance-savvy that it's frightening. But he wears it well.

> Being a celebrity is probably the closest to being a beautiful woman as you can get.
>
> KEVIN COSTNER

Capricorn guy is unassuming and subtle. Not flashy like Leo, or attention-starved like Gemini, or talk, talk, blah, blah, like Aquarius. He's stable, sturdy, and like a prisoner getting ready for a prison break, he's waiting to bolt if you mess up.

I'm not saying that Capricorn guy doesn't *appear* open. Ask him something—he's an open book. It's just that he may always keep something distant from the whole process. Sex? It suits him. As long as it doesn't get too emotional, at first.

He's also judgmental—people are guilty until proven innocent, not the other way around. Be careful. His most ardent pursuit besides making money and conquering nations is labeling people. He

> The trouble with having dames on board is you can't pee over the side.
>
> HUMPHREY BOGART

analyzes and puts people on different shelves, categorizing them: "Psycho" goes here; "tramp" goes here; "nice girl/potential" goes here. Truly, he can't see all sides, the three-dimensional you. You're either this way or that. That's what works for him.

Truth is, though, you can trick him. If you get him to believe you're one way in the beginning, he's not likely to change his mind quickly. Capricorn hates being wrong. He believes in first impressions—like a kid just out of a college in a first-time interview for an important job—and will likely keep referring back to it. He thinks he knows you. Does he?

An excellent father. A disciplinarian. Devoted husband. A good breadwinner. He feels more in control when *he's* the one earning the moola. Gruff, but has a soft spot for those he loves.

His bedside manner leaves much to be desired—he can be as warm as Cruella De Vil. Or as tender as a nurse who's just been assigned to empty your bedpan.

It's not that he doesn't care. He really doesn't know how to demonstrate it sometimes. It's also a power thing. He senses he can have the upper backhand swing if he identifies your weaknesses (and uses them against you).

A parade is a parade—and a trumpet is a strumpet. Too much advertising in a thirty-minute show annoys the crap out of him. He'll fast-forward through the commercials. To him, they're gratuitous.

Drama does not play well with Capricorn. Unless, of course, it's his own.

CAPRICORN TONGUE LASHING

"I'll bet you aren't," Capricorn mumbles.

You're probably taken aback. He's just implied that you aren't that great in business, aren't all that good in finances, suck in . . . (whatever you've just admitted to him) . . . or just plain suck (insert sexual term here).

His sarcasm stings you. His directness surprises you. His harshness depresses you. He takes the air out of your tires. Slooooowllly. It's how he controls.

> I don't know if I even have an aura, man. I just try to win.
>
> TIGER WOODS

Sure, he's testing you. So don't tell him your faults off the bat. DO NOT. Modesty doesn't fly well here. To him, there's no such thing. State what you're good at. Again, it's either this way or that. *He'll interpret it as truth.* And refer back to it (for years to come), using that information as a power chip.

In fact, don't try to decipher Capricorn's meaning. Unless he's got his Venus in Scorpio, he's pretty straightforward, even if it hurts *you*.

Speaking of straightforward: Win. Win. Win. Win. Win!!! Cappy must have what he wants—and if that's you, he'll get it. Just don't play games. He'll see right through 'em. And you. His intuition is pretty on the money. He's a decent judge of character.

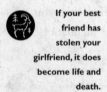

> Men are motivated and empowered when they feel needed. Women are motivated and empowered when they feel cherished.
>
> **JOHN GRAY**

You'll probably have to meet him more on his side than in the middle. Cap's a "cardinal" sign, which means this Goat wants to rule the roost. He wants to come out on top.

Right. Missionary position may work. (He can be pretty traditional in, ahem, bed—depending on whether he's repressed or unleashed. If he's the latter, prepare for Mr. Toad's Horny Ride.)

> If your best friend has stolen your girlfriend, it does become life and death.
>
> **BEN KINGSLEY**

Make him laugh. Capricorn, like the rest of him, has a refined, ironic sense of humor. Just show him your grounded, intelligent side. If you're a bit capricious, whimsical, or self-involved, he'll think you're going to leave him hanging out to dry emotionally. That's a no-no.

He has only so much to give, and if he believes that you're about to drain him like a plumber on an all-too-important Draino mission, he'll put on his AT&T shoes . . . and Sprint.

CAPRICORN: IS HE *INTO* YOU?

How difficult is this to tell? Not very. Capricorn won't keep you around just for the sake of it. He has no need for ego-boosting. Comes out with his guns, ahem, blazing. He has a hard time faking it. In fact, if he falls out of love, you'll be the first to notice. Maybe even before he does. First, he'll stop calling like he used to. Then, he won't go out of his way for you. Maybe he'll even get a little nasty or pick a fight.

Cappy guy will probably date two women in the beginning, then choose. He adores amusing, semi-neurotic women who make him feel alive. Then he'll always pick the more stable one. Capricorn guy will often single out Aquarius woman. This can only work if she doesn't put other friendships and agendas first. One thing's for sure: Capricorn guy will weigh everything out. He doesn't let his heart necessarily dictate who he should be with.

He's probably socially ambitious and will charm those he wants to, "needs" to. Like a mountain goat, he's an uphill climber (yes, this can translate as opportunist, too). Your "important" status—good profession, wealthy family— might be the brick that tips the scales in your favor.

Just sayin'.

> Nothing interferes with my concentration. You could put on an orgy in my office and I wouldn't look up. Well, maybe once.
>
> **ISAAC ASIMOV**

But is he into you? Oh, you'll know it. If he's playing games, the answer is no. Unlike Gemini, who plays even more when he likes you—like a little boy pulling that poor little girl's pigtails on the playground—Cap only plays when he's unsure. Like Cancer guy, Cappy will probably wait to confide in you until he trusts you completely. If he's already gone there, he's made himself vulnerable.

And that, my friends, means he wants you bad.

ADVICE TO THE FUTURE MRS. CAPRICORN

Here's a story of Cap success for you. Elena met Jonathan, a Cappy. He was more poetic and romantic than many other Caps.

(But that's the thing about Caps—they cover a wider range than a lot of other signs.) He swept her off her feet. One night she finally encountered the not-so-ex girlfriend, in a restaurant with him. Remember, Cap usually has two chicks in the beginning—then narrows it down to one (and/or keeps the other as backup).

To succeed with the opposite sex, tell her you're impotent. She can't wait to disprove it.

CARY GRANT

Jonathan "broke it off" with the Other Woman. After a couple of blissful months, Elena and he finally decided to have sex. (Aw. They were waiting for the right moment.) Now, the night they were about to consummate, the ex-girlfriend shows up *in* Jonathan's apartment. Why? She still had the key. (Talk about open-door policy.) After Jon got rid of the ex from his house, he and Elena went on for a few months with a wonderful relationship— until the ex showed up again.

WAIT. With the same key. (Turns out, he never took that key away.)

This time, Elena stopped believing that he had stopped seeing the ex (as, um, all her friends kept telling her) and wised up. She did not give him an ultimatum—that never would have worked.

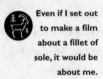

Even if I set out to make a film about a fillet of sole, it would be about me.

FEDERICO FELLINI

Instead, when she caught him "hanging" with the ex, "just helping her out with some money issues," she took back her pride. Just like in the movies, she said to him, "Take one good, long look at my face. 'Cause it's the last time you'll ever see it." And meant it. Got into her car and left him standing there, mouth agape.

He called. And called. And called. He was devastated. Finally figured out that she was The One.

She even packed up and left the city he lived in. It took months and months of calling, pleading, and wooing for him to get her back.

He never cheated again.

And asked her to marry him a year later.

(She said no.)

ADVICE TO THE EX MS. CAPRICORN

Be forewarned. Like a really bad kitchen pan, everything sticks with this guy. He'll remember if you've done something bad. It'll stay in his head, like grease after cooking sausages. And it'll take him a long time to forgive and forget.

More likely than not, though, it's probably a behavioral issue with Cap if he's running away. In other words, it's not one specific thing. For example, he thinks you're too high-maintenance. Too neurotic or needy. If you break up, he might call once or twice, to "check up" on you. That's a good sign. He sometimes wonders if he can make it work after all. When this happens, have friends over. Or, more precisely, act like you're busy and can't really talk. Tell him you'll call him back. Then wait a week to do it. Call when you least want to—not when you feel like you can't live without the bastard.

> I always had a
> repulsive need
> to be something
> more than
> human.
>
> **DAVID BOWIE**

I know. I know. Game playing. But there wouldn't be so many dating advice books out there if there weren't somethin' to it.

Truth is, if you can show him your fun, happy, secure side—namely, the real you—you may just have a chance. Just don't revert to psychodom and show up at his window throwing rocks. Or sneak into his e-mail to check who he's been talking to. If he catches you—or sees a truly scary neurotic side, it's over for good.

Don't, don't, *don't* sleep with him until you're back together.

Respect is a serious issue for Capricorn. He can separate himself from sex and "making love" like an exhibitionist from his Calvin Kleins on a nude beach (unlike Brooke Shields from hers).

SUN/VENUS COMBINATIONS:
THE TRUE LOVE POTENTIAL TEST

Capricorn Sun, Venus in Scorpio

For this guy, pride is his biggest downfall. If he doesn't have the upper hand, he can be touchy and sensitive, like a prick . . . ly pear.

I'm an instant star. Just add water and stir.

DAVID BOWIE

Then he moans and whines or huffs and holes up in his private space until he's ready to come out.

He'll make you work for it, too. Crafty, this one is.

However, he truly believes in family and can be a surprisingly good father/husband if he was cut from a good mold. He'll likely follow in his 'rents' footsteps, so just look to see if his childhood was a happy one. And that he had good role-model trend-setters.

I try to do the right thing with money. Save a dollar here and there, clip some coupons. Buy ten gold chains instead of twenty. Four summer homes instead of eight.

L. L. COOL J

At his best, this guy can rock your disco world. He'll claim he can't read your mind, but he knows exactly what makes you purr. Sure he's modest— like a three-hundred-pound girl turned thin. He's unsure of his moves, but will do more to woo you and make you happy if he knows you appreciate his efforts. If not, he'll never do anything for you ever again. Right. Be careful. He'll remember how you treated him five years ago and bring it up at the most awkward moment.

BUT. He usually does what he says and says what he does. Security goes a long way. Don't underestimate this.

To him, words are law. But here's the calamine rub: If you say something, then go back on your word, you're now about as trustworthy as a bungee jump with a three-dollar jump rope used as the cord.

You're a really crappy flotation device . . . made of lead.

He won't respect you. And here's the cincher—Cap is more serious than Aretha Franklin. R-E-S-P-E-C-T. He doesn't sing it. He brands you with it like a multimillion-dollar advertising agency. With this Cappy, it's all about authority. Most times, he is absolutely, positively, supercalifragilistically sure that he knows the answer: to everything. In other words, if you ask his opinion, then don't listen, you've broken one of *his* ten commandments: Thou Shalt Not Take the Lord's Word in Vain.

Lying is like alcoholism. You are always recovering.

STEVEN SODERBERGH

BOYFRIEND POTENTIAL RATING: High if you have a degree in psychology and can beat him at his Home-player's advantage game. Low if the intense, raw, quiet, and staid power-thing gives you the creeps.

CELEBRITY CORRESPONDENTS
WITH CAPRICORN SUN, VENUS IN SCORPIO

Val Kilmer (December 31, 1959) Dated Cindy Crawford, Drew Barrymore, Ellen Barkin, and Cher; wrote poetry for Michelle Pfeiffer. Has married and divorced.

Denzel Washington (December 28, 1954) Married since 1983.

Jon Voight (December 29, 1938)

Ralph Fiennes (December 22, 1962) Married once; dated a woman eighteen years older than him that ended when the tabloids reported he was having an affair on her.

Tiger Woods (December 30, 1975)

Conrad Hilton (December 25, 1887) Creator of the Hilton Hotel chain and had three wives, including Zsa Zsa Gabor.

John Gray (December 28, 1951) Both he and Barbara DeAngelis, whom he married and divorced, write relationship books.

Jimmy Buffett (December 25, 1946)

Ben Kingsley (December 31, 1943)

Isaac Asimov (January 2, 1920)

Kevin Weisman (December 29, 1970)

John Denver (December 31, 1943)

Tom Weir (December 29, 1914)

Capricorn Sun, Venus in Sagittarius

A rake. A cad. A dashing, daring specimen. Women adore him. Men respect him. So here's my advice, kitten. Listen. This guy's all over the map. He travels so much (or wants to), that the airlines have named happy meals, after women, in his honor:

Karen-so-much. Lauren-her-in.

The question isn't at what age I want to retire, it's at what income.

GEORGE FOREMAN

Polly, want a cracker? Aaaaack.

Do this: Let him seek you out. Don't look for him. *Ever.* But when he calls, see him. Look like a pretty thang. Tell him how wonderful he is. Praise him and the way he thinks. Tell him you're so happy to hear from him (after you've been missing in action for a few days—that'll really confuse him).

This guy's used to getting what he wants. So don't give it to him. Um. Yeah. Make him think the ball's in his court. Or, rather, that his balls truly want to be in *your* court.

But wait. Don't contradict him: at first.

Janet Jackson's breast has gotten me into a whole bunch of trouble.

HOWARD STERN

Be arm candy. Speak in a Marilyn Monroe voice. Sing *"Happy Birthday, Mr. President . . . Happy Birthday to you."*

It'll take him about fifteen years to figure out that you're The One, but when he does, you can finally stop sucking your stomach in and breathe.

BOYFRIEND POTENTIAL RATING: High, if you don't have any feminism issues. Higher if you resemble a young Bo Derek. Higher still if you and he have the age difference of Bo and her late husband—twenty to thirty years. Perfect if you're a water sign (Scorpio, Cancer, or Pisces), or if you're prone to saying things like "My man. Look how handsome he is"; cooing in a voice that would make the rest of us utterly revolted and want to throw up all over you.

CELEBRITY CORRESPONDENTS
WITH CAPRICORN SUN, VENUS IN SAGITTARIUS

Kevin Costner (January 18, 1955)

Jude Law (December 29, 1972) Cheated with the nanny on wife and girlfriend.

Al Capone, aka "Scarface" (January 18, 1899)

Cary Grant (January 18, 1904) Married five times and rumored to be bisexual.

Gerard Depardieu (December 27, 1948)

David Bowie (January 8, 1947) Still with second wife, came out as bisexual, then took it back.

Howard Hughes (December 24, 1905) Notorious ladies' man; married three times.

Michael Stipe, of R.E.M. (January 4, 1960)

Lyle Menendez (January 10, 1968) Sentenced to life in prison in '92 for killing his parents with brother Erik (Scorpio); both brothers managed to meet women and get married, all from jail.

Eddie Vedder, of Pearl Jam (December 23, 1964)

Jimmy Page (January 9, 1944) Was fascinated with the occult. He had astrological symbols on his clothes—Capricorn, Scorpio, and Cancer (his sun, ascendant, and moon signs).

Federico Fellini (January 20, 1920)

Kid Rock (January 17, 1971) Married Pamela Anderson in 2006.
   They divorced six months later.

Rasputin (January 10, 1869)

Chad Lowe (January 15, 1968)

Chet Baker (December 23, 1929) Married three times.

Frank Sinatra, Jr. (January 10, 1944)

Albert Schweitzer (January 14, 1875)

Rowan Atkinson (January 6, 1955)

Simon Wiesenthal (December 31, 1908)

Rudyard Kipling (December 30, 1865)

Joey McIntyre (December 31, 1972)

L.L. Cool J (January 14, 1968) Married since '95 with four
   children.

James Denton (January 20, 1963)

John DeLorean (January 6, 1925) He married three times, once
   to model Christina Ferrare.

George Foreman (January 10, 1949)

Rip Taylor (January 13, 1931)

Christopher Durang (January 2, 1949)

Victor Borge (January 3, 1909)

Walter Mondale (January 5, 1928)

Sean Paul (January 8, 1973)

Steven Soderbergh (January 14, 1963) On second marriage, to
   Jules Asner.

Stanley Tucci (January 11, 1960)

Cuba Gooding, Jr. (January 2, 1968)

Oliver Platt (January 12, 1960) A distant cousin of Princess Di,
   he married in 1993 and has three children.

Capricorn Sun, Venus in Capricorn

This guy doesn't really give himself a break. He's as tough on himself as he is on others (unlike Virgo—who doesn't judge others as

harshly as he kicks his own butt). He can be slightly masochistic, even—abusing himself with alcohol or pain pills if his self-esteem ranks low on the charts.

He's got a curious nature. He reads other people well and can be ultra-charming in a distinct, odd, complex way. There's always some mystery shrouding his M.O. That's no car accident. As the song goes, he likes it like that.

Sometimes, this guy has a thing for younguns. Girls. School uniforms. He loves to start from scratch; mold and shape. There's always a purity thing with women and him. Not that they have to be virgins, but there must be something upstanding and good about the women he chooses. He's not about overstated glam or fake eyelashes; it's more Abercrombie and Fitch than Versace. He likes a down-home girl who's pretty but more wholesome than vamp. *He* can be a little dirty (read: perverted). You can't. He'll grill you with questions, like Barbara Walters with Fidel Castro— thoroughly. He only wants to make sure you're right for him. Don't try to answer according to what you think he wants to hear. He'll sense if you're censoring.

> I know a lot of gay males who I work with that are fantastic people and I love hanging out with them. But because I hang out and bring gay men into my life, does that mean that I'm gay? I promise you that I very much love women.
>
> RYAN SEACREST

Creative and intelligent, this guy has a keen eye and a practical nature, though his patience may wear thin easily. If he's got any Scorpio in his chart (which he might), he's probably fascinated by the news and a little obsessed with death.

That said, he's a pretty cheery guy when he's not off being tragic and isolated.

BOYFRIEND POTENTIAL RATING: Very high if the last book you read was *Curious George Goes to School* (a youngun, get it?). (See

Howard Stern with wife. See Howard run. See Howard with extra-young *Playboy* centerfold.) Extra-high if you meet at an AA meeting and are determined to keep him off the wagon. Okay, if he's really, truly in love—and considers you an equal. Or a superior. Low if you leave him before he gets his act together. Which may take a while.

CELEBRITY CORRESPONDENTS
WITH CAPRICORN SUN, VENUS IN CAPRICORN

Elvis Presley (January 8, 1935) Wouldn't have sex with Priscilla until she turned eighteen. Was happy to do it with everyone else, though.

Anthony Hopkins (December 31, 1937) Married three times.

Jim Carrey (January 17, 1962) Went public that he suffers from depression. Was married twice; once to Lauren Holly. Dated Renée Zellweger.

Louis Pasteur (December 27, 1822)

Syd Barrett, of Pink Floyd (January 6, 1946)

Humphrey Bogart (December 25, 1899) Was actually married four times but best known for his stellar marriage with Lauren Bacall.

Jay Kay, aka Jamiroquai (December 30, 1969)

Benjamin Franklin (January 17, 1706)

Andy Kaufman (January 17, 1949) Interesting: same birth date as Jim Carrey (January 17, 1962), who played him in *Man on the Moon*; he expounded on the virtues of older women because they're grateful.

Frank Langella (January 1, 1938)

Robert Palmer (January 19, 1949)

J. D. Salinger (January 1, 1919)

Philippe Starck (January 18, 1949)

J. Edgar Hoover (January 1, 1895)

Ryan Seacrest (December 24, 1974)

Howard Stern (January 12, 1954) Longtime marriage; famous because he was surrounded by nude models and porn stars. Wife left him not for being unfaithful, but because he was a workaholic. Now with model nineteen years younger than him.

Mario Van Peebles (January 15, 1957)

Don Maclean (January 16, 1970)

Eddie Cahill (January 15, 1978)

Lawrence Kasdan (January 14, 1949)

Cab Calloway (December 25, 1907)

Danny Thomas (January 6, 1914) Married to same woman from 1936 to 1991, when he died.

Brandon Tartikoff (January 13, 1949)

Capricorn Sun, Venus in Aquarius

This guy can have a sex appeal that is undeniable. It's all that air (Aquarius) mixed with earth (Capricorn). The air lightens him up so that he can exude sensuality without being too heavy about it. His charisma is subtle, though, which only makes him more sincere and appealing.

He believes in causes bigger than himself. Wants to help the world and all of its victims abounding.

He's a peaceful storm. A light hurricane. Drizzle with a bit of thunder. A cool cat. An intelligent, too-sweet guy who grows into his own—and becomes a very respectable, solid charmer.

He's a touch psychic and can read people's motives (which can be scary for you).

> After about twenty years of marriage, I'm finally starting to scratch the surface of what women want. And I think the answer lies somewhere between conversation and chocolate.
>
> MEL GIBSON

Although he's sturdy, he's got a creative mind that balances his sometimes too-practical nature. Only problem—he can back away from a love situation if he believes it's the best thing to do. He doesn't latch on for dear life like Cancer, Taurus, or even Sagittarius, when he's fallen over the edge.

Ego plays a strong part in this. It's like: Leggo my Eggo. He wants what he wants. Like a kid in an ice cream shop who's severely diabetic, he'll order a pint of mint chocolate chip, anyway.

BOYFRIEND POTENTIAL RATING: High, but only once he knows himself. Pretty faithful, too, unless he changes his mind about you. Not saying he's fickle. Just saying he's got to be sure.

CELEBRITY CORRESPONDENTS
WITH CAPRICORN SUN, VENUS IN AQUARIUS

Mel Gibson (January 3, 1956) Married to same woman for more than twenty years; they have seven kids together.

Ricky Martin (December 24, 1971)

Nicolas Cage (January 7, 1964) Lisa Marie Presley's dad, Elvis, was a Cappy, too. She's an Aquarius.

Olivier Martinez (January 12, 1966)

Nostradamus (December 14, 1503)

Taye Diggs (January 2, 1972) Happily married since 2003.

Patrick Dempsey (January 13, 1966) On his second marriage since 1999.

Marc Blucas (January 11, 1972)

Michael Schumacher (January 3, 1969) Likes to keep private life private. Married since 1995 and has two children.

Muhammad Ali (January 17, 1942)

Carlos Castaneda (December 25, 1925)

Sir Isaac Newton (January 4, 1643)

Jared Leto (December 26, 1971)

Henrí Matisse (December 31, 1869)

Paul Cézanne (January 19, 1839)

Ted Danson (December 29, 1947) Was dating Whoopi Goldberg while he was married to his first wife. Married to Mary Steenburgen since 1995.

Bob Denver (January 9, 1935)

Tim Matheson (December 31, 1947)

Rush Limbaugh (January 12, 1951)

Donald Fagen (January 12, 1951)

Capricorn Sun, Venus in Pisces

Sweet. Sweet. A good catch who likes to show his dark, strange side so you don't think he's a total pansy. He's not necessarily a goofball, maybe just a little mysterious. (Though he opens up a lot when you get to know him.)

There's always a layer, however, that you might not uncover till the ring's on your finger. He distances himself like a restraining order. Comes close—then pulls away, like Courtney Love trying to go completely sober, cold turkey. It's inevitable.

He's ambitious, though. And he rotates his focus. For a period, he'll concentrate on you and family. Then work. Multitasking rattles his nerves. In fact, he needs calm and de-stressing in order to function and be his kind, caring self. He can be more sensitive than the other Cappys—again, he may not show this side at first. He hides behind a persona, agenda, or creed. His public face is usually different from his private one.

He's good at faking it and throws you for Froot Loops. It's unlikely that he'll come out and say what he needs or wants. After a while, though, you'll get the hang of it. Just don't get hung up too soon or you'll get hung out to dry. He needs to work for it and conquer you.

BOYFRIEND POTENTIAL RATING: Mezzo-high, but he's frequently misunderstood. If he lets you into his private world and shares, he may just gravitate back to you, always. If he gets into self-pitying mode, though, just make sure not to drown in whatever tragedy he's living out at the moment.

CELEBRITY CORRESPONDENTS
WITH CAPRICORN SUN, VENUS IN PISCES

Orlando Bloom (January 13, 1977) Was on/off with Kate Bosworth until 2006.

Marilyn Manson (January 5, 1969) His name comes from a mix of two names: Marilyn Monroe and Charles Manson; married in 2005. Dita Von Teese filed for divorce a year later.

Martin Luther King, Jr. (January 15, 1929)

Dave Grohl, of Nirvana (January 14, 1969)

Rod Stewart (January 10, 1945) Divorced twice, last marriage was to supermodel Rachel Hunter.

Edgar Allan Poe (January 19, 1809) The master of horror married his thirteen-year-old cousin; she died a few years later. He attempted suicide many times, and was found dead in a gutter at forty.

Malcolm Young, of AC/DC (January 6, 1953)

Molière (January 15, 1622)

Richard Nixon (January 9, 1913)

David Caruso (January 17, 1956) Divorced three times.

Jason Bateman (January 14, 1969) Married to singer Paul Anka's daughter since 2001.

CAPRICORN DIC*-TIONARY

FAITHFUL <FAYTH-FULL> You can count on him.

Translation for potential girlfriend: Even though he has the bedside manner of Dr. Kevorkian.

EXPERT <EHKS-PERT> Has many skills and much knowledge.

Translation for potential girlfriend: Knows it—and may just have a serious I AM GOD complex.

FAIR <FARE> Fights for what's right and sticks up for you when you need it.

Translation for potential girlfriend: So competitive, it makes those nasty bitches on reality dating shows look tame.

FACTUAL <FAAAHK-TOO-ALL> Has a good grasp of the situation, which makes him sincere and a good catch.

Translation for potential girlfriend: So goddamn literal, he'll argue that "High Hopes" is false because there ain't no way that ant coulda moved that rubber tree plant. So literal, he'll slam Dr. Seuss because there t'aint no such thing as green eggs and ham.

REALISTIC <REE-ALL-HIS-TICK> Stable and grounded; down-to-earth.

Translation for potential girlfriend: Has the patience of a cop on line for donuts if things get too emotional.

BALANCED <BAHHH-LANCED> Knows how to stay calm in stressful situations.

Translation for potential girlfriend: 'Cause he can be as removed as acetate on nail polish.

CHAPTER 11

Aquarius, Ex or Next
(the Water Bearer, January 20–February 18)

AQUARIUS RUDE-IMENTS

Be a Bond girl. Be a Robert Palmer girl in "Addicted to Love." Be Catwoman—without the claws. (Ouch!)

Hey, that's all you have to do to get this one. You need mystery, a foreign accent, diplomatic plates . . . and a pilot's license. That's all. That's all he wants. Then you'll get him.

See? It's not so hard. Aquarius guy likes quirky. Out of the mold. Breaking new ground. Strange, maybe. Fascinating (to him). It could just be that you're incredibly organized and together, unlike him. This will intrigue him—you're *different*.

> Marriage is about the most expensive way for the average man to get laundry done.
>
> BURT REYNOLDS

Aquarius guy needs lots of stimuli. Like Carrie Bradshaw shoe shopping at Payless, he's easily bored.

If there's nothing fun for him to do, he gets lazy. Sure, he's social (and has acquaintances coming out of the woodwork). You say you have twenty weddings to attend in the next few months? Slow year. Like Dalmatians, he has 101 "best" friends. In fact, he never rents a tux. He owns one. (He needs it.)

He's also happiest when he's discovering a new culture, a new outlook on life; new rules to follow—so he can break them.

I deserve respect for the things I did not do.

DAN QUAYLE

Aquarius guy is never a snob—not ever. He can mix with people from all walks of life, rub shoulders with the best of them. Rub other things, too.

Here's the thing. Aquarius likes sex. But he can remove himself. If he thinks you're on the down-low, he'll do it, too. Even Steven. Tit for tat. If you've cheated (or have treated him badly), he'll need to even the score. Aquarius can be scary that way. He's attached. Attached. And then he's not.

I have a BMW. But only because BMW stands for Bob Marley and the Wailers, and not because I need an expensive car.

BOB MARLEY

This guy can separate sex from making love, like a good journalist, real tears from Visine-manufactured.

Incidentally, the best talk-show hosts—who are better speaking to the masses than one-on-one—are always Aquarius. Oprah Winfrey. Ellen Degeneres.

Hell, even Jerry Springer is an Aquarius. (Though David Letterman and Conan O'Brien are both Aries.)

Oh. Wait. Ex–talk show host Arsenio Hall is also an Aquarius.

Aquarius men usually feel more than they show. They go for dominant, bold types, and don't mind being grabbed. They also need to respect their woman tremendously. You can sneak up on Aquarius by getting him addicted to you. It creeps up, up on him, like the boogeyman in a kid's nightmare.

I was married at sixteen, a father at seventeen, and divorced at eighteen.

PLACIDO DOMINGO

Sex can be used. He may have the tool . . . You've got the weapon.

AQUARIUS TONGUE LASHING

"Show me your panties."

You're sitting on the rooftop of a glamorous hotel, and Aquarius guy shoots off this one. He likes to stir the pot. Is he romantic? Depends. Does this turn you on? If it does, you

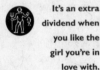

> Dream as if you'll live forever; live as if you'll die tomorrow.
>
> JAMES DEAN

may have found the Kurt Cobain to your Courtney Love.

You have to be verbally whip-smart to tongue-lash him back. Ironic, subtle humor works best. If you get a chuckle, you're in. A guffaw means you've delighted him, utterly. Like music to the ears.

Oh. The act of sex culminates in one blissful moment of groaning, not talking. This is a feat for him because he probably rarely stops yapping.

> It's an extra dividend when you like the girl you're in love with.
>
> CLARK GABLE

Bragging and being praised for his accomplishments is the best foreplay for him. (Poor, insecure thing. That's what I'm saying.)

If you play hard to get, he'll always be, uh, hard for you.

That's how it works.

AQUARIUS: IS HE *INTO* YOU?

He can be raunchy and direct—it's not often that he's sweet and sensual. If he is, he's yours. Truly. He's opened up his heart to you.

Showing his vulnerable side is akin to a turtle being happy with his hard shell facing down. His poor little swimmer things flail about. He can't move. Can't do anything but try to "right himself."

Ego and pride, like with Gemini guy, take on the form of showing he's just fine without you, thank you very much. He'll walk away just to prove he can (then whine to his friends that it's not that he *needs* you, he just wants the scoop of what's really going on).

See, Aquarius guy is convinced he can live without you. He's as independent as a low-budget art film.

However, if you've done your job, he'll stick around like a mosquito to flypaper. Basically, if Aquarius is spending lots of time with you, he's *into you.* Why else would he keep all his other fans waiting?

He can be a taker, not a giver, with money and almost everything. If he's spending on you, he's truly, truly fixated. And that, my friend, is a rare thing, indeed. (What, did you drug him?)

He won't be a show-off, like Anna Nicole Smith and her famed medicine cabinet filled with, ah, VitaSlim (or whatever)—and her hilariously drunk "Like my body?" commercials. It's more like Paris Hilton draping her gremlin-like weird rat-thing kinkajou leisurely over her shoulder. She's not asking for publicity or attention. (Nah. If she wanted that, she would have done it One Night in Paris.)

I don't have anything that I treasure at all. They're just things. I tend to buy an awful lot of stuff, like clothes and things. But I wouldn't be bothered if my house burns down tomorrow.

ROBBIE
WILLIAMS

I could really care less about what they think about me, but at the same time, I do have something to prove.

BOBBY
BROWN

ADVICE TO THE FUTURE MRS. AQUARIUS

Here 'tis.

One Capricorn woman worked with a typical Aquarius man. He was so good at what he did—took names, kicked butt. A creative type who could work his contacts and move up the food chain quickly.

> The hippies wanted peace and love. We wanted Ferraris, blondes, and switchblades.
>
> ALICE COOPER

Yes, Cappy girl was impressed. But was she convinced of his romantic-wooing skills? Not entirely.

He went after her. Drew her in with light-hearted teasing. Hinted about the two of them going out. Honed his strategy to test what was working on her. (Yup, Aquarius guy has an innate sense of when to move forward and when to draw back. Especially in the beginning.)

She played it very, very cool. Which is exactly how you get Aquarius guy. He has to know you're saner and more stable than he is. That you're solid. That there's none of the desperate wannabe diva in you. (*That* will send him running for dear life.)

> If you get murdered—what a great thing. What a great publicity thing.
>
> ALICE COOPER

Anyway, long story short. She always kept her cool, even when they started dating. Never stepped it up and looked for more than he was offering. (With some guys, *you* have to move it forward. Not with Aquarius guy. He has to be the one to take the next step.)

Aquarius guy asked her to move in. They lived together. She still remained sturdy. (See? You can't fake this. Either you're this type—not looking for rainbows and puppies—or you're not.)

The two main problems were Aquarius guy's many "best friends" and the way he handled his finances. She gave him an ultimatum for both. He couldn't quite meet them. She left him.

He called her for a year begging her to marry him.

No, this is not a happy ending. She wanted to be numero uno, not an RSVP on a hundred wedding invites from his "closest friends" a year. But . . . three years later, she could still call him and he'd hire a good wedding photographer and, very happily, pop the question. That's powah.

> The key to immortality is first living a life worth remembering.
>
> **BRANDON LEE**

ADVICE TO THE EX MS. AQUARIUS

Precarious. Aquarius is not the chasee. And he's not necessarily the chas*er*, either (unless he's gotten so used to you that he'd rather keep ya than start all over again).

Here's the thing about Aquarius guy they don't tell you: He's lazy. Once he's worked to capture a love interest in his grab-bag, he's not gonna want to go out and find another. Like everything else in his life, he wants it to be *easy.* Calm. Tranquil. Set. That way, he can go off and earn his bucks, shake hands, take names, kick butt.

> It's sad and upsetting when you see somebody crying hysterically, but at the same time it's real funny.
>
> **SETH GREEN**

If he's actually broken up with you, it's for a reason. He just doesn't see it. The experience hasn't moved him, and he's off to deeper waters to look for other fish in the sea.

Don't despair. You'll likely find a better catch.

A little masochistic, are you? Sleep with him. If he gets attached again (he can, sometimes), he'll stick around for a while. But, for you, it'll be like that construction guy who's hanging by his helmet with crazy glue, five hundred feet up. Move an inch and you fall from grace.

And he might just take off like Orville and Wilbur, afterward.

Again, this guy can leave you sleeping peacefully in bed, go out, have sex, come back, get into bed again, and accuse you of hogging the covers.

When dealing with an Aquarius ex, watch your back like a goodfella in an Italian restaurant.

SUN/VENUS COMBINATIONS: THE TRUE LOVE POTENTIAL TEST

Aquarius Sun, Venus in Sagittarius

One day Alice came to a fork in the road and saw a Cheshire cat in a tree. Which road do I take? she asked. Where do you want to go? was his response. I don't know, Alice answered. Then, said the cat, it doesn't matter.

LEWIS CARROLL

Unconventional. Strangely pious. Possibly hung up on his special moral code. This Aquarius/Sag has an outwardly optimistic view of life—yet may suffer privately. Consider Alan Alda: devout Catholic when he was younger, zealous feminist when he was older. Or Dan Quayle, persecuted by the media for his public denouncement of TV character Murphy Brown having a child out of wedlock. Or Neil Bush, joining Cardinal Ratzinger (now Pope Benedict XVI) in the crusade to publish original religious texts.

BUT, the joke's on him. He's fallible like the rest of us mortals. (Neil Bush was caught having sex with prostitutes in Thailand when he was still married.)

He has a strange approach for living the high

> I firmly believe in marriage. It's a real important decision that takes a lot of dedication and time. If you're thinking about divorce, you shouldn't get married.
>
> SETH GREEN

life, but it works for him. He's got the I-want-a-soul-mate thing going (his Sag Venus) yet can rationalize and distance himself, too (Aquarius Sun). Therefore, he may have several "soul mates" over the course of his life, depending on how quickly he matures. (Right, little brother Bush?)

> The problem is with men. I know I shouldn't say this, but they've shrouded and hidden women to hide their incompetence.
>
> JOHN GALLIANO

Problem is, does he hold himself accountable? Take responsibility for his actions? Or does he claim "victim," swearing up and down that he didn't drink the last of the milk in the fridge (when he's got a thick white mustache on his upper lip)? Be brutally honest—like a plain ol' housewife being harshly interrogated by the FBI. (Ever see *True Lies* and that mirthful scene between Arnold Schwarzenegger and Jamie Lee Curtis??)

George Burns (Aquarius/Sag) once said, "Look to the future, because that is where you'll spend the rest of your life." Good advice, but how can this guy enjoy the present when he's always two steps ahead of everyone else?

> Any girl that's got a $500,000 table and $5 shoes, I'm in love with.
>
> JAMES BROLIN

BOYFRIEND POTENTIAL RATING: High if he's truly committed. He'll make you his lifelong art project. Low if his idea of being a grown-up is putting on a snazzy suit and just making it to work on time every day.

CELEBRITY CORRESPONDENTS
WITH AQUARIUS SUN, VENUS IN SAGITTARIUS

Eddie Van Halen (January 26, 1955) Married to Valerie Bertinelli; she filed for divorce in 2005.

Rutger Hauer (January 23, 1944)

Alan Alda (January 28, 1936)

George Burns (January 20, 1896) His first marriage was in name only; he was married to Gracie Allen from 1926 until her death in '64.

Dan Quayle (February 4, 1947)

Conrad Bain (February 4, 1923)

Lewis Carroll (January 27, 1832) Rumored (but not proven) to have written *Alice in Wonderland* due to his creepy obsession with the twelve-year-old neighbor, Alice.

William McKinley (January 29, 1843)

Rip Torn (February 6, 1931)

Ugo Calvelli Gucci (January 24, 1899)

Stonewall Jackson (January 20, 1824)

Neil Bush (January 22, 1955)

Pope Clement IX (January 28, 1600)

Walter Miller (January 23, 1923) This science fiction author was a recluse until he shot himself in 1996.

Jeff Koons (January 21, 1955)

Curtis Strange (January 30, 1955)

Troy Donahue (January 27, 1936) Had problems with drug addiction and alcoholism. This teen idol married twice.

Michael Hutchence (January 22, 1960)

Urs Buhler, of Il Divo (January 29, 1971)

Aquarius Sun, Venus in Capricorn

This guy has it, with a serious edge. No matter which way you slice it, he exudes some kind of raw power. Like he was born to it. People trust him because he has a startling air of respectability (even when he's being bad). He garners respect with his easy smile, ironic humor, and admirable dedication to the people he loves.

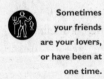

Sometimes your friends are your lovers, or have been at one time.

AXL ROSE

In fact, this guy has more friends than he knows what to do with. He sets the tone. His dry cleaner guy loves him. So do the waiter, the bartender, and the manager of the hotel he stays at. Like Hilary Duff in a world full of Lindsay Lohans and Paris Hiltons, he somehow manages to keep it clean.

Yet he doesn't get close and truly open himself up to many.

The woman he does choose, though, gets the royal treatment. He's built for longevity. Although he's very cunning, he uses his superpowers for good. If he waits until he knows what he truly wants from a woman, you can open up an account at his bank. 'Cause he's into fidelity.

> I don't believe that old cliché that good things come to those who wait. I think good things come to those who want something so bad they can't sit still.
>
> **ASHTON KUTCHER**

BOYFRIEND POTENTIAL RATING: Pretty darn high, especially if he's got his career together and involves you in it. Low if you're even a little insecure. Or don't handle social get-togethers gracefully. He shuns neediness like a groom getting hit on by the female wedding photographer.

> I had lived a charmed life, and then I lost a beautiful woman I loved with all my heart.
>
> **ROBERT WAGNER**

CELEBRITY CORRESPONDENTS
WITH AQUARIUS SUN, VENUS IN CAPRICORN

James Dean (February 8, 1931)

Paul Newman (January 26, 1925) After a brief early marriage, has been married to Joanne Woodward for almost fifty years.

James Spader (February 7, 1960)

Clark Gable (February 1, 1901) He was married five times. The third one, seemingly the marriage made in heaven, ended in tragedy when Carole Lombard was killed in a plane crash.

Justin Timberlake (January 31, 1981) Ex-flame Britney's a Sag (fire), which doesn't go with Justin's sun (air) or Venus (earth); ex Cameron Diaz is a Virgo (earth) and Jessica Biel is a Pisces (water).

Christian Bale (January 30, 1974)

Robbie Williams (February 13, 1974)

Elijah Wood (January 28, 1981)

Burt Reynolds (February 11, 1936) Was married and divorced twice; very noisy divorce from Loni Anderson. He also had relationships with Sally Field and Dinah Shore.

Michael Jordan (February 17, 1963) Divorced after twelve years of marriage.

Brandon Lee (February 1, 1965)

Franz Schubert (January 31, 1797)

David Lynch (January 20, 1946) Has been married twice and has three children with three different women.

Placido Domingo (January 21, 1941)

Dick Cheney (January 30, 1941)

John Belushi (January 23, 1949)

Chris Rock (February 7, 1966) He's been married since 1996 and has two daughters.

Neil Diamond (January 24, 1941)

Alan Cumming (January 27, 1965) Was married for eight years but describes himself as bisexual.

Jerry Springer (February 13, 1944)

Franco Zeffirelli (February 12, 1923)

James Ingram (February 16, 1952)

Giorgio Gucci (February 8, 1928)

Buzz Aldrin (January 20, 1930)

John Galliano (January 28, 1960)

Edward Burns (January 29, 1968) Married to model Christy Turlington since 2003.

Seth Green (February 8, 1974)

Jerry O'Connell (February 17, 1974)

Josh Brolin (February 12, 1968)

John Grisham (February 8, 1955)

Gary Coleman (February 8, 1968)
Mike Farrell (February 6, 1939)
Stephen Cannell (February 5, 1941) Married since 1964 to same woman.
Gregory Louganis (January 29, 1960)
Sinclair Lewis (February 7, 1885)
Fats Domino (February 16, 1928)
Ernest Borgnine (January 24, 1917)

Aquarius Sun, Venus in Aquarius

This guy can be a good beau, but he's looking for the unusual. The exceptionally powerful. The woman who *can* live without him. He wants a grounded type, someone who can calm his fears, wipe his brow, tell him he's wonderful . . . and wipe his tush when he can't reach. She's got to be Mother Nature, Gloria Steinem, Sophia Loren, Audrey Hepburn, Madonna (and whore), an open book, a closed auction, and everything in between. He must respect her, respect her lifestyle choices, respect the way she handles people, respect the way she deals with children (he wants some). And she has to keep herself looking good (the superficial aspect is not lost on Aquarius/Aquarius). He wants it all.

> I only go out to get me a fresh appetite for being alone.
>
> **LORD BYRON**

Yup. He's a perfectionist. But if he's not sucked into the wrong marriage, wooed simply by beauty, he'll be as content as a pig in a blanket. He just has to know himself. To have done a little soul searching. And, truthfully, it's better if he's suffered a bit. He'll rise to the occasion like a sixty-year-old on Viagra.

> Like the measles, love is most dangerous when it comes late in life.
>
> **LORD BYRON**

Aquarius/Aquarius men are survivors. They do what they

need to do to get ahead (even if it means cutting the line). If you fit *all* the requirements on his list, though, burp and pamper him—you're good. That's not asking much, right?

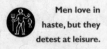

Men love in haste, but they detest at leisure.

LORD BYRON

BOYFRIEND POTENTIAL RATING: High if you vex him and fit into his strange idealization of strong, paradoxical women. What he wants is unattainable love. He lives between romantic fantasy and disillusionment, and yearns for the holy grail of a partner. Low if you're just short of perfect— spelled with a *k*.

CELEBRITY CORRESPONDENTS
WITH AQUARIUS SUN, VENUS IN AQUARIUS

Ashton Kutcher (February 7, 1978) Demi Moore is a double whammy, too: Scorpio/Scorpio.

Phil Collins (January 30, 1951) On his third marriage.

Peter Gabriel (February 13, 1950)

Lorenzo Lamas (January 20, 1958) Divorced four times.

Wolfgang Amadeus Mozart (January 27, 1756)

Axl Rose (February 6, 1962)

Lovers may be—and indeed generally are— enemies, but they never can be friends, because there must always be a spice of jealousy and a something of Self in all their speculations.

LORD BYRON

Franklin D. Roosevelt (January 30, 1882) Wife, Eleanor, was constantly pregnant. They had six children. He had a mistress outside the marriage. They remained married in name only.

Nick Nolte (February 8, 1941) Has married and divorced three times.

Paco Rabanne (February 18, 1934)

Robert Wagner (February 10, 1930) Was married four times—twice to Natalie Wood. She left him for Warren Beatty and was back with him at the time of her mysterious death.

Leslie Nielsen (February 11, 1926)

Lord Byron (January 22, 1788) Known for his
love poems, he led a hedonistic life with many
affairs. Though he was gay, he wrote "she"
instead of "he" so he wouldn't offend anyone.
He was said to have been flamboyant, eccentric, and out of control.

I'm free of all
prejudices. I
hate everyone
equally.

W. C. FIELDS

Bill Bixby (January 22, 1934)

Gene Hackman (January 30, 1930)

William Burroughs (February 4, 1914)

James Joyce (February 2, 1882)

W. C. Fields (January 29, 1879)

John Barrymore (February 14, 1882) Drew's grandfather was a
notorious alcoholic and philanderer. He married four times.

Jack Lemmon (February 8, 1925)

George Segal (February 13, 1934)

Emmanuel Ungaro (February 13, 1933)

Garth Brooks (February 7, 1962) Divorced
Sandy Brooks but remains friendly for
children's sakes. Now with Trisha Yearwood,
he retired so that he can spend more time with
his family.

It was a woman
who drove me
to drink, and I
never had the
courtesy to
thank her for it.

W. C. FIELDS

Robert Klein (February 8, 1942)

Graham Nash (February 2, 1942)

Yakov Smirnoff (January 24, 1951)

Mike Bloomberg (February 14, 1942)

Dr. Dre (February 18, 1965)

Ice-T (February 16, 1958)

Sidney Sheldon (February 17, 1917)

Aquarius Sun, Venus in Pisces

It's easy to make a buck. It's a lot tougher to make a difference.

TOM BROKAW

I've been married twenty-nine years to the same girl, never
cheated on her once. I've got three kids, who've never been
in trouble. I live a real different life. But when I become Alice
I get to be that guy, I get to be him. It's like Anthony Hopkins
playing Hannibal Lechter—you get to be Hannibal Lechter,
and all of a sudden it's a different character and it's fun.

ALICE COOPER

Not your average Joe Bear. (Hey, Boo, Boo!) This guy, besides having a true genius, creative side, knows how to get people to work
for him, not against him. He's a manager. A contact guy. A nice
guy. People love 'im. (Even if he goes the sad way
of being a jerk, he still manages to earn everyone's
respect and they eventually wind up doing his bid-
ding.)

> I suspect that
> Helen and I are
> still together
> because of this
> unspoken
> acknowledgment
> that I needed
> this lively mental
> life.
>
> GEORGE
> SEGAL

He can go the way of saint, too, when he's in
love. Especially when his friends don't need him
at the moment.

Right. Here's the thing. This guy is a true
friend. To many. I mean, too many. If he's a rare
breed of Aquarius/Pisces, and doesn't have fans
clamoring at the door, you've found yourself a
keeper. But hey, there are worse things.

Of all the Aquarius men, this guy's most likely to settle down
early. Plus, he's a faithful sort.

See? That's not so bad.

He's also interested in the world, at large. Has high standards and interesting political ideals. He likes to go against the grain, yet always "gets" what's important in life. (And loves to be admired for his generous spirit, though doesn't like to brag about it.) He wants his actions to speak louder than his words, yet doesn't lack for the appropriate words—ever.

Does he make a good potential? Well. If he can control his finances (they tend to slip away from him like a one-night stand) and you can put up with all his shenanigans with work buddies (who he calls friends), then yes. He's a good catch and a home run.

> To conceal anything from those to whom I am attached, is not in my nature. I can never close my lips where I have opened my heart.
>
> **CHARLES DICKENS**

BOYFRIEND POTENTIAL RATING: High, if you don't mind when he's off in four directions at the same time. Basically high. Low, if you're the ex-publicist to his Tom Cruise. He'll take your advice in work and money, then resent you for it.

CELEBRITY CORRESPONDENTS
WITH AQUARIUS SUN, VENUS IN PISCES

John Travolta (February 18, 1954) Has been married to Kelly Preston since '91.

Jules Verne (February 8, 1828)

Thomas Edison (February 11, 1847)

Nick Carter (January 28, 1980)

Tom Selleck (January 29, 1945) Married twice; first, to actress/model; then, in '87 to current wife.

John McEnroe (February 16, 1959) Divorced Tatum O'Neal in '92; married rocker Patty Smyth in '97; has full custody of his three children with Tatum, two with Patty, and one from Patty's previous marriage.

Sir Francis Bacon (January 22, 1561)

Enzo Ferrari (February 18, 1898)

Christian Dior (January 21, 1905)

Alice Cooper (February 4, 1948)

Ronald Reagan (February 6, 1911)

Charles Lindbergh (February 4, 1902)

Charles Dickens (February 7, 1812) He had ten children with his wife and they separated. He maintained her in a house until she died.

Sonny Bono (February 16, 1935) Married three times; once to Cher.

Wayne Gretzky (January 26, 1961)

Joe Pesci (February 9, 1943)

Mikhail Baryshnikov (January 27, 1948) Doesn't believe in marriage. Had one child with Jessica Lange and three with Lisa Rinehart.

Bill Maher (January 20, 1956)

Benny Hill (January 21, 1924)

Nathan Lane (February 3, 1956)

Babe Ruth (February 6, 1895)

John Hurt (January 22, 1940)

Tom Brokaw (February 6, 1940)

Harvey Korman (February 15, 1927)

Christopher Marlowe (February 6, 1564)

Thomas Paine (January 29, 1737)

Henry VII (January 28, 1457)

Joey Fatone (January 28, 1977) Married his longtime girlfriend in 2004.

Jack Nicklaus (January 21, 1940)

Lou Diamond Phillips (February 17, 1962)

Stan Getz (February 2, 1927) Had problems with substance abuse.

Jack Palance (February 18, 1919)

Rick James (February 1, 1948) Was convicted of assaulting two women; had serious problems with cocaine and other drug use.

Aquarius Sun, Venus in Aries

Rasta no abide amputation.
I don't allow a mon ta be dismantled.

> BOB MARLEY, after being told that he had skin cancer on his
> toe and they needed to amputate it for him to live. (After
> refusing, he died a few years later. He had twelve children—
> three with his wife—and was buried with his Gibson guitar,
> a bud of marijuana, and a Bible.)

Scary. Scary. Scary. Not half as scary as Aries/Aquarius but a terrifying sort nevertheless. It's all that air (Aquarius) blowing big gusts of wind on that fire (Aries). He's a ticking time bomb.

Sure, so he may have a bit of a temper. He's stubborn and sensitive and wants a mommy/partner to boss him around and kick his ass. Only strong fiery women who are never doormats need apply.

> With affection beaming in one eye, and calculation shining out of the other.
>
> CHARLES DICKENS

When he's not off licking his wounds, he can be romantic. It's kinda sad, though. He needs people to notice him when he walks into a room. And he'd rather go the route of bad boy to get that attention—it's more immediate—than to work hard and chat everyone up to get it.

He picks his mate. Not the other way around. Women who go after him might as well slather themselves in baby oil and sit out in the blazing sun—they'll get burned. His attention span is almost nil, though, so if you meet him and immedi-

> I can be shy when I talk to women. I'm a shy dude.
>
> NICK CARTER

ately go to the ladies' room, you might come back to find him with another prospect. Don't go powder your nose. It's fine; just a little shiny. He won't even notice. He's probably already consumed half the vodka in Russia.

You can tell a lot about a fellow's character by his way of eating jelly beans.

RONALD
REAGAN

However, if he behaves more like a got-it-together guy and less like a spoiled rock star on a death mission, you may have found a good one. Just be sure to look for the signs. Unless, of course, the man-child thing works for ya.

BOYFRIEND POTENTIAL RATING: High if you have the patience of a saint—and a bit of a broken BS meter. Low if you're truly grounded in any way, shape, or form. And don't crave excitement like a bipolar gal off her usual dose of lithium.

CELEBRITY CORRESPONDENTS
WITH AQUARIUS SUN, VENUS IN ARIES

Bobby Brown (February 5, 1969) He fathered three children with two different women before he wed Whitney Houston.

Bob Marley (February 6, 1945)

Matt Dillon (February 18, 1964)

George Stephanopoulos (February 10, 1961)

Chris Farley (February 15, 1964) Struggled with drug addiction and obesity; died of cocaine overdose at age thirty-three—the same age as John Belushi, fifteen years prior, who died the same way. John was an Aquarius, too.

Jimmy Hoffa (February 14, 1913)

Arsenio Hall (February 12, 1956)

Charles Darwin (February 12, 1809)

Louis XV (February 15, 1710)

Abraham Lincoln (February 12, 1809)

Billie Joe Armstrong, of Green Day (February 17, 1972)
Taylor Hawkins, of Foo Fighters (February 17, 1972)
Phoenix, aka David Farrell, of Linkin Park (February 8, 1977)

AQUARIUS DIC*-TIONARY

ANALYTICAL <AH-NAH-LIH-TEE-CAHL> Can separate all the facts.
Translation for potential girlfriend: Can separate himself from you, love, and sex.

GREGARIOUS <GREH-GARE-EE-US> Fun and frolicky with friends.
Translation for potential girlfriend: Has *so many* fans that you sometimes need binoculars to get a glimpse of him.

FREE <FREEEEEE> Optimistic and open.
Translation for potential girlfriend: Always sees the good in people—which makes him a bad judge of character.

FINANCIALLY SOLVENT <FY-NAN-SHUH-LEE SAHL-VENT> Can make it.
Translation for potential girlfriend: Spends it on a dollar, not a dime.

EASYGOING <EEEZYGOHING> Knows how to relax.
Translation for potential girlfriend: Mentally or physically lazy. If it's the latter, he'll watch bad TV 'cause the remote control is on the other side of the room.

CHAPTER 12

Pisces, Ex or Next
(the Fish, February 19–March 20)

PISCES RUDE-IMENTS

Never met a Pisces who wasn't smart—boy or girl. In fact, Pisces guy can be a *genius with an inventive mind.* Albert Einstein, Alexander Graham Bell, Nicolas Copernicus, Galileo . . . Jesus Christ (no, I'm not cursing. Rumor has it that Christ arrived during the Age of Pisces). All Pisces masterpiece theater men.

> My wife heard me say I love you a thousand times, but she never once heard me say sorry.
>
> BRUCE WILLIS

Also, many of the top CEOs in the country are Pisces: Steve Jobs, Michael Eisner, and Rupert Murdoch, for example. Powerhouses.

See? It all depends on whether or not he lives up to his potential. And therein lies *el problemo.*

Here 'tis, sistah. Pisces. Pisces. He's the culmination of every sign before him—the good stuff . . . and the rotten fruit, too. Aries, for example, is the first sign of the zodiac. He represents birth. Pisces is an old soul, even when he's born, and represents death and eternity.

Pretty heavy sack of potatoes to carry 'round.

Pisces guy can get weighed down by life *and take you with him.* He's never violent (well, it happens, but it's rare). And he tries to preserve the peace by acknowledging your requests whenever possible.

However, he can be judgmental—whether he truly believes he's better than someone else . . . or just putting down so he can, in stark comparison, look good. Either way, it doesn't really show his evolved side, which he *does* have, *n'est-ce pas?*

Talk about beating around the burning bush, Pisces excels. In fact, unlike the other water signs—Cancer and Scorpio—he can distance himself when he needs to in order to get the job done. That's why so many successful CEOs are Pisces men. When they combine their imaginations with ambition, it's a delicious recipe for stardom.

> I would love to do a comedy. The primary thing is complexity. The reason I play so many dark characters is because there is room for the unexpected.
>
> **BILLY ZANE**

Though some don't go that way at all.

He's a composite shot of all the signs who've come before him. Has the curiosity of Aries, the stubbornness of Taurus, the flakiness of Gemini, the sensitivity of Cancer, the happy disposition of Leo, the analytical mind of Virgo, the judiciousness of Libra, the secrecy of Scorpio, the ironic humor of Sag, the organizational skills of Cappy, and the ability to fit into any situation, like Aquarius.

> Frankly, I don't mind not being President. I just mind that someone else is.
>
> **EDWARD KENNEDY**

Summed up, Pisces men would make amazing secret agents. They listen. They decipher. They're excellent judges of character. They're intuitive. And they're crafty with the coded messages. (Pisces guy will let you hang yourself with the rope he's handed you before he'll ever call you on something.)

But. BUT. They may be also good hubbys to groom.
And that's a horse of a different color.

PISCES TONGUE LASHING

Don't let this guy drink. It's more pathetic than watching Anna Nicole Smith pretend she's sober on national TV. There's a very self-destructive side with this guy. If he manages to stay the course, you might just be okay.

> Men are like steel. When they lose their temper, they lose their worth.
>
> CHUCK NORRIS

"Can I have your number again? I lost it," Pisces guy tells you.

"If you're going to use it this time, I'll give it to you. If you're not, don't bother," you must answer.

This works whether you're just starting out in a relationship or waiting behind your bridesmaids to walk down that aisle. You have to be direct with Pisces at all times. If not, he'll mull it over and be indecisive about you. Like relationship ADD.

Just don't be *aggressive*. There's a difference. Be straightforward. Don't suffocate. Or chase. He'll squirm away like a puppy who'd rather go play with the ten-year-old fat cat (who abhors him) down the hall.

> I have other obligations now—the show, my family, my life . . . though I know that without my sobriety I wouldn't have any of those things.
>
> ROB LOWE

Again. There's that whole she-doesn't-want-me-so-I-love-her sob story with Pisces men. Before they're ready to truly settle down, they worship women from afar and try for the "biggest catch" of the county—as they see it.

(Admittedly, superficiality and looks, unfortunately, can play a big part in this.)

Good news is, they usually wind up with the right gal for them because *they're just so difficult.* Not in a normal way. No, no. They're so bendy to your ways, like those accordion-straw thingies. But their true natures come out, eventually.

Nice, yes. High maintenance? Definitely. Pisces guy knows the difference between the good stuff and not-so-good stuff. Quality. With women, with home decorating—you name it—Pisces guy considers every possible strategy and outcome. The planning and research part of it is almost more fun for Fish guy than the actual *doing*.

> I had fears of the dark, you know. I didn't like being in the dark.
>
> **BILLY CRYSTAL**

And therein lies Pisces' M.O. Like an overdoing-it mother who makes her kid wear galoshes when it's fifty degrees out and partially cloudy:

Pisces always needs to be prepared.

PISCES: IS HE *INTO* YOU?

Just make sure he doesn't burn the place down with all those candles lit around you—during. He surely won't notice if the bed catches on fire. It'll just confirm what he's suspected all along: that he's *really good*.

Chances are, he's not gonna want a *wham, bam, thank you*. He'll convince himself he's into you—until he's not anymore and just can't get it up.

> I'd rather be hated for who I am than loved for who I am not.
>
> **KURT COBAIN**

That's right. He'll schtup and schtup till he can schtup no more. Then he'll find another victim to woo with all his talk of soul mates and Sleeping Beauty (waking with *his* kiss) and living happily ever after.

This one, though he means well, can be so idealistic (and looking for Ms. Perfect) that, when the real thing comes along, it makes him run scared. Once he settles down, though, it can be for good.

Just make sure you're into him, too. He'll put you up on a

pedestal so high, it'll be a rough fall to the next guy—from the top of the Empire State Building.

Oh, he tends to be frugal but will spend extra on the quality paper he uses to make all those neat drawings he wants you to hang on your wall.

I'm too busy acting like I'm not naïve. I've seen it all, I was here first.

KURT COBAIN

Above your bed.

So he can stare at them and sigh at what a good job he's done while he's *into* you.

ADVICE TO THE FUTURE MRS. PISCES

Here's a bite that might smart: Again Pisces guy can be all over the map. He's charming, charismatic, bright as all the galaxies together, and an excellent master in persuasion. Remember, Pisces guys are leaders because they're sooo unassuming. Everything is gone about so diplomatically; in such a nice, respectful fashion. People follow him willingly. However, he doesn't always know what's good for him—and this can be dangerous when he lets himself play out little idyllic fantasies in love.

I've always had a problem with the average macho man— they've always been a threat to me.

KURT COBAIN

If that's you: good.

If not, you're in for a rowboat-without-a-paddle-in-a-sea-of-crocodiles trip.

When a Pisces guy commits, truly commits— and not 'cause he's locked up in a rehabilitation center at the moment—he *can* be a good partner: faithful, loving, generous, and loyal. He's got all those traits in him. Pisces women are sometimes better catches, though. They know themselves well, and aren't as tempted to play the money card in order to woo a mate.

Basically, Pisces guy is a grab-bag gift at Christmastime. You can get a good one—or a really sucky one. Or, ahem—on the devastating side—a cruel joke. Peek and check the merchandise, first. You won't be sorry.

Summed up. It's not difficult to tell which Pisces man you've got. It'll be the difference between Norman Bates and a Norman Rockwell painting.

(Just perfect.)

And that ain't bad.

I wanted to be successful, not famous.

GEORGE HARRISON

ADVICE TO THE EX MS. PISCES

Pisces guy may be the only guy in the zodiac where you can show up on his doorstep and he's just *too nice* to turn you away. Oh, he'll try. But he'll finally give up and take the bait.

I'm not saying this is the best way to deal with him. But, if it comes to it, attack the problem head-on, not with psychotic phone calls or e-mails. Disruption, to him, is a four-letter word. He needs his space and "me" time.

Actually, Pisces, after a fight, will want to go off by himself and sulk. This is part emotional overload, part control factor. Give him just a little time—then go talk to him. You must be thoroughly, genuinely sorry if you've done wrong. Pisces will smell it like cabbage in a closed kitchen if you're not sincere.

Just be forewarned. Pisces knows that he holds the strings. You're the puppet.

A good friend of mine always said, "Those who manipulate can easily be manipulated." Basically, that means you can handle him right back. Learn the moves, kids. Get smart.

We were talking about the space between us all and the people who hide themselves behind a wall of illusion. Never glimpse the truth—then it's far too late when they pass away.

GEORGE HARRISON

In the end, Pisces eventually becomes aware of his own brand of strangeness, especially where love is concerned. If he's in love, he'll be back no matter what. If he's not, he'll be a big bag of chocolate bars in a room full of kiddies.

Gone.

SUN/VENUS COMBINATIONS: THE TRUE LOVE POTENTIAL TEST

Pisces Sun, Venus in Capricorn

There's a stillness to this guy. A big, powerful force that emanates from him. He doesn't always speak with words. It's a facial expression, an eyebrow raised, a deep chuckle from his gut that affects all those around him.

> The only thing I like more than my wife is my money, and I'm not about to lose that to her and her lawyers, that's for damn sure.
>
> JON BON JOVI

He resists evolving, though, because he knows it's inevitable. Little boy Pisces/Cappy wants what he wants, and that's that.

He's an enigma, though. His social status is *muy importante,* though he can be recklessly antisocial at times. When he's turned his light on, though, and is ready to move about the crowd (um, actually—among the underlings, as he sees them), he collects fans and starry-eyed admirers like the Pied Piper. Even somewhat of a cult following.

> You know these love letters mix with whisky, just don't light a match when you kiss me.
>
> JON BON JOVI

People respect his words and follow him without hesitation. It's a commanding, elegant, diplomatic thing he's got. Even if it is, well, a bit fake sometimes. No one suspects. His well-timed humor smooths over the rough spots.

Charismatic. Persuasive. Smart as a whip and terrifying to those who can't live up to his standards. This Pisces guy believes in himself—and you should, too. Only problem with women is that he wants the best (*his definition*). Like a guy who drives the fire-engine-red Ferrari to get *even more* attention, Pisces/Cap will look for the youngest, fastest, and most powerful model.

> I am the character you are not supposed to like.
>
> **ALAN RICKMAN**

Or supermodel.

'Cause that's what he thinks he deserves.

BOYFRIEND POTENTIAL RATING: Very high if you just reached legal drinking age and have the face and body of an angel. Higher if your dad owns the company he works for. Lower if he owns it and you work for him. This guy won't mind if you're a stay-at-home mom. As long as you come with a trust fund—or, at least . . . a really good, uh, rack.

CELEBRITY CORRESPONDENTS
WITH PISCES SUN, VENUS IN CAPRICORN

Steve Jobs (February 24, 1955)

Karl Jaspers (February 23, 1883)

Edward James Olmos (February 24, 1947) Divorced from Lorraine Bracco in 2002.

Prince Andrew, the Duke of York (February 19, 1960) Married and divorced Fergie. When he was away, a tabloid showed her in a compromising position with her financial advisor.

Mikhail Gorbachev (March 2, 1931)

Billy Baldwin (February 21, 1963) Met Chynna Phillips on a plane flight. Married her in 1995.

Seal (February 19, 1963) In 2004, overtook duties as father to Heidi Klum's baby with absent father/ex Flavio Briatore. He married her in 2005.

Sean Astin (February 25, 1971)

Jules Renard (February 22, 1864)

Billy Zane (February 24, 1966)

Alan Thicke (March 1, 1947) Married twice; second wife, *much* younger.

Pope Clement VIII (February 24, 1536)

Jeff Daniels (February 19, 1955) Married to high school sweetheart since 1979.

Dave Gorman (March 2, 1971)

Tommy Tune (February 28, 1939)

Kelsey Grammer (February 21, 1955) Married three times: to a dance instructor for eight years; to a stripper for one year; currently to a former nude model.

Bob Mackie (March 2, 1939)

Zero Mostel (February 28, 1915)

Charles Durning (February 28, 1923)

Ryan Cassidy (February 23, 1966)

Pisces Sun, Venus in Aquarius

This guy has a sense of humor about himself. His ironic, warped idea of what's funny keeps him constantly chuckling, even if the jokes are just between him and him. He loves when people get it, though, and will fall for a woman who can share in the private affair of, what he considers to be, the dark recesses of his mind.

> I don't mind seducing as long as at the end of the seduction there's an idea or a shock.
>
> ALAN RICKMAN

His charm, easy smile, and natural wit serve him well. People trust him, even when they shouldn't—always. He's psychic, by the way, so tread softly.

Though he resists, this guy is best when he has a partner. If he doesn't, or if he has even slight mental problems, he can be scary with a capital S.

Pisces is emotional but can distance himself. Aquarius can just plain psycho-separate himself, totally. Therefore, Pisces/Aquarius can go the way of frightening-dom (John Wayne

Gacy, the clown serial killer of Chicago—who killed more than thirty boys and was revered and trusted by all—was a Pisces/Venus in Aquarius).

But. That's extreme.

Truth is, the majority of these guys are built for marriage, the long haul. Pisces/Aquarius is a wonderful father. A devoted, loving husband. A good role model—even if he likes to play the bad boy sometimes. So *sweet,* he can give in to it or risk losing his soul. He's incredibly sensitive; a poet.

If his emotions don't frighten him into retreating and turning to Evil Spawn, he's as good as gold.

Summed up, if this guy's given the freedom to express himself and pursue the hobbies he loves, he'll be a homing pigeon, always coming back to base: you.

> A woman who is very secure in herself, what she's about, what she wants to do, who probably figures that she's a prize catch. . . . Sooner or later he's going to come around.
>
> SPIKE LEE

BOYFRIEND POTENTIAL RATING: High if he's the norm for this sign. He only stays and marries when he's in love. And, since he knows himself well, he usually picks right. This guy makes up his own mind and doesn't listen to what others tell him about who he should be with. Good for him. Low if he's had a particularly bad childhood, has even slight issues about his sexuality, or is just plain starring in the remake of *American Psycho.*

CELEBRITY CORRESPONDENTS
WITH PISCES SUN, VENUS IN AQUARIUS

Bruce Willis (March 19, 1955) Both Bruce and Ashton Kutcher have their Venuses in Aquarius; Demi Moore is a Scorpio/Scorpio.

Albert of Monaco (March 14, 1958)

Adam Levine, of Maroon 5 (March 18, 1979)

Daniel Craig (March 2, 1968)

Josh Groban (February 27, 1981)

John Wayne Gacy (March 17, 1942)

Chuck Norris (March 10, 1942)

Freddie Prinze, Jr. (March 8, 1976) Married Sarah Michelle
   Gellar in 2002.

Jerry Lewis (March 16, 1926)

Cyrano de Bergerac (March 6, 1619)

Michael Eisner (March 7, 1942)

Aaron Eckhart (March 12, 1968)

Ed McMahon (March 6, 1923)

Alexis Denisof (February 25, 1966) Married to Alyson Hannigan
   since 2003.

Zeppo Marx (February 25, 1901)

Wyatt Earp (March 19, 1848)

Enrico Coveri (February 26, 1952)

John Turturro (February 28, 1957)

David Niven (March 1, 1910) Married both wives within two
   weeks of meeting them. The first wife had an accidental death.

Roger Daltrey, of the Who (March 1, 1944)

Lou Reed (March 2, 1942)

James Redfield (March 19, 1950)

Falco (February 19, 1957)

George Frideric Handel (March 5, 1685)

Ralph Nader (February 27, 1934)

John Steinbeck (February 27, 1902)

Bobby McFerrin (March 11, 1950)

Adam Clayton, of U2 (March 13, 1960)

Johnny Knoxville (March 11, 1971)

Andy Gibb (March 5, 1958) The teen idol had one marriage, a
   drug addiction, numerous affairs (including one with Victoria
   Principal), and died at age thirty.

Mark-Paul Gosselaar (March 1, 1974)

Rupert Murdoch (March 11, 1931)

Brian Jones, of the Rolling Stones (February 28, 1942) Known for his drug and sexual escapades, he had two children with different women (out of wedlock) starting at age sixteen. He was found dead in his swimming pool at age twenty-seven.

Tony Randall (February 26, 1920) Fathered a child at the age of seventy-nine with his second wife.

William Hurt (March 20, 1950)

Chris Klein (March 14, 1979)

Gary Sinise (March 17, 1955)

Heinrich Steinway (February 22, 1797)

John Irving (March 2, 1942)

Desi Arnaz (March 2, 1917) Married to Lucille Ball for twenty years and notoriously unfaithful; was with second wife for twenty-two years, until she died.

Ja Rule (February 29, 1976)

Robert Altman (February 20, 1925)

Claude Lévi-Strauss (February 26, 1829)

William H. Macy (March 13, 1950) Has been happily married to Felicity Huffman since 1997.

Glenn Miller (March 1, 1904)

Jonathan Demme (February 22, 1944)

Pisces Sun, Venus in Pisces

Cursed. Afflicted. A martyr to the nth degree. He can go the way of saint—or throw a bonfire party with the devil.

His way of seeing the world is so uniquely his; no one can change it. To him, his ideals are real, and he'll do anything in his power to accomplish them.

He needs, wants, must have an outlet for leaving his creative (though sometimes deranged) mark on humankind. He's all over the place and needs a grounding plug.

He can be dark, too. Quietly pensive and repressed. Mild-mannered. Unassuming. Insecure (though he tries desperately not to show it).

Fearless of death.

Whether he chooses to unleash his troubled-soul righteousness onto himself or the rest of us—only your guess.

Either way. He turns it in or out. Like Kevin Kline in the film.

Hmm. *Interesting* how there's that gay reference there. It ties in.

Here's why: Pisces is a feminine sign. Pisces/Pisces, double feminine. Now, that doesn't mean *effeminate*. It's a mutable sign. Always changing. Thinking. Modifying. Influencing circumstances around him.

> Love is the ultimate expression of the will to live.
>
> TOM WOLFE

A harsh critic, one moment. Nurturing the next. Puzzling. A work in progress, like Lego, the toy. He builds up his walls to be a ship. Then tears them down. Next. A big skyscraper. Ditto.

Though, his visions are warped, sometimes. Like Carly Simon's clouds in your coffee. Only much more delusional.

If you're still reading this, there is hope, however. (Knew you were waiting for that.) This guy can idealize the woman he's with, too. She becomes his tour de force. His glimmering light of hope (in an otherwise bleak world. Sigh. Double sigh.). His *soul mate*. Yup. It's true. This guy believes in it. And you? You're either "it," or you're not.

No Oreo cream-filling in the middle.

If he makes you his star, for example, you'll still be tortured. But he may just torture *only you*.

See? That's not bad, right?

BOYFRIEND POTENTIAL RATING: High, if you accept drama like a newcomer to L.A. And revel in bad choices like Courtney Love to breaking and entering (Kurt Cobain: Pisces/Pisces). This guy, though he seems sweet, can be actually (Jon Bon Jovi) or manufactured-ly (Osama bin Laden). Please. Choose wisely.

CELEBRITY CORRESPONDENTS
WITH PISCES SUN, VENUS IN PISCES

Kurt Cobain (February 20, 1967) Courtney Love is a Cancer; they were both water signs.

Osama bin Laden (March 10, 1957) Has approximately five wives and at least twenty-four children.

Victor Hugo (February 26, 1802)

Jon Bon Jovi (March 2, 1962)

Galileo Galilei (February 15, 1564)

George Harrison (February 24, 1943) His wife, model Pattie Boyd, left him for Eric Clapton, who she then married. George married again and had one child.

Frédéric Chopin (March 1, 1810)

Prince Ernst August of Hannover (February 26, 1954)

Edgar Cayce (March 18, 1877)

Sidney Poitier (February 20, 1927)

Alan Rickman (February 21, 1946)

Michael Caine (March 14, 1933) Married since 1973; second marriage.

Patrick Duffy (March 17, 1949)

George Washington (February 22, 1732)

Bugsy Siegel (February 28, 1906) Married his childhood sweetheart but was a legendary womanizer and had many affairs.

Kyle MacLachlan (February 22, 1959)

Quincy Jones (March 14, 1933) He has seven children with three different women; was married three times, and lived with Nastassja Kinski from '91–'97.

Ron Howard (March 1, 1954)

Buffalo Bill Cody (February 26, 1846)
Victor Garber (March 16, 1949)
Spike Lee (March 20, 1957) Married since 1993.
Tom Wolfe (March 2, 1930)

Pisces Sun, Venus in Aries

Brilliant, with an analytical mind. A philosopher. A dreamer, but all with a specific intent at the end of his Finian's Rainbow. So intent to prove his beliefs that his personal life (i.e.: you) can suffer for it.

He takes his work to an obsessive-compulsive level. He *must* be the best at what he does and be, at least, greatly respected and admired. At least.

I would advise you to keep your overhead down; avoid a major drug habit; play every day; and take it in front of other people. They need to hear it, and you need them to hear it.

JAMES TAYLOR

Facts must be proven. Unlike most other Pisces, he doesn't necessarily believe in the otherworldly. He's got to see the proof in the pudding.

He's as stubborn as a mule and can revere the woman he's with, but she has to be whip-smart and fiery. That's what he'll look for.

He can be old-fashioned . . . to the point of being downright anti-feminist. (In other words, he wants an "equal" partner in love, but he may never consider her truly an equal. If he does, congratulations on your find.) On this far end of the spectrum, he can be caveman in his thinking.

He's the boss and his word is law. Creepy, right?

I'm not going to lie to you. This guy is intense. He can be tormented (Johnny Cash) and fall into the womanizer category (Ted Kennedy . . . and even Albert Einstein, who had a string of lovers when he was married (including his, uh, cousin, Elsa). Or prejudiced (Bobby Fischer was rumored to be an extreme anti-Semite) or terribly misguided (Arthur Schopenhauer, the philosopher, waxed poetic on the virtues of women: only to serve men).

To give you a better idea, on the woman side of it, Elizabeth Taylor and Liza Minnelli are both Pisces/Venus in Aries. Right. Train wrecks. (Eva Longoria, of *Desperate Housewives,* too. Look out.)

And it's rare that the men of this sign escape their powerful bad destiny in amor. Kurt Russell, who's been with Goldie Hawn for more than twenty years, is an exception. But notice—he's not married to her. See? He made it work. Cool beans.

Time will take your money, but money won't buy time.

JAMES TAYLOR

But that's the thing. This guy shouldn't be praised for being a decent mate. *Something's not right.*

It can be a heady ride, though. Powerful, tumultuous, exciting. But like even the best Space Mountain roller coasters, sometime it's gotta stop, and you've gotta get off. And not in a good way.

BOYFRIEND POTENTIAL RATING: High if he's defeated the law of gravity, Murphy's law, all rules of physics, and his inherent compulsion to create a tidal wave (and walk away while people flail for dear life around him). Einstein's wife wound up in an insane asylum. Get the picture? Otherwise, low. Period. But you never know.

CELEBRITY CORRESPONDENTS
WITH PISCES SUN, VENUS IN ARIES

Albert Einstein (March 14, 1879)

Josef Mengele (March 16, 1911) The sadistic doctor at Auschwitz tortured and killed many Jews for his experiments. He divorced his wife and married his brother's widow.

Nicolaus Copernicus (February 19, 1473)

Antonio Vivaldi (March 4, 1678)

Mike Wallace (March 10, 1959)

Carl Reiner (March 20, 1922)

Bobby Fischer (March 9, 1943)

Ted Kennedy (February 22, 1932) After his brothers John and Robert were assassinated, he took on the role as father to their thirteen children. He's been married twice and has three children from his first marriage.

Chris Martin, of Coldplay (March 2, 1977) Married to Gwyneth Paltrow.

Johnny Cash (February 26, 1932)

Auguste Renoir (February 25, 1841)

Arthur Schopenhauer (February 22, 1788)

Alexander Graham Bell (March 3, 1847)

Kurt Russell (March 17, 1951) Was married for five years but has found happiness with Goldie without the wedding papers.

Shaquille O'Neal (March 6, 1972)

Michael Bolton (February 26, 1953) Had three children with wife, Maureen, 1975–1990. With Nicolette Sheridan. He has a foundation since '93 to assist impoverished, abused women and children.

Peter Fonda (February 23, 1940)

Nat King Cole (March 17, 1919)

Gabriel García Márquez (March 6, 1927)

Fabio (March 15, 1959)

John Garfield (March 4, 1913)

Rex Harrison (March 5, 1908) Heartbreaker Rex was married six times. His affair with actress Carole Landis is thought to have led to her suicide.

Jordan Taylor Hanson, of the Hanson Brothers (March 14, 1983)

Harry Belafonte (March 1, 1927)

Prince Gabriele d'Annunzio (March 12, 1863)

Mitch Gaylord (March 10, 1961)

Jackie Gleason (February 26, 1916)

Christopher Atkins (February 21, 1961) This teen idol was married once and has two children.

Tom Arnold (March 6, 1959) Ex Roseanne Barr is a Scorpio; they're both water signs (but with Scorpio and Pisces, there are sometimes problems with who gets the power in the relationship—e.g., Demi Moore, Scorpio, and Bruce Willis, Pisces).

Kato Kaelin (March 9, 1959)

James Van Der Beek (March 8, 1977)

Vincente Minnelli (February 28, 1903) Was married four times; first marriage to Judy Garland for six years.

Andrew Jackson (March 15, 1767)

Ronan Keating (March 3, 1977)

Perry Ellis (March 3, 1940)

Terence Trent d'Arby (March 15, 1962)

John Heard (March 7, 1945)

Pisces Sun, Venus in Taurus

This Pisces has the beating-around-the-bush thing down pat. Like Cancer, he can't help but try to manipulate and control happenings around him. It's how he (thinks he) stays grounded. He needs the security. Desperately.

He also despises vulgar speech even more than Libra guy. It makes him depressed, like a Democrat who's forced to attend an NRA meeting.

He's looking for perfect. *If he only knew what that was. Boohoo.* However, when he starts looking outside the box and considers women who aren't too flaky or beyond his reach, he can do very well, indeed.

Yet, there's somewhat of a mental masturbation that goes on

with this guy. He's self-mocking and ironic. Though, insecure waters run deep—and his jests (when he says "kidding, kidding") always have some truth to them.

He can be rock-solid when he's calm. He works hard to maintain the peace. His ambitions are great—and he'll look for a partner who loves him for himself (his ultimate desire) and will accept him with all the faults he knows he has.

Just be careful not to blow smoke up his ass when he doesn't deserve it. He'll love it. Crave it. Stick with you for a while just to hear it.

But. Like the Donald. He'll eventually take you for granted like you're Marla Maples. *Yeah. Whatever happened to her? She sired his kid and then disappeared like a magician's assistant.*

BOYFRIEND POTENTIAL RATING: High, if you stick to your guns and never use an automatic (too powerful; choose the old-fashioned kind kept in a holster. Only take it out when you need it). Low, if you don't let him know you're packing.

CELEBRITY CORRESPONDENTS
WITH PISCES SUN, VENUS IN TAURUS

Rob Lowe (March 17, 1964) Married his hairdresser in '91 after a scandal in '88—a video of him having sex with two women, one underage.

Billy Crystal (March 14, 1948)

James Taylor (March 12, 1948) Was married to Carly Simon, a Cancer; they're both water signs.

Al Jarreau (March 12, 1940)

Amerigo Vespucci (March 9, 1451)

Dane Cook (March 18, 1972)

Raul Julia (March 9, 1940)

Oliver Wendell Holmes (March 8, 1841)

Charles LeClerc, French general (March 17, 1772)
Walter Cunningham, America's second civilian astronaut
  (March 16, 1932)
John Updike (March 18, 1932) He has four children and is still
  with his second wife.

PISCES DIC*-TIONARY

CEREBRAL <SUH-REE-BRAHL> Exceptionally, ridiculously pensive.
Translation for potential girlfriend: Devious, actually; he's always one step
ahead of you.

SWEET <SWEET> Like sugah, honey.
Translation for potential girlfriend: Albeit like diabetic chocolate. It tastes
great, but you have to run to the bathroom, after, 'cause the fakeness
makes you sick.

INTELLIGENT <IN-TELL-I-GENT> Really smart.
Translation for potential girlfriend: Though, a snob about it. He can't help
himself.

ADEPT <ADD-DEHPT> Always knows the best way to handle a situation.
Translation for potential girlfriend: . . . to work in *his* favor.

DIPLOMATIC <DIP-LOW-MAH-TICK> Who better than Pisces to lead the
masses *and* engage in an intimate one-on-one pep talk?
Translation for potential girlfriend: Can fib like Pinocchio in order to
smooth out a situation, except his nose doesn't grow, unfortunately. So it's
hidden like his motives.

Quick Looker-Upper Sun Signs

 ARIES, THE RAM, March 21–April 19: masculine, fire, cardinal

 TAURUS, THE BULL, April 20–May 20: feminine, earth, fixed

 GEMINI, THE TWINS, May 21–June 20: masculine, air, mutable

 CANCER, THE CRAB, June 21–July 22: feminine, water, cardinal

 LEO, THE LION, July 23–August 22: masculine, fire, fixed

 VIRGO, THE VIRGIN, August 23–September 22: feminine, earth, mutable

LIBRA, THE SCALES, September 23–October 22: masculine, air, cardinal

SCORPIO, THE SCORPION, October 23–November 21: feminine, water, fixed

SAGITTARIUS, THE ARCHER, November 22–December 21: masculine, fire, mutable

CAPRICORN, THE GOAT, December 22–January 19: feminine, earth, cardinal

AQUARIUS, THE WATER BEARER, January 20–February 18: masculine, air, fixed

PISCES, THE FISH, February 19–March 20: feminine, water, mutable

Cusp sign dates fall within two days of the cutoff mark to the other sign. For example, someone who's born September 22 may have the stubborn tenaciousness of Virgo and the annoying indecisiveness of Libra. Both.

His Venus

1925

January 1–14	Sagittarius
January 15–February 7	Capricorn
February 8–March 3	Aquarius
March 4–27	Pisces
March 28–April 20	Aries
April 21–May 15	Taurus
May 16–June 8	Gemini
June 9–July 3	Cancer
July 4–27	Leo
July 28–August 21	Virgo
August 22–September 15	Libra
September 16–October 11	Scorpio
October 12–November 16	Sagittarius
November 17–December 5	Capricorn
December 6–31	Aquarius

1926

January 1–April 5	Aquarius
April 6–May 6	Pisces
May 7–June 2	Aries
June 3–28	Taurus
June 29–July 23	Gemini
July 24–August 17	Cancer
August 18–September 11	Leo
September 12–October 5	Virgo
October 6–29	Libra
October 30–November 22	Scorpio
November 23–December 16	Sagittarius
December 17–31	Capricorn

1927

January 1–9	Capricorn
January 10–February 1	Aquarius
February 2–26	Pisces
February 27–March 22	Aries
March 23–April 16	Taurus
April 17–May 11	Gemini
May 12–June 7	Cancer
June 8–July 7	Leo
July 8–November 9	Virgo
November 10–December 8	Libra
December 9–31	Scorpio

1928

January 1–3	Scorpio
January 4–28	Sagittarius
January 29–February 22	Capricorn
February 23–March 17	Aquarius
March 18–April 11	Pisces
April 12–May 5	Aries
May 6–29	Taurus
May 30–June 23	Gemini
June 24–July 17	Cancer
July 18–August 11	Leo
August 12–September 4	Virgo
September 5–28	Libra
September 29–October	Scorpio
October 24–November 16	Sagittarius
November 17–December 11	Capricorn
December 12–31	Aquarius

1929

January 1–5	Aquarius
January 6–February 2	Pisces
February 3–March 7	Aries
March 8–April 19	Taurus
April 20–June 2	Aries
June 3–July 7	Taurus
July 8–August 4	Gemini
August 5–30	Cancer
August 31–September 25	Leo
September 26–October 19	Virgo
October 20–November 12	Libra
November 13–December 6	Scorpio
December 7–30	Sagittarius
December 31	Capricorn

1930

January 1–23	Capricorn
January 24–February 16	Aquarius
February 17–March 12	Pisces
March 13–April 5	Aries
April 6–30	Taurus
May 1–24	Gemini
May 25–June 18	Cancer
June 19–July 14	Leo
July 15–August 9	Virgo
August 10–September 6	Libra
September 7–October 11	Scorpio
October 12–November 21	Sagittarius
November 22–December 31	Scorpio

1931

January 1–3	Scorpio
January 4–February 6	Sagittarius
February 7–March 4	Capricorn
March 5–31	Aquarius
April 1–25	Pisces
April 26–May 20	Aries
May 21–June 13	Taurus
June 14–July 8	Gemini
July 9–August 2	Cancer
August 3–26	Leo
August 27–September 19	Virgo
September 20–October 13	Libra
October 14–November 6	Scorpio
November 7–30	Sagittarius
December 1–24	Capricorn
December 25–31	Aquarius

1932

January 1–18	Aquarius
January 19–February 11	Pisces
February 12–March 8	Aries
March 9–April 3	Taurus
April 4–May 5	Gemini
May 6–July 12	Cancer
July 13–27	Gemini
July 28–September 8	Cancer
September 9–October 6	Leo
October 7–November 1	Virgo
November 2–25	Libra
November 26–December 20	Scorpio
December 21–31	Sagittarius

1934

January 1–April 5	Aquarius
April 6–May 5	Pisces
May 6–June 1	Aries
June 2–27	Taurus
June 28–July 22	Gemini
July 23–August 16	Cancer
August 17–September 10	Leo
September 11–October 4	Virgo
October 5–28	Libra
October 29–November 21	Scorpio
November 22–December 15	Sagittarius
December 16–31	Capricorn

1933

January 1–13	Sagittarius
January 14–February 6	Capricorn
February 7–March 2	Aquarius
March 3–26	Pisces
March 27–April 19	Aries
April 20–May 28	Taurus
May 29–June 8	Gemini
June 9–July 2	Cancer
July 3–26	Leo
July 27–August 20	Virgo
August 21–September 14	Libra
September 15–October 10	Scorpio
October 11–November 15	Sagittarius
November 16–December 4	Capricorn
December 5–31	Aquarius

1935

January 1–7	Capricorn
January 8–31	Aquarius
February 1–25	Pisces
February 26–March 21	Aries
March 22–April 15	Taurus
April 16–May 10	Gemini
May 11–June 6	Cancer
June 7–July 6	Leo
July 7–November 8	Virgo
November 9–December 7	Libra
December 8–31	Scorpio

1936

January 1–2	Scorpio
January 3–27	Sagittarius
January 28–February 21	Capricorn
February 22–March 16	Aquarius
March 17–April 10	Pisces
April 11–May 4	Aries
May 5–28	Taurus
May 29–June 22	Gemini
June 23–July 16	Cancer
July 17–August 10	Leo
August 11–September 4	Virgo
September 5–27	Libra
September 28–October 22	Scorpio
October 23–November 15	Sagittarius
November 16–December 10	Capricorn
December 11–31	Aquarius

1937

January 1–5	Aquarius
January 6–February 1	Pisces
February 2–March 8	Aries
March 9–April 13	Taurus
April 14–June 3	Aries
June 4–July 6	Taurus
July 7–August 3	Gemini
August 4–29	Cancer
August 30–September 24	Leo
September 25–October 18	Virgo
October 19–November 11	Libra
November 12–December 5	Scorpio
December 6–29	Sagittarius
December 30–31	Capricorn

1938

January 1–22	Capricorn
January 23–February 15	Aquarius
February 16–March 11	Pisces
March 12–April 4	Aries
April 5–28	Taurus
April 29–May 23	Gemini
May 24–June 18	Cancer
June 19–July 13	Leo
July 14–August 8	Virgo
August 9–September 6	Libra
September 7–October 13	Scorpio
October 14–November 14	Sagittarius
November 15–December 31	Scorpio

1939

January 1–3	Capricorn
January 4–February 5	Aquarius
February 5–March 4	Pisces
March 5–30	Aries
March 31–April 24	Taurus
April 25–May 19	Gemini
May 20–June 13	Cancer
June 14–July 8	Leo
July 9–August 1	Virgo
August 2–25	Libra
August 26–September 19	Scorpio
September 20–October 13	Cancer
October 14–November 6	Leo
November 7–30	Virgo
December 1–24	Libra
December 25–31	Scorpio

1940

January 1–18	Aquarius
January 19–February 11	Pisces
February 12–March 7	Aries
March 8–April 3	Taurus
April 4–May 5	Gemini
May 6–July 4	Cancer
July 5–31	Gemini
August 1–September 8	Cancer
September 9–October 5	Leo
October 6–31	Virgo
November 1–25	Libra
November 26–December 19	Scorpio
December 20–31	Sagittarius

1942

January 1–April 5	Aquarius
April 6–May 5	Pisces
May 6–June 1	Aries
June 2–26	Taurus
June 27–July 22	Gemini
July 23–August 16	Cancer
August 17–September 9	Leo
September 10–October 3	Virgo
October 4–27	Libra
October 28–November 20	Scorpio
November 21–December 14	Sagittarius
December 15–31	Capricorn

1941

January 1–12	Sagittarius
January 13–February 5	Capricorn
February 6–March 1	Aquarius
March 2–26	Pisces
March 27–April 19	Aries
April 20–May 13	Taurus
May 14–June 6	Gemini
June 7–July 1	Cancer
July 2–26	Leo
July 27–August 20	Virgo
August 21–September 14	Libra
September 15–October 9	Scorpio
October 10–November 5	Sagittarius
November 6–December 4	Capricorn
December 5–31	Aquarius

1943

January 1–7	Capricorn
January 8–31	Aquarius
February 1–24	Pisces
February 25–March 20	Aries
March 21–April 14	Taurus
April 15–May 10	Gemini
May 11–June 6	Cancer
June 7–July 6	Leo
July 7–November 8	Virgo
November 9–December 7	Libra
December 8–31	Scorpio

1944

January 1–2	Scorpio
January 3–27	Sagittarius
January 28–February 20	Capricorn
February 21–March 16	Aquarius
March 17–April 9	Pisces
April 10–May 3	Aries
May 4–28	Taurus
May 29–June 21	Gemini
June 22–July 16	Cancer
July 17–August 9	Leo
August 10–September 2	Virgo
September 3–27	Libra
September 28–October 21	Scorpio
October 22–November 15	Sagittarius
November 16–December 10	Capricorn
December 11–31	Aquarius

1945

January 1–4	Aquarius
January 5–February 1	Pisces
February 2–March 10	Aries
March 11–April 6	Taurus
April 7–June 3	Aries
June 4–July 6	Taurus
July 7–August 3	Gemini
August 4–29	Cancer
August 30–September 23	Leo
September 24–October 18	Virgo
October 19–November 11	Libra
November 12–December 5	Scorpio
December 6–29	Sagittarius
December 30–31	Capricorn

1946

January 1–21	Capricorn
January 22–February 14	Aquarius
February 15–March 10	Pisces
March 11–April 4	Aries
April 5–28	Taurus
April 29–May 23	Gemini
May 24–June 17	Cancer
June 18–July 12	Leo
July 13–August 8	Virgo
August 9–September 6	Libra
September 7–October 15	Scorpio
October 16–November 7	Sagittarius
November 8–December 31	Scorpio

1947

January 1–4	Scorpio
January 5–February 5	Sagittarius
February 5–March 4	Capricorn
March 5–29	Aquarius
March 30–April 24	Pisces
April 25–May 19	Aries
May 20–June 12	Taurus
June 13–July 7	Gemini
July 8–August 1	Cancer
August 2–25	Leo
August 26–September 18	Virgo
September 19–October 12	Libra
October 13–November 5	Scorpio
November 6–29	Sagittarius
November 30–December 23	Capricorn
December 24–31	Aquarius

1948

January 1–17	Aquarius
January 18–February 10	Pisces
February 11–March 7	Aries
March 8–April 3	Taurus
April 4–May 6	Gemini
May 7–June 28	Cancer
June 19–August 2	Leo
August 3–September 7	Cancer
September 8–October 5	Leo
October 6–31	Virgo
November 1–25	Libra
November 26–December 19	Scorpio
December 20–31	Sagittarius

1950

January 1–April 5	Aquarius
April 6–May 4	Pisces
May 5–31	Aries
June 1–26	Taurus
June 27–July 21	Gemini
July 22–August 15	Cancer
August 16–September 9	Leo
September 10–October 3	Virgo
October 4–27	Libra
October 28–November 20	Scorpio
November 21–December 13	Sagittarius
December 14–31	Capricorn

1949

January 1–12	Sagittarius
January 13–February 5	Capricorn
February 6–March 1	Aquarius
March 2–25	Pisces
March 26–April 19	Aries
April 20–May 13	Taurus
May 14–June 6	Gemini
June 7–30	Cancer
July 1–25	Leo
July 26–August 19	Virgo
August 20–September 14	Libra
September 15–October 9	Scorpio
October 10–November 5	Sagittarius
November 6–December 5	Capricorn
December 6–31	Aquarius

1951

January 1–7	Capricorn
January 8–31	Aquarius
February 1–24	Pisces
February 25–March 21	Aries
March 22–April 15	Taurus
April 16–May 10	Gemini
May 11–June 6	Cancer
June 7–July 7	Leo
July 8–November 9	Virgo
November 10–December 7	Libra
December 8–31	Scorpio

1952

January 1–2	Scorpio
January 3–27	Sagittarius
January 28–February 20	Capricorn
February 21–March 16	Aquarius
March 17–April 9	Pisces
April 10–May 4	Aries
May 5–28	Taurus
May 29–June 21	Gemini
June 22–July 16	Cancer
July 17–August 9	Leo
August 10–September 3	Virgo
September 4–27	Libra
September 28–October 21	Scorpio
October 22–November 15	Sagittarius
November 16–December 10	Capricorn
December 11–31	Aquarius

1953

January 1–5	Aquarius
January 6–February 1	Pisces
February 2–March 13	Aries
March 14–31	Taurus
April 1–June 5	Aries
June 6–July 7	Taurus
July 8–August 3	Gemini
August 4–29	Cancer
August 30–September 24	Leo
September 25–October 18	Virgo
October 19–November 11	Libra
November 12–December 5	Scorpio
December 6–29	Sagittarius
December 30–31	Capricorn

1954

January 1–22	Capricorn
January 23–February 15	Aquarius
February 16–March 11	Pisces
March 12–April 4	Aries
April 5–28	Taurus
April 29–May 23	Gemini
May 24–June 17	Cancer
June 18–July 13	Leo
July 14–August 8	Virgo
August 9–September 6	Libra
September 7–October 22	Scorpio
October 23–27	Sagittarius
October 28–December 31	Scorpio

1955

January 1–6	Scorpio
January 7–February 5	Sagittarius
February 6–March 4	Capricorn
March 5–30	Aquarius
March 31–April 24	Pisces
April 25–May 19	Aries
May 20–June 13	Taurus
June 14–July 7	Gemini
July 8–August 1	Cancer
August 2–25	Leo
August 26–September 18	Virgo
September 19–October 13	Libra
October 14–November 5	Scorpio
November 6–30	Sagittarius
December 1–24	Capricorn
December 25–31	Aquarius

1956

January 1–17	Aquarius
January 18–February 11	Pisces
February 12–March 7	Aries
March 8–April 4	Taurus
April 5–May 7	Gemini
May 8–June 23	Cancer
June 24–August 4	Gemini
August 5–September 8	Cancer
September 9–October 5	Leo
October 6–31	Virgo
November 1–25	Libra
November 26–December 19	Scorpio
December 20–31	Sagittarius

1957

January 1–12	Sagittarius
January 13–February 5	Capricorn
February 6–March 1	Aquarius
March 2–26	Pisces
March 26–April 19	Aries
April 20–May 13	Taurus
May 14–June 6	Gemini
June 7–July 1	Cancer
July 2–26	Leo
July 27–August 19	Virgo
August 20–September 14	Libra
September 15–October 19	Scorpio
October 20–November 5	Sagittarius
November 6–December 6	Capricorn
December 7–31	Aquarius

1958

January 1–April 6	Aquarius
April 7–May 5	Pisces
May 6–31	Aries
June 1–26	Taurus
June 27–July 22	Gemini
July 23–August 15	Cancer
August 16–September 9	Leo
September 10–October 3	Virgo
October 4–27	Libra
October 28–November 20	Scorpio
November 21–December 14	Sagittarius
December 15–31	Capricorn

1959

January 1–7	Capricorn
January 8–31	Aquarius
February 1–24	Pisces
February 25–March 20	Aries
March 21–April 14	Taurus
April 15–May 10	Gemini
May 11–June 6	Cancer
June 7–July 8	Leo
July 9–September 20	Virgo
September 21–24	Leo
September 25–November 9	Virgo
November 10–December 7	Libra
December 8–31	Scorpio

1960

January 1–2	Scorpio
January 3–27	Sagittarius
January 28–February 20	Capricorn
February 21–Mach 15	Aquarius
March 16–April 9	Pisces
April 10–May 5	Aries
May 6–28	Taurus
May 29–June 21	Gemini
June 22–July 15	Cancer
July 16–August 9	Leo
August 10–September 2	Virgo
September 3–26	Libra
September 27–October 21	Scorpio
October 22–November 15	Sagittarius
November 16–December 10	Capricorn
December 11–31	Aquarius

1961

January 1–5	Aquarius
January 6–February 2	Pisces
February 3–June 5	Aries
June 6–July 7	Taurus
July 8–August 3	Gemini
August 4–29	Cancer
August 30–September 23	Leo
September 24–October 17	Virgo
October 18–November 11	Libra
November 12–December 4	Scorpio
December 5–28	Sagittarius
December 29–31	Capricorn

1962

January 1–21	Capricorn
January 22–February 14	Aquarius
February 15–March 10	Pisces
March 11–April 3	Aries
April 4–28	Taurus
April 29–May 22	Gemini
May 23–June 17	Cancer
June 18–July 12	Leo
July 13–August 8	Virgo
August 9–September 6	Libra
September 7–December 31	Scorpio

1963

January 1–6	Scorpio
January 7–February 5	Sagittarius
February 6–March 4	Capricorn
March 5–29	Aquarius
March 30–April 23	Pisces
April 24–May 18	Aries
May 19–June 12	Taurus
June 13–July 7	Gemini
July 8–31	Cancer
August 1–25	Leo
August 26–September 18	Virgo
September 19–October 12	Libra
October 13–November 5	Scorpio
November 6–29	Sagittarius
November 30–December 23	Capricorn
December 24–31	Aquarius

1964

January 1–16	Aquarius
January 17–February 10	Pisces
February 11–March 7	Aries
March 8–April 4	Taurus
April 5–May 9	Gemini
May 10–June 17	Cancer
June 18–August 5	Gemini
August 6–September 8	Cancer
September 9–October 5	Leo
October 6–31	Virgo
November 1–24	Libra
November 25–December 19	Scorpio
December 20–31	Sagittarius

1966

January 1–February 6	Aquarius
February 7–25	Capricorn
February 26–April 6	Aquarius
April 7–May 5	Pisces
May 6–31	Aries
June 1–26	Taurus
June 27–July 21	Gemini
July 22–August 15	Cancer
August 16–September 8	Leo
September 9–October 2	Virgo
October 3–26	Libra
October 27–November 19	Scorpio
November 20–December 13	Sagittarius
December 14–31	Capricorn

1965

January 1–12	Sagittarius
January 13–February 5	Capricorn
February 6–March 1	Aquarius
March 2–26	Pisces
March 26–April 18	Aries
April 19–May 12	Taurus
May 13–June 6	Gemini
June 7–30	Cancer
July 1–25	Leo
July 26–August 19	Virgo
August 20–September 13	Libra
September 14–October 9	Scorpio
October 10–November 5	Sagittarius
November 6–December 7	Capricorn
December 8–31	Aquarius

1967

January 1–6	Capricorn
January 7–30	Aquarius
January 31–February 23	Pisces
February 24–March 20	Aries
March 21–April 14	Taurus
April 15–May 10	Gemini
May 11–June 6	Cancer
June 7–July 8	Leo
July 9–September 9	Virgo
September 10–October 1	Leo
October 2–November 9	Virgo
November 10–December 7	Libra
December 8–31	Scorpio

1968

January 1	Scorpio
January 2–26	Sagittarius
January 27–February 20	Capricorn
February 21–March 15	Aquarius
March 16–April 8	Pisces
April 9–May 3	Aries
May 4–27	Taurus
May 28–June 20	Gemini
June 21–July 15	Cancer
July 16–August 8	Leo
August 9–September 2	Virgo
September 3–26	Libra
September 27–October 21	Scorpio
October 22–November 14	Sagittarius
November 15–December 9	Capricorn
December 10–31	Aquarius

1969

January 1–4	Aquarius
January 5–February 2	Pisces
February 3–June 6	Aries
June 7–July 6	Taurus
July 7–August 3	Gemini
August 4–28	Cancer
August 29–September 22	Leo
September 23–October 17	Virgo
October 18–November 10	Libra
November 11–December 4	Scorpio
December 5–28	Sagittarius
December 29–31	Capricorn

1970

January 1–21	Capricorn
January 22–February 14	Aquarius
February 15–March 10	Pisces
March 11–April 3	Aries
April 4–27	Taurus
April 28–May 22	Gemini
May 23–June 16	Cancer
June 17–July 12	Leo
July 13–August 8	Virgo
August 9–September 7	Libra
September 8–December 31	Scorpio

1971

January 1–7	Scorpio
January 8–February 5	Sagittarius
February 6–March 4	Capricorn
March 5–29	Aquarius
March 30–April 23	Pisces
April 24–May 17	Aries
May 18–June 12	Taurus
June 13–July 6	Gemini
July 7–31	Cancer
August 1–24	Leo
August 25–September 17	Virgo
September 18–October 17	Libra
October 18–November 5	Scorpio
November 6–29	Sagittarius
November 30–December 23	Capricorn
December 24–31	Aquarius

1972

January 1–16	Aquarius
January 17–February 10	Pisces
February 11–March 7	Aries
March 8–April 3	Taurus
April 4–May 10	Gemini
May 11–June 11	Cancer
June 12–August 6	Gemini
August 7–September 7	Cancer
September 8–October 4	Leo
October 5–30	Virgo
October 31–November 24	Libra
November 25–December 18	Scorpio
December 19–31	Sagittarius

1974

January 1–29	Aquarius
January 30–February 28	Capricorn
March 1–April 6	Aquarius
April 7–May 4	Pisces
May 5–31	Aries
June 1–25	Taurus
June 26–July 21	Gemini
July 22–August 14	Cancer
August 15–September 8	Leo
September 9–October 2	Virgo
October 3–26	Libra
October 27–November 19	Scorpio
November 20–December 13	Sagittarius
December 14–31	Capricorn

1973

January 1–11	Sagittarius
January 12–February 4	Capricorn
February 5–28	Aquarius
March 1–24	Pisces
March 25–April 18	Aries
April 19–May 12	Taurus
May 13–June 5	Gemini
June 6–30	Cancer
July 1–25	Leo
July 26–August 19	Virgo
August 20–September 13	Libra
September 14–October 9	Scorpio
October 10–November 5	Sagittarius
November 6–December 7	Capricorn
December 8–31	Aquarius

1975

January 1–6	Capricorn
January 7–30	Aquarius
January 31–February 23	Pisces
February 24–March 19	Aries
March 20–April 13	Taurus
April 14–May 9	Gemini
May 10–June 6	Cancer
June 7–July 9	Leo
July 10–September 2	Virgo
September 3–October 4	Leo
October 5–November 9	Virgo
November 10–December 7	Libra
December 8–31	Scorpio

1976

January 1	Scorpio
January 2–26	Sagittarius
January 27–February 19	Capricorn
February 20–March 15	Aquarius
March 16–April 8	Pisces
April 9–May 2	Aries
May 3–27	Taurus
May 28–June 20	Gemini
June 21–July 14	Cancer
July 15–August 8	Leo
August 9–September 1	Virgo
September 2–26	Libra
September 27–October 20	Scorpio
October 21–November 14	Sagittarius
November 15–December 9	Capricorn
December 10–31	Aquarius

1977

January 1–4	Sagittarius
January 5–February 2	Capricorn
February 3–June 6	Aquarius
June 7–August 2	Pisces
August 3–28	Aries
August 29–September 22	Taurus
September 23–October 17	Gemini
October 18–November 10	Cancer
November 11–December 4	Leo
December 5–27	Virgo
December 28–31	Libra

1978

January 1–20	Capricorn
January 21–February 13	Aquarius
February 14–March 9	Pisces
March 10–April 2	Aries
April 3–27	Taurus
April 28–May 22	Gemini
May 23–June 16	Cancer
June 17–July 12	Leo
July 13–August 8	Virgo
August 9–September 7	Libra
September 8–December 31	Scorpio

1979

January 1–7	Scorpio
January 8–February 5	Sagittarius
February 6–March 3	Capricorn
March 4–29	Aquarius
March 30–April 23	Pisces
April 24–May 18	Aries
May 19–June 11	Taurus
June 12–July 6	Gemini
July 7–30	Cancer
July 31–August 24	Leo
August 25–September 17	Virgo
September 18–October 11	Libra
October 12–November 4	Scorpio
November 5–28	Sagittarius
November 29–December 22	Capricorn
December 23–31	Aquarius

1980

January 1–16	Aquarius
January 17–February 9	Pisces
February 10–March 6	Aries
March 7–April 3	Taurus
April 4–May 12	Gemini
May 13–June 5	Cancer
June 6–August 6	Gemini
August 7–September 7	Cancer
September 8–October 4	Leo
October 5–30	Virgo
October 31–November 24	Libra
November 25–December 18	Scorpio
December 19–31	Sagittarius

1982

January 1–23	Aquarius
January 24–March 2	Capricorn
March 3–April 6	Aquarius
April 7–May 4	Pisces
May 5–30	Aries
May 31–June 25	Taurus
June 26–July 20	Gemini
July 21–August 14	Cancer
August 15–September 7	Leo
September 8–October 2	Virgo
October 3–26	Libra
October 27–November 19	Scorpio
November 19–December 12	Sagittarius
December 13–31	Capricorn

1981

January 1–11	Sagittarius
January 12–February 4	Capricorn
February 5–28	Aquarius
March 1–24	Pisces
March 24–April 17	Aries
April 18–May 12	Taurus
May 13–June 5	Gemini
June 6–29	Cancer
June 30–July 24	Leo
July 25–August 18	Virgo
August 19–September 12	Libra
September 13–October 8	Scorpio
October 9–November 5	Sagittarius
November 6–December 8	Capricorn
December 9–31	Aquarius

1983

January 1–5	Capricorn
January 6–29	Aquarius
January 30–February 22	Pisces
February 23–March 19	Aries
March 20–April 13	Taurus
April 14–May 9	Gemini
May 10–June 6	Cancer
June 7–July 10	Leo
July 11–August 27	Virgo
August 28–October 5	Leo
October 6–November 9	Virgo
November 10–December 6	Libra
December 7–31	Scorpio

1984

January 1	Scorpio
January 2–25	Sagittarius
January 26–February 19	Capricorn
February 20–March 14	Aquarius
March 15–April 7	Pisces
April 8–May 2	Aries
May 3–26	Taurus
May 27–June 20	Gemini
June 21–July 14	Cancer
July 15–August 7	Leo
August 8–September 1	Virgo
September 2–25	Libra
September 26–October 20	Scorpio
October 21–November 13	Sagittarius
November 14–December 9	Capricorn
December 10–31	Aquarius

1985

January 1–4	Aquarius
January 5–February 2	Pisces
February 3–June 6	Aries
June 7–July 6	Taurus
July 7–August 2	Gemini
August 3–28	Cancer
August 29–September 22	Leo
September 23–October 16	Virgo
October 17–November 9	Libra
November 10–December 3	Scorpio
December 4–27	Sagittarius
December 28–31	Capricorn

1986

January 1–20	Capricorn
January 21–February 13	Aquarius
February 14–March 9	Pisces
March 10–April 2	Aries
April 3–26	Taurus
April 27–May 21	Gemini
May 22–June 15	Cancer
June 16–July 11	Leo
July 12–August 7	Virgo
August 8–September 7	Libra
September 8–December 31	Scorpio

1987

January 1–7	Scorpio
January 8–February 5	Sagittarius
February 6–March 3	Capricorn
March 4–28	Aquarius
March 29–April 22	Pisces
April 23–May 17	Aries
May 18–June 11	Taurus
June 12–July 5	Gemini
July 6–30	Cancer
July 31–August 23	Leo
August 24–September 16	Virgo
September 17–October 10	Libra
October 11–November 3	Scorpio
November 4–28	Sagittarius
November 29–December 22	Capricorn
December 23–31	Aquarius

1988

January 1–15	Aquarius
January 16–February 9	Pisces
February 10–March 6	Aries
March 7–April 3	Taurus
April 4–May 17	Gemini
May 18–27	Cancer
May 28–August 6	Gemini
August 7–September 7	Cancer
September 8–October 4	Leo
October 5–29	Virgo
October 30–November 23	Libra
November 24–December 17	Scorpio
December 18–31	Sagittarius

1990

January 1–16	Aquarius
January 17–March 3	Capricorn
March 4–April 6	Aquarius
April 7–May 4	Pisces
May 5–30	Aries
May 31–June 25	Taurus
June 26–July 20	Gemini
July 21–August 13	Cancer
August 14–September 7	Leo
September 8–October 1	Virgo
October 2–25	Libra
October 26–November 18	Scorpio
November 19–December 12	Sagittarius
December 13–31	Capricorn

1989

January 1–10	Sagittarius
January 11–February 3	Capricorn
February 4–27	Aquarius
February 28–March 23	Pisces
March 24–April 16	Aries
April 17–May 11	Taurus
May 12–June 4	Gemini
June 5–29	Cancer
June 30–July 24	Leo
July 25–August 18	Virgo
August 19–September 12	Libra
September 13–October 8	Scorpio
October 9–November 5	Sagittarius
November 6–December 8	Capricorn
December 11–31	Aquarius

1991

January 1–5	Capricorn
January 6–29	Aquarius
January 30–February 22	Pisces
February 23–March 18	Aries
March 19–April 13	Taurus
April 14–May 9	Gemini
May 10–June 6	Cancer
June 7–July 11	Leo
July 12–August 21	Virgo
August 22–October 6	Leo
October 7–November 9	Virgo
November 10–December 6	Libra
December 7–31	Scorpio

1992

January 1–25	Sagittarius
January 26–February 18	Capricorn
February 19–March 13	Aquarius
March 14–April 7	Pisces
April 8–May 1	Aries
May 2–26	Taurus
May 27–June 19	Gemini
June 20–July 13	Cancer
July 14–August 7	Leo
August 8–31	Virgo
September 1–25	Libra
September 26–October 19	Scorpio
October 20–November 13	Sagittarius
November 14–December 8	Capricorn
December 9–31	Aquarius

1994

January 1–19	Capricorn
January 20–February 12	Aquarius
February 13–March 8	Pisces
March 9–April 1	Aries
April 2–26	Taurus
April 27–May 21	Gemini
May 22–June 15	Cancer
June 16–July 11	Leo
July 12–August 7	Virgo
August 8–September 7	Libra
September 8–December 31	Scorpio

1993

January 1–3	Aquarius
January 4–February 2	Pisces
February 3–June 6	Aries
June 7–July 6	Taurus
July 7–August 1	Gemini
August 2–27	Cancer
August 28–September 21	Leo
September 22–October 16	Virgo
October 17–November 9	Libra
November 10–December 2	Scorpio
December 3–26	Sagittarius
December 27–31	Capricorn

1995

January 1–7	Scorpio
January 8–February 4	Sagittarius
February 5–March 2	Capricorn
March 3–28	Aquarius
March 29–April 22	Pisces
April 23–May 16	Aries
May 17–June 10	Taurus
June 11–July 5	Gemini
July 6–29	Cancer
July 30–August 23	Leo
August 24–September 16	Virgo
September 17–October 10	Libra
October 11–November 3	Scorpio
November 4–27	Sagittarius
November 28–December 21	Capricorn
December 22–31	Aquarius

1996

January 1–15	Aquarius
January 16–February 9	Pisces
February 10–March 6	Aries
March 7–April 3	Taurus
April 4–August 7	Gemini
August 8–September 7	Cancer
September 8–October 4	Leo
October 5–29	Virgo
October 30–November 23	Libra
November 24–December 17	Scorpio
December 18–31	Sagittarius

1998

January 1–9	Aquarius
January 10–March 4	Capricorn
March 5–April 6	Aquarius
April 7–May 3	Pisces
May 4–29	Aries
May 30–June 24	Taurus
June 25–July 19	Gemini
July 20–August 13	Cancer
August 14–September 6	Leo
September 7–30	Virgo
October 1–25	Libra
October 26–November 17	Scorpio
November 18–December 11	Sagittarius
December 12–31	Capricorn

1997

January 1–10	Sagittarius
January 11–February 3	Capricorn
February 4–27	Aquarius
February 28–March 23	Pisces
March 24–April 16	Aries
April 17–May 10	Taurus
May 11–June 4	Gemini
June 5–28	Cancer
June 29–July 23	Leo
July 24–August 17	Virgo
August 18–September 12	Libra
September 13–October 8	Scorpio
October 9–November 5	Sagittarius
November 6–December 12	Capricorn
December 13–31	Aquarius

1999

January 1–4	Capricorn
January 5–28	Aquarius
January 29–February 21	Pisces
February 22–March 18	Aries
March 19–April 12	Taurus
April 13–May 8	Gemini
May 9–June 5	Cancer
June 6–July 12	Leo
July 13–August 15	Virgo
August 16–October 7	Leo
October 8–November 9	Virgo
November 10–December 5	Libra
December 6–31	Scorpio

2000

January 1–24	Sagittarius
January 25–February 18	Capricorn
February 19–March 13	Aquarius
March 14–April 6	Pisces
April 7–May 1	Aries
May 2–25	Taurus
May 26–June 18	Gemini
June 19–July 13	Cancer
July 14–August 6	Leo
August 7–31	Virgo
September 1–24	Libra
September 25–October 19	Scorpio
October 20–November 13	Sagittarius
November 14–December 8	Capricorn
December 9–31	Aquarius

2001

January 1–3	Aquarius
January 4–February 2	Pisces
February 3–June 6	Aries
June 7–July 5	Taurus
July 6–August 1	Gemini
August 2–August 26	Cancer
August 27–September 20	Leo
September 21–October 15	Virgo
October 16–November 8	Libra
November 9–December 2	Scorpio
December 3–December 26	Sagittarius
December 27–December 31	Capricorn

2002

January 1–January 18	Capricorn
January 19–February 11	Aquarius
February 12–March 7	Pisces
March 8–April 1	Aries
April 2–25	Taurus
April 26–May 20	Gemini
May 21–June 14	Cancer
June 15–July 10	Leo
July 11–August 7	Virgo
August 8–September 7	Libra
September 8–December 31	Scorpio

2003

January 1–January 7	Scorpio
January 8–February 4	Sagittarius
February 5–March 2	Capricorn
March 3–March 27	Aquarius
March 28–April 21	Pisces
April 22–May 16	Aries
May 17–June 9	Taurus
June 10–July 4	Gemini
July 5–July 28	Cancer
July 29–August 22	Leo
August 23–September 15	Virgo
September 16–October 9	Libra
October 10–November 2	Scorpio
November 3–November 26	Sagittarius
November 27–December 21	Capricorn
December 22–December 31	Aquarius

2004

January 1–January 14	Aquarius
January 15–February 8	Pisces
February 9–March 5	Aries
March 6–April 3	Taurus
April 4–August 7	Gemini
August 8–September 6	Cancer
September 7–October 3	Leo
October 4–October 28	Virgo
October 29–November 22	Libra
November 23–December 16	Scorpio
December 17–December 31	Sagittarius

2006

January 1	Aquarius
January 2–March 5	Capricorn
March 6–April 5	Aquarius
April 6–May 3	Pisces
May 4–May 29	Aries
May 30–June 23	Taurus
June 24–July 18	Gemini
July 19–August 12	Cancer
August 13–September 6	Leo
September 7–September 30	Virgo
October 1–October 24	Libra
October 25–November 17	Scorpio
November 18–December 11	Sagittarius
December 12–December 31	Capricorn

2005

January 1–January 9	Sagittarius
January 10–February 2	Capricorn
February 3–February 26	Aquarius
February 27–March 22	Pisces
March 23–April 15	Aries
April 16–May 9	Taurus
May 10–June 3	Gemini
June 4–June 28	Cancer
June 29–July 22	Leo
July 23–August 16	Virgo
August 17–September 11	Libra
September 12–October 7	Scorpio
October 8–November 5	Sagittarius
November 6–December 15	Capricorn
December 16–December 31	Aquarius

2007

January 1–January 3	Capricorn
January 4–January 27	Aquarius
January 28–February 21	Pisces
February 22–March 17	Aries
March 18–April 11	Taurus
April 12–May 8	Gemini
May 9–June 5	Cancer
June 6–July 14	Leo
July 15–August 8	Virgo
August 9–October 8	Leo
October 9–November 8	Virgo
November 9–December 5	Libra
December 6–December 30	Scorpio
December 31	Sagittarius

2008

January 1–January 24	Sagittarius
January 25–February 17	Capricorn
February 18–March 12	Aquarius
March 13–April 6	Pisces
April 7–April 30	Aries
May 1–May 24	Taurus
May 25–June 18	Gemini
June 19–July 12	Cancer
July 13–August 5	Leo
August 6–August 30	Virgo
August 31–September 23	Libra
September 24–October 18	Scorpio
October 19–November 12	Sagittarius
November 13–December 7	Capricorn
December 8–December 31	Aquarius

2010

January 1–January 18	Capricorn
January 19–February 11	Aquarius
Feburary 12–March 7	Pisces
March 8–March 31	Aries
April 1–April 25	Taurus
April 26–May 19	Gemini
May 20–June 14	Cancer
June 15–July 10	Leo
July 11–August 6	Virgo
August 7–September 8	Libra
September 9–November 7	Scorpio
November 8–November 29	Libra
November 30–December 31	Scorpio

2009

January 1–January 3	Aquarius
January 4–February 2	Pisces
February 3–June 6	Aries
June 7–July 5	Taurus
July 6–July 31	Gemini
August 1–August 26	Cancer
August 27–September 20	Leo
September 21–October 14	Virgo
October 15–November 7	Libra
November 8–December 1	Scorpio
December 2–December 25	Sagittarius
December 26–December 31	Capricorn

Sex columnist and love astrology expert **JENNI KOSARIN** is a native New Yorker who has lived, too, in Florence, Cancún, and Mexico City, where she learned from the wisdom passed down from generations of astrologers, the real deal. Her techniques are singular. Kosarin's predictions have also been seen in *OK!* magazine, *US Weekly*, Page Six of the *New York Post*, *Yahoo!*, and *Seventeen* magazine. She is the author of eight other nonfiction books, has contributed to magazines such as *First for Women*, *YM*, *Reader's Digest*, *Self*, and *Glamour*. She is a graduate of Cornell University and currently resides in New York City.

www.jennikosarin.com
www.notinthestars.com

Jenni Kosarin